PROGRESSIVE ANONYMITY

PROGRESSIVE ANONYMITY

From Identity Politics to Evidence-Based Government

Naomi Zack

ROWMAN & LITTLEFIELD
Lanham • Boulder • New York • London

Published by Rowman & Littlefield
An imprint of The Rowman & Littlefield Publishing Group, Inc.
4501 Forbes Boulevard, Suite 200, Lanham, Maryland 20706
www.rowman.com

6 Tinworth Street, London SE11 5AL, United Kingdom

Copyright © 2021 by The Rowman & Littlefield Publishing Group, Inc.

All rights reserved. No part of this book may be reproduced in any form or by any electronic or mechanical means, including information storage and retrieval systems, without written permission from the publisher, except by a reviewer who may quote passages in a review.

British Library Cataloguing in Publication Information Available

Library of Congress Cataloging-in-Publication Data

Names: Zack, Naomi, 1944– author.
Title: Progressive anonymity : from identity politics to evidence-based government / Naomi Zack.
Description: Lanham, Maryland : Rowman & Littlefield, 2020. | Includes bibliographical references and index. | Summary: "Continuing her visionary work in social-political philosophy, Zack critiques identity politics as perpetuating damaging essentialist perspectives and policies. The antidote to identity group egoism is anonymity based on relevant shared interests and a meritocracy led by experts chosen without preference for group affiliation or political charisma"— Provided by publisher.
Identifiers: LCCN 2020031251 (print) | LCCN 2020031252 (ebook) | ISBN 9781538136034 (cloth) | ISBN 9781538136041 (epub) | ISBN 9781538174104 (pbk)
Subjects: LCSH: Identity politics—United States. | Political participation—Social aspects—United States. | Equality before the law—United States.
Classification: LCC JK1764 .Z34 2020 (print) | LCC JK1764 (ebook) | DDC 320.5—dc23
LC record available at https://lccn.loc.gov/2020031251
LC ebook record available at https://lccn.loc.gov/2020031252

To Alex, Bradford, Jessica, Cloe, and Winona, with love.

CONTENTS

Preface and Acknowledgments ix
Introduction and Chapter Overview 1

1 Political Diagnoses in the Post–World War II Era and the Need for Identity Politics 13
2 From Society to Government: Problems with Identity Politics 33
3 Universalism or Force: Inclusion or Domination 57
4 White Supremacy and Status: The Racism of Race 77
5 Evidence-Based Government and Its Obstacles 99
6 The Problems with Evidence and Universal Basic Income 121

Conclusion: Progressive Anonymity: Review and Loose Ends 141
Postscript 149
Notes 153
Select Bibliography 179
Index 191

PREFACE AND ACKNOWLEDGMENTS

I didn't realize until I finished the penultimate draft of the manuscript for this book how compatible it is with my last book, *Reviving the Social Compact: Inclusive Citizenship in an Age of Extreme Politics* (2018). In that work, I offered new concepts for understanding and acting through political and social upheaval and distress post-2016. Politics as contest has become turbo-charged—it is boosted by its own exhaust in an expanding, closed system. In that book, I considered how, in our now very agonistic two-party system, candidates and then elected officials and the public become more focused on winning than governing and holding government accountable for the benefit of the people, as the social contract requires. My main idea then was that the people had to do for themselves what government dysfunction was allowing to fall by the wayside. It was a call for good citizenship. In this book, I consider the best form of government for our time, given the enthusiasm for group identities or identity politics, while the culture writhes in discord. My general conclusion is that, because government remains necessary, it is important to delineate government from society. The strife in society will have to work itself out, but the conflicts caused by identities ought not to be brought into government. Government should be boring and evidence-based. The electorate is not overly fond of evidence (to say the least), and democracy allows for populism in times of great social change (such as the browning of America), but evidence and democracy nonetheless remain our best structural hopes for the organization of the ultimate force that government is.

I have been working on the ideas herein for more than a year and in my daily conversations and travels have shared the major themes with more people—colleagues, students, friends, family members—than I can recall. When people asked me what the book I was working on was about, I tended to give them answers from the perspective of the chapter I was working on at the time. The general response was positive, although not without skepticism. Of course, I do not know that all or most of these people would agree with the final result, but I hope they will let me know either way. I generally thank them all, because interest in one's work is always a great motivator. Still, specific thanks are due to members of the Philosophy Department at the University of Wisconsin–Madison, where I gave a talk based on what is now chapter 4, "White Supremacy and Status." Parts of chapters 4 and 5 were to be included in my second and third Romanell-PBK lectures, "A Philosophical Approach to Intersectionality," at Lehman College on March 18, 2020. However, COVID-19 quickly became urgent in early March and those lectures were cancelled, to be rescheduled. In my final revision of the manuscript I have found that the governmental response to this disaster sadly confirms the reasoning in this book, as well as my 2018 *Reviving the Social Compact*. This is not a book about COVID-19, but where immediate relevance is evident, I have added brief comments to the final manuscript. They lack the usual scholarly apparatus, which I will develop in *The Pandemic and the Police: Early COVID-19 Politics and Society in the United States* (forthcoming 2021).

I am grateful to Robert Farrell and Lisa Estreich, with whom I participated in a Levinas reading group at Lehman, during the fall of 2019. Both know more about Levinas than I ever will, and I appreciate their agreement and disagreement with my interpretations that occur in chapters 1 and 3.

Thanks to Simon Rackham for meticulous copyediting of the final manuscript.

I'm extremely grateful to Natalie Mandziuk, my editor at Rowman & Littlefield, for her open mind to new ideas, and to her team as well, for expert book production guidance. Special thanks to Patricia Stevenson for taking over as production editor after Karen Ackermann's tragic death, as well as posthumous thanks to Karen.

Naomi Zack
The Bronx, NY
April 2020

INTRODUCTION AND CHAPTER OVERVIEW

In the United States, there are problems with contemporary identity politics as a way to allocate power in political domains, although not necessarily in social domains, such as educational institutions, or in expressive domains, such as art and entertainment. The main problem concerns the nature of democratic government, which is supposed to apply to members of all identity groups in its domain; laws and the decisions of political officials are ultimately backed up by force, which must prevail for government to persist. In political domains, identity politics entails that individuals or groups with certain identities receive entitlements or have official political power that is based on their group identities. If these groups are opposed by other groups, whether represented in government or not, the result can be extreme political and social division, resulting in government dysfunction or, in extreme cases, revolution or civil war. Identity groups are typically based on distinctions and differences in race, ethnicity, gender, and social class. In extremely politicized situations, political party strife may itself be a kind of identity warfare, particularly when, as now, the Democrats and Republicans are lined up with different factions in what has come to be known as a "culture war."

In social (societal) domains, the inclusion of minorities through a value of diversity is more easily accomplished, although after gaining entry, minorities may find that power within organizations or institutions is not equally shared with them. This disparity in power may be experienced as "political," for instance, in the sense of "academic politics." The official, governmental presence of identity politics and its social presence are often confused. Quite often, theorists do not distinguish between society and its institutions that are apart from government, and government itself. This is because many analyses of identities are discussions of power differences and allocations, and power is assumed to be "political." But not everything that is political in the sense of power is, or should be, political in the sense of government. This confusion between society and government through ambiguity in the meaning of "power" can lead to an assumption that valid demands for recognition and respect in social institutions will automatically translate into changes in law and government. By the same token, formal changes in law and government are assumed to somehow automatically translate into changes in life outside of government within society—but this does not happen unless effective public policies are designed, government officials obey the law, and the people accept the law. Obedience to the law is particularly important in a democracy. The punitive apparatus may be straightforward in sentencing, incarceration, or fines for criminal law breakers. But simple noncompliance with law, especially law that (if complied with) would change society, is more difficult to address. A prime example is the persistence of racial discrimination in housing that has resulted in ongoing residential racial segregation. Housing discrimination is itself against the law but difficult to prove. And living in or profiting from the sale or rental of real estate in racially segregated neighborhoods is, of course, entirely within the law.

Ideally, the goal is for society to be morally good and government to be just, but all too often the two domains are not well aligned. As a result, theorists and activists fill gaps by working on the side that seems to need the greater correction—that is, changes in law or compliance with law. However, filling in such gaps becomes unnecessarily contentious and controversial when the generality of social needs and problems is overlooked in favor of specific identity advocacy. All identities are valuable and disadvantaged identities may deserve special attention. But on a governmental political level, it is important that proposals for change be inclusive of both disadvantaged and advantaged identities. Failures of inclusivity result in unnecessary partisan conflicts, increasing government dysfunction. Government exists to solve problems, and it is important that the problems for democratic government to solve be broadly understood as problems that people share across identities.

Society consists of life outside of government or over which government has little substantive control or regulation, because everything is permitted which is not against the law. Government, by contrast, is an official structure that issues decisions such that their implementations are backed up by legitimate force. There is also the area of discourse in which theorists might propose how to approach changes in government, and it is in that space or on that conceptual level—namely, social-political theory—that this book should be considered.

I begin with an assumption that sociology is not politics and society is not government. On that basis, I argue in chapter 1 that identity politics was necessary after a mainly diagnostic progressive reaction to the Third Reich following World War II. But identity politics is not a coherent approach to egalitarian governmental change in the early twenty-first century—at least not in the United States. Instead, the progressive focus should be on the contemporary interests of large segments of the electorate, composed of all identity groups. Even if it is understood that one or another group may benefit more from a particular policy, the groups that will not benefit as much nevertheless will receive some benefit. This benefit to all constituents should be immediately specific and transparent. It will not do to speak of the good of society in the long run. For example, society would generally benefit if homeless people benefited from a program that simply housed them, because society would become less unequal and public life in urban areas would have come closer to an appearance of convenience and ease for all. But such programs are likely to be opposed by the housed. What would work, instead, would be a program that provided everyone with a universal housing allowance.[1]

I suggest that government itself should be mixed or flexible regarding what can be called socialism or capitalism, because each system has specialized merits in terms of distribution, and both systems are compatible with democracy if used for appropriate purposes. A pragmatic but rights-based interpretation of evidence-based government is presented in chapters 5 and 6; in chapter 6 and the conclusion, the reduced importance of government is also entertained.

The foundation for both capitalistic and socialistic forms of government or motivations for public policy is social compact theory. Social compact theory assumes that primary political power belongs to the people, outside of government, who get to choose their form of government. Ultimate power over the nature of social institutions and the form of government remains with the people, who shape government through voting, reactions during administrations to those candidates who are elected, and varied kinds of influence over government, through moral suasion and lobbying.[2] It may be that our present consumer-based economy has already reached the point where it makes sense to view citizen-consumers as choosing one or the other ideological macrosystem, without consistency or even more than superficial understanding of the ideologies involved. Consumers now demand some form of socialistic policy through safety nets (e.g., Social Security), but they also demand a vast array of products and services that cannot be delivered by government.

The goal of political rule through progressive anonymity would be progress in the well-being of all who are governed. This could require an agreed-upon base level of minimal well-being in health, education, income, and other necessities for progressing in a specific society. Below a base level, progress is not possible, because people in some groups may be living hand to mouth, their children unable to get a good education, with adequate health care out of reach. Bare existence itself thus becomes a challenge. Those who do not have the base level might therefore require remedial assistance before the entire collectivity can progress. Or those below the basic level of income may have a humanitarian right to the base level. Conservatives and libertarians have also supported universal basic income, presumably not motivated by ideas of collective progress or humanitarian rights, but by hopes to shrink the existing welfare state and with it the federal budget. Universal basic income public policy is discussed in chapter 6 and the conclusion, with uneven results.

Progress beyond the base level of minimal well-being does not require economic redistribution above that minimum. Indeed, the most exciting, ambitious, and strongly motivated aspects of life in society occur after minimal well-being is achieved and there is no good argument against such trajectories. This is a strong modification of John Rawls's difference principle that change is acceptable provided that the disadvantaged are not less well off as a result. Instead, we might entertain the idea that *before* unequal progress occurs, none may be worse off below a minimum.[3]

Raymond Williams posed the classic modern dilemma about economic systems: "We seem reduced to a choice between speculator and bureaucrat and while we do not like the speculator, the bureaucrat is not exactly inviting either."[4] Without avowed ideology, the main ideas for government reduce to public policy ideas and proposals. This allows for greater flexibility for choosing government forms such as capitalism or socialism. Both are compatible with representative democracy. Economic inequality is usually associated with capitalism. Remedial assistance is associated with socialism. US democracy has functioned with a mixed capitalistic and socialist economy since changes introduced during the 1930s Great Depression. This historical reality should be better recognized by critics and advocates of both capitalism and socialism. Both have and can coexist: socialism would enable a more comprehensive minimal baseline, added to existing "safety nets" such as Social Security, Medicare, Medicaid, education, highways, and regulatory systems; capitalism would continue for distributing goods above minimal levels. The choice of system—capitalism or socialism—should not be viewed as a form of government but as a choice of how to govern—namely, a choice of public policy, which is pragmatically determined on the level of *public* policy, rather than ideologically decided as a holistic form of society. Examples: tax-funded goods such as national highways and Social Security require central government production, while cars and luxury goods do not; addressing food insecurity requires government resources, while choosing a restaurant for a fine meal does not. For a greater example, Republicans and Democrats united to pass unemployment and small business support in response to the economic effects of "stay-home" directives in response to COVID-19 during the spring of 2020. This legislation would have been viewed as extreme socialism in normal times, but conservatives joined progressives in supporting it and looking ahead to further federal support. The virtue of a mixed economy is that capitalists and socialists can constantly provide checks on each other's specialized policies. Without ideology, they would be required to do that in terms of what each system can offer society.

The historical experience of the electorate supports a mixed economy that is ideologically "lite." There has been a utilitarian dreariness in the public sector. This may be because central planning does not reward creativity about end products as incentives for employees. The end products tend to be plain and lacking in aesthetic variation and sources of pleasure. The causes of this may be related to requirements for survival and advancement among government employees. Within bureaucracies, workers need to be focused on the psychological and political interiors of their institutions, more than on the appeal of its end products. At the same time, such institutions may not be fully attentive to those who receive their outputs (a situation that public policy critics have identified as a problem within the US educational system).[5] By contrast, employees in capitalistic enterprises, especially in a consumer-dependent economy, are attuned to the appeal of the retail product, in a competitive environment. Indeed, capitalism has been able to excite and please consumers to an extent that government products have never been able to do.

In a secular society, neither capitalism nor socialism, as functional distributional policies, require ideology if we remember that all government action is problem-driven and we prioritize problems that require solutions that government is able and suited to provide. Capitalism has been so successful as an economic and aesthetic distributional system that it threatens the functioning of representative democratic government when business interest lobbying is allowed unchecked. But the influence of business in government can be checked if we remember that the problems solved by capitalism in our present consumer-driven economy[6] concern the production and distribution of material goods, for which wants and needs are ever more optional, personally aspirational, individualized, and nonvital.

When given a choice, the majority of people globally have selected some form of what progressives would call capitalism, from micro-loans in the third world to state-controlled capitalism in China. The arguments for capitalism since Adam Smith have stressed the efficiency of the marketplace, the importance of profit motives, and the satisfaction of human wants and needs. In contemporary economies that are mainly consumer-driven, both in the US and globally, capitalism or free enterprise has resulted in a vast array of consumer goods that consumers want and value. In this last sense, capitalism is the ultimate form of economic democracy. The abuses of capitalism result from crony capitalism (undue influence of private companies over government policy—

e.g., disaster capitalism) and insufficient government regulation (e.g., the financial industry causes of the 2008 Great Recession). Capitalism need not mean lack of regulation or unbridled destruction of natural environments, exploitation of labor, and abuse of end consumers. In addition, mitigation of the effects of climate change could be a government function in terms of its regulation of capitalism for the common good. Ideological support of capitalism may be based on idealized myths of individualism. But capitalism viewed as a distribution system for consumers can motivate individuals to demand distributions that benefit them, by demanding government regulation and prevention of exploitation of people and unbridled exploitation of natural resources.

The arguments for socialism as a macro-system are based on idealizations of groups as abstract entities. But, in practice, socialism does not require an ideology either, once it becomes evident that certain basic, functional human and environmental needs require state regulation and distribution. Socialism without ideology is the necessary commons, what people need beyond private consumption, which they can only get if others get it, too. Since Marx, socialism has been accompanied with an ideology of its utopian benefits and normative imperatives, such as the evils of capitalism and the miseries of alienation (workers do not recognize themselves in their work products). Socialism without ideology is a means for distributing services and material goods (including money) and, in some cases, administrative organization (e.g., defense, war, diplomacy, infrastructure, emergency response, taxation, and entitlements and minima payments). This requires no vision of utopia but instead a fulfillment of the social compact insofar as government benefits all of those governed, often acting in a humanitarian role as the benefactor of last resort.

Both the capitalist and the socialist ideologies accompanying political rhetoric can be understood as persuasive, motivational, and ministerial legacies of historical religious leadership. These ideologies distract from the practical needs and functions of government and require deconstruction as obstacles to secular democratic political life. As an aside, political messaging through social media has developed such insidious skill at getting people fired up and ready to act in certain ways that it may be clearing the way for genuine political ideas and activism to shed the hoopla of ideology. That is, it may soon be time for a mass movement toward just letting the show people put on the show, while concerned citizens attend to effective and fair government.

Getting to a political situation that is free of ideology, as well as unencumbered by identities as we now know them through identity politics, would require massive reeducation and a kind of sobriety in public life that has not been seen for a very long time. It may be that the excesses of present identity politics and ideology are the result of relative global prosperity that can support frivolity and decadence on the big stage. Or these excesses may be ephemera, a kind of historical episode that will soon pass on its own or go out of fashion. Government is necessary when there are problems. When enough people become aware of collective urgent problems, democratic structures may reintroduce serious demand for effective solutions. Of course, we are not there yet, because public ideas about the nature of democracy have degenerated into simple numerical majority rule and political practices neither appeal to reason nor conform to ideals of evidence-based anything, much less evidence-based government. Evidence alone is not a panacea, because it cannot substitute for human choices and decisions. Evidence in any area of human life and knowledge is context dependent, usually imperfect, and in need of skillful interpretation. Nonetheless, it is important to maintain standards of common rationality and empiricism. (The state and left wing media reactions to the US federal government response to COVID-19 have bypassed this numerical idea of democracy to call for greater federal response on moral, more basic social contract levels. Calls for activation of the Defense Production Act have simply assumed that the federal government is obligated to benefit the people.)

The critique of identity politics in favor of inclusive identity-neutral egalitarianism is pragmatic, but not at the expense of principles. The purpose of the critique of individually based identities is to address the tension between the use of identities to achieve equality and the very broadly based standing requirement that democratic government as we know it remain neutral regarding identities. Large parts of the US white population are adverse to any policies that selectively help minorities. The strong reaction against school busing as a means to achieve integration is one example of such aversion, and the rejection of affirmative action policies, all the way through to the US Supreme Court, is another.[7] While the defeat of school integration measures and affirmative action are taken by many to be grounds for pessimism about racial egalitarianism, we need to remember that these policies were means and not ends. There may be other means that address current needs without futile conflict. For instance, the large part of the white population that remains vigilant against any "favoritism" of minorities is not generally averse to Social Security, Medicare, or even Medicaid.[8] The theoretical task is to determine the differences between the various kinds of entitlements or distribution, those that are inclusive and those that are targeted.

The big problem with identity politics in early twenty-first-century US political life is that identity groups that are imagined to be composed of individuals who share common traits motivate opposition from other identity groups. This process is intensified when different degrees of status are imagined to be uniformly and permanently attached to different identities. Such attachments and perceptions of status are not uniform: people of color have lower status than whites most of the time, but other times they are imagined to be privileged; anti-Semites condemn Jews but also think that Jewish people belong to a secret elite that oppresses them; people of color believe they have lower status than whites, but their champions are often obviously privileged and high in status; men dominate women, who thereby have lower status, but women are feared and demonized when they show that they do not have the traits used to justify domination and cannot be dominated. Nevertheless, status accompanies racial identities in favor of whites, and chapter 4 can be read as a suggestion that much of discourse about racism be supplemented, if not replaced, by discourse about status.

The political goal for any identity group is to win, but winning now strangely depends on the skill with which a group can persuade itself and others that it has been victimized. Political life and ideology have thus become self-contradictory battles to prove which side is more oppressed and deprived and for that reason entitled to dominate. That is, the current popular path to justice requires an initial establishment of victimization, followed by proposals to correct it. Like progressives, reactionaries presume a universal value of justice (although of course they mean different things by it). However, their language of victimization is mere rhetoric offered as justification for demands or aggression. No one thinks that those truly victimized are able to dominate. There are no principled arguments showing why the severely victimized should dominate. Their victimization should cease, and many are entitled to compensation—only their oppressors would call that domination.

The contemporary opposition to identity politics has been accompanied by a huge unmarked change in the arena of identity politics. Before White Supremacist/White Nationalist political groups became an explicit part of mainstream politics within the United States and internationally in the twenty-first century, many advocates of identity groups struggled against what they considered *implicit* white supremacy, as part of their general struggles against an oppressive system.[9] Until recently, it was customary to study White Supremacy mainly sociologically, as demography or descriptions of the ethnicity of people who were in power. But now White Supremacy has, through legitimate political processes, become part of explicit official politics, not only in the United States but also throughout the world, and its internal connections have expanded through social media.[10]

Liberatory scholars of race insisted for decades that whites are a race in societies when and where only nonwhites have racial problems. But now, some whites are asserting their white racial identity in order to claim superiority, entitlement, and political power. Few expected this "How do you like me now?" moment, and now that it has erupted, fewer still on the "left" recognize the extent to which it is an appropriation of progressive methodology previously deployed by nonwhites, insofar as its ideology stems from claims of oppression and protests against perceived injustice.[11]

Violent white supremacism within the United States has sharply increased as a percentage of domestic terrorist attacks since 2016.[12] Although small in numbers, such extremists have a major disruptive effect and it remains to be seen whether such terrorism will obstruct or support the politically legitimized rise of the White Right. Will more racially temperate citizens support them or oppose them? Is there a natural limit to the number of such terrorists in a majority white population, or could anti-nonwhite terrorism become normalized within that whole population? We know from history (e.g., the "blood libel" of Jews[13]) that ideas about nonwhite inferiority and dangerousness remain a resource for current white-right radicals, even though they have been long since discredited in legitimate scholarship and public morality. But such ideas do not have agency on their own. Once resurrected, they need to be applied to contemporary contexts in ways that make sense to contemporary audiences. And the valorization of identities—although not identity-based violence and terrorism—has been ready-to-hand for almost three-quarters of a century. A public discourse of competing racial and ethnic identities forms a volatile atmosphere for hatred, which can spark violence.

A prospective progressive presidential candidate for the 2020 election has spoken against identity politics, exactly because of current White Right ascendancy.[14] But more theoretical context and intellectual history is needed before the necessity for actions that are immediately prudent can be fully understood, and some of that forms the content of this book. Evaluations of which identities have better claims about injustice does little to forestall such violence and may even feed it when racial and ethnic identities are already set up against one another. Identity competitions and wars are too bitter and recalcitrant to be rationally adjudicated. But neither can they be evaded once in play. The general theme of chapter 3 is that they should be avoided by exclusion from legitimate politics. Although individuals are the ultimate political unit for voting, they often approach politics through group membership. Progressive scholars would do well to increase attention paid to the nature of groups that can become political groups. It is important to rethink progressive assumptions that every difference in power within society should be a political issue within government.

Groups based on ideas about who their individual members *are* find it difficult or impossible to cooperate and compromise with opposing identity groups. The alternative proposed here is political recognition of the interests of very large groups that may not have much history, beyond pressing concerns that "pop up" to constitute them. The overarching political goal should be to serve the interests of all groups in terms of the common interests of all groups in a greater political whole. The dynamics of conflict among identity groups is an obstacle to consideration by all groups of what would be good for the members of all groups in the entire collective that is presumed to be democratic.

Political egoism is often perceived to be organized by similarities of race, class, and gender among voters and between groups of voters and selected candidates. But such similarities are often superficial compared to the actual goals and needs of voters. The identification with leaders that politically fuels identity groups is a kind of aspirational magical thinking that a candidate encourages by saying, "If I can do it, so can you," thereby inspiring a voter to prefer a candidate who "looks like me." Both the self-appointed role model and the appearance model may have little in common with their followers beyond superficial resemblance. Such problems with groups are anchored in deeper theoretical issues, which are addressed in chapter 2.

The antidote to identity group egoism is anonymity based on relevant shared interests, within and between groups, a form of politics led not by charismatic or tribally approved leaders, but by experts who are experienced and knowledgeable about common goals and problems. Meritocracy would replace popularity in the choice of leaders. This rational, positivist approach to government, which becomes evidence-based government, is not as doomed to failure as our spectacle-focused, scandal-obsessed era might suggest. Successful leadership is already gauged by accomplishments after candidates assume office. People choose and follow their leaders ideologically and emotionally, but those who voted based on identities, rather than their interests, are often conned and feel disappointed. Expertise should be assessed before candidates are elected. Instead of deciding who they would prefer to have a beer with, voters would decide who is most qualified for the job they need to get done, given candidates' proven skills and past experience. This would be a kind of algorithmic "people learning" (in contrast to machine learning), because new experiences determine future choices. Whether algorithms for selecting leaders are put together by the deliberations of individual voters or even constructed through machine learning, final selections would be made by assessing candidates in terms of the problem-solving expertise of proffered candidates, when and where there are problems that government can solve. Government is fused to some problems in society insofar as the solution of such problems is its raison d'être.

I

POLITICAL DIAGNOSES IN THE POST–WORLD WAR II ERA AND THE NEED FOR IDENTITY POLITICS

I think it [Nazism] has a *signification*, at least it shows that what happened once can happen again, and this indeed, I believe is entirely true. You see, tyranny has been discovered very early, and identified very early as an enemy. Still, it has never in any way prevented any tyrant from becoming a tyrant. It has not prevented Nero, and it has not prevented Caligula. And the cases of Nero and Caligula have not prevented an even closer example of what the massive intrusion of criminality can mean for the political process.

—Hannah Arendt, interview by Roger Errera[1]

But in the relationship of cruelty, the point of view of the victimizer is of only minor importance; it is the point of view of the victim that is authoritative. The victim feels the suffering in his own mind and body, whereas the victimizer, like Himmler's "hard" and "decent" Nazi, can be quite unaware of the suffering. The sword does not feel the pain that it inflicts. Do not ask it about suffering.

—Philip Hallie[2]

Progressive or egalitarian thought, like other traditions, occurs historically. Different stages are rooted in reaction to experiences of oppression in life. Conceptual tools for cultural analysis build over time. The innocence or clumsiness of thinkers from any given time may only be visible through the lenses of tools for analysis that happen later. That is, while progressive thought seeks progress in the world, it is itself an integral part of its own intellectual history—we hope that this history itself is progressive. Such progress inevitably results in the criticism of hindsight, which is difficult to pursue without anachronism, because methodological tools of today are used to critique insights of the past.

Identity politics developed mainstream attention well after World War II, during the 1960s. Its focus was on victims of oppression, the oppressed, and it has served to fill an important void in critical intellectual discourse that had previously been confined to abstract generalities. It is important to get a sense of that void, before criticizing identity politics. When thinkers in the 1930s and 1940s reflected on the political world, they focused on oppressors instead of the oppressed and the result was often diagnosis without prescription. This chapter will be occupied by some of that philosophical focus on political evil, augmented by less abstract considerations of the time.

During the era of World War II, many European thinkers were up against ugly, brutal realities and their subject was not what came to be known as "ideal theory" after John Rawls—that is, not an ideal of justice for societies that were already law abiding, with shared democratic values. Instead, the most influential progressive thinkers often provided psychological moral analyses of the nature of individual consciousness that contributed to systemic oppression and bad government. Intellectual critiques of the core ideas driving oppressive ideologies also assumed great importance. Political utopia was not imagined, social contract theory for citizens was not invoked, and compensation for victims and survivors was not an intellectual topic. Preventative measures against the Nazi genocide happening again were rarely explored and discussed. There were two practical exceptions to this characterization: the formation of the state of Israel and the establishment of the United Nations as a humanitarian organization to support human rights and promote peace. But our present subject is the intellectual history of progressivism. The first section addresses the post–World War II identity void, and in section 2 the entrance of identity is recognized.

THE POST–WORLD WAR II IDENTITY VOID

The post–World War II literature is vast, but here it will be excerpted to key insights by Emmanuel Levinas (1906–1975), Hannah Arendt (1906–1975), and Jean Paul Sartre (1905–1980). Karl Popper (1902–1994), who thought from a different philosophical tradition, is relevant for his practical, empirical political concerns that included prescription, as well as diagnosis. These four were contemporaries, all progressive thinkers, and their birth dates from 1902 to 1906 meant that they were in their thirties and forties from about 1935 to 1945. The contemporary audiences of Levinas and Sartre would have known exactly what they were talking about when they did not name it—German Nazism. But it is easy, after so many decades of their widespread influence, to forget that historical particularity. However, Arendt and Popper do bring us more explicitly to urgency, for their own time and perhaps for those concerned with racial and ethnic violence at this time.

Levinas

We begin with Levinas, the most dense, possibly the most profound, but actually the most pointed, because at times he seems to talk directly to the villainous perpetrators of crimes against humanity. But if he considers victims, it is from the viewpoint of their oppressors. Levinas did not think that the closed circle of consciousness-as-intentional was an ultimate experience, or that it encompassed all experience. His critique of the Husserlian turn toward the analysis of objects of consciousness that "brackets" their existence was to insist on a deeper level of awareness through nonintentional consciousness. Specifically in this regard, Levinas took issue with Husserl's treatment of the Other, which followed from his theory of intentionality.[3]

For Levinas, intentional consciousness, as the Western historical searcher and grasper of truth and knowledge, is a free, active, successful, and happy subject. Because consciousness is *intentional* in its basic, universal structure, this subject always has an object. Levinas seeks to bypass intentional consciousness, which he accuses of seeming to appropriate the entire world into itself, in favor of metaphysics. We could say that for Levinas, the tradition of Husserlian intentionality was epistemological and that he tried to break out of that into a more realist approach via his idea of metaphysics. Metaphysics for Levinas is prior to the ontology of subject-object or even subject-subject. The subject-object relation has the sweep of Western philosophical epistemology and the subject-subject relation shows how unavoidable this epistemology is, in even Martin Buber's I-thou analysis that purported to not objectify the other.[4] If metaphysics is prior to ontology and ontology is the study of being, of what there is, then Levinas also brushes Heidegger aside, for Heidegger is, of course, the premier ontologist in the Husserlian legacy. Heidegger said he wanted to overthrow traditional subject-object metaphysics by placing the human being *in* Being,[5] but for Levinas, Heidegger is still an ontologist, because he is talking about what there *is* for the subject. And the subject, as subject, cannot help but spin an all-encompassing web or blow an all-containing bubble.[6] The subject is egotistically self-engrossed.

Levinas seeks to describe a mode of awareness that, to an early twenty-first-century reader, resembles a Buddhist goal of dissolving the ego, assuming that this ego is the center of intentional consciousness.[7] He seeks the nonintentional counterpart to intentional freedom and epistemological success is a vague and empty, passive state. But instead of tranquility while adrift from the ego, Levinas's nonintentional subject experiences fear for what will happen to the generalized Other. Levinas's suggests that normal intentional consciousness is likely to be oblivious to this deeper reality, but it may be brought ("invited") to an awareness of it:

> The intentional consciousness of reflection, in taking as its object the transcendental ego, along with its mental acts and states, may also thematize and grasp supposedly implicit modes of nonintentional lived experience. It is invited to do this by philosophy in its fundamental project which consists in enlightening the inevitable transcendental naivety of a consciousness forgetful of its horizon, of its implicit content and even of the time it lives through.[8]

Levinas, in inviting normal intentional consciousness to attend to nonintentional consciousness, is proposing a radical shift from the tradition stemming from Husserl, which held that consciousness is always intentional and at the same time aware of itself as "intending" something other than itself.

Levinas's invitation can be read as a philosophical call to attend to a particular historical time, although he acknowledges that he has to show how implicit lived experience is a source of knowledge:

> Does the "knowledge" of pre-reflective self-consciousness really know? As a confused, implicit consciousness preceding all intentions—or as duration freed of all intentions—it is less an act than a pure passivity.[9]

As purely passive and without the ego implied by intentional consciousness, nonintentional consciousness is timid. It is *mauvaise conscience* on account of the Other's displacement and it must justify itself, its right to be:

> One has to respond to one's right to be, not by referring to some abstract and anonymous law, or judicial entity, but because of one's fear for the Other. My being-in-the-world or my "place in the sun", my being at home, have these not also been the usurpation of spaces belonging to the other man whom I have already oppressed or starved, or driven out into a third world; are they not acts of repulsing, excluding, exiling, stripping, killing? Pascal's "my place in the sun" marks the beginning of the image of the usurpation of the whole earth. A fear for all the violence and murder my existing might generate, in spite of its conscious and intentional innocence.[10]

There are leaps here. Levinas's analysis seems highly speculative. He is simply positing a fundamental reality that consciousness is obligated to experience, the face of the Other whom the ego has unjustly harmed. And he assumes a concern for, or possibly identification with, the Other, so that the ego takes harm of the other to heart.

The face of the Other, which is not an actual individual face, but the other side of an encounter or a response to my fear, provides the knowledge that belongs to unintentional consciousness. This fear for the Other arises before I am confronted with the face of the Other. Therefore, before I experience the face, I am already close to the other. Levinas is here describing an extraordinary experience of overcoming dissociation as a normal state. The Other must already be close to me for me to recognize that closeness, but I need to see the face of the Other in order to realize this fact. That we might normally harm the Other without realizing that the Other is close suggests that this closeness is more sameness or similarity than physical proximity. In other words, I harm the Other as though the Other is an object to my ego/subject, but when I let down my subject-object stance, I experience fear for the Other. Then I see the Other's face, and perhaps the fact that I now know the Other has a face is what tells me that the Other is like me, because I have a face. This is knowledge of the Other's vulnerability, for which I, as the ego, am responsible. I am responsible because of what I have done and will do to the Other. Thus, the meaning of this Other's "face" is that the Other is close to me:

> The proximity of the other is the face's meaning, and it means from the very start in a way that goes beyond those plastic forms which forever try to cover the face like a mask of their presence to perception. But always the face shows through these forms. Prior to any particular expression and beneath all particular expressions, which cover over and protect with an immediately adopted face or countenance, there is the nakedness and destitution of the expression as such, that is to say extreme exposure, defencelessness, vulnerability itself. This extreme exposure—prior to any human aim—is like a shot "at point blank range." Whatever has been invested is extradited, but it is a hunt that occurs prior to anything being actually tracked down and beaten out into the open. From the beginning there is a face to face steadfast in its exposure to invisible death, to a mysterious forsakenness. Beyond the visibility of whatever is unveiled, and prior to any knowledge about death, mortality lies in the Other. . . . True self-expression stresses the nakedness and defencelessness that encourages and directs the violence of the first crime: the goal of a murderous uprightness is especially well-suited to exposing or expressing the face.[11]

Violent action reveals the vulnerability of one who is close.

> The first murderer probably does not realize the result of the blow he is about to deliver, but his violent design helps him to find the line with which death may give an air of unimpeachable rectitude to the face of the neighbour; the line is traced like the trajectory of the blow that is dealt and the arrow that kills.[12]

Violent action has preceded both fear for the Other in the nonintentional state and the Other's face.

POLITICAL DIAGNOSES IN THE POST-WORLD WAR II ERA

The passive, nonintentional consciousness is aware of the dire future awaiting the Other. This self is responsible for the Other's death and its own right to be is thereby unjustified. I know about the Other's death before the Other knows.

> The other man's death calls me into question, as if, by my possible future indifference, I had become the accomplice of the death to which the other, who cannot see it, is exposed; and as if, even before vowing myself to him, I had to answer for this death of the other, and to accompany the Other in his mortal solitude. The Other becomes my neighbour precisely through the way the face summons me, calls for me, begs for me, and in so doing recalls my responsibility, and calls me into question.[13]

Finally, the result is that

> The right to be and the legitimacy of this right are not finally referred to the abstraction of the universal rules of the Law—but in the last resort are referred, like that law itself and justice—or for the other of my non-indifference, to death, to which the face of the Other—beyond my ending—in its very rectitude is exposed. Whether he regards me or not, he "regards" me. In this question being and life are awakened to the human dimension. This is the question of the meaning of being: not the ontology of the understanding of that extraordinary verb, but the ethics of its justice. The question par excellence or the question of philosophy. Not "Why being rather than nothing?", "but how being justifies itself."[14]

Levinas here deploys the experience, or idea of the experience, of non-intentional pre-reflective consciousness, as a bad conscience. Given what he has already said about murderous intent and violence, one can imagine a concentration camp official or administrator while off duty or at home from work, for whom a face of a murdered inmate intrudes into consciousness. Again, that the Other has a face means that the Other is like me, as opposed to a faceless object. This realization creates awareness of one's own injustice and with it the need to justify one's existence. The passiveness of this consciousness opens up awareness of itself as unjust. Fear *for* the Other signals that one is unjust.

It is not clear whether, or to what extent, Levinas intends this analysis to apply to all human beings when they let go of their intentionality, which is to say, their egos, or if he is performing a kind of thought experiment that is specifically about the minds of fascist killers and their enablers. If he is positing a structure of consciousness and existence, such that each of us implicitly knows that we usurp or murder the Other, he has not provided a sufficient range of human life and experience to support such universality. Does he mean that every one of us who is not a victim of oppression has a passive bad conscience and a felt need to justify their existence? Because he refers specifically to violence and historical horizons, it seems more likely that he is referring to the evil doers of his day and others like them. But that raises the question of whether those with mauvaise conscience are capable of having their desire for self-affirmation (i.e., justification of their right to be) questioned through realization of the vulnerability of their actual and potential victims. They may never put aside their intentional consciousness so as to enter the passive nonintentional state in the first place. Levinas posits ethical epiphany at the heart of awareness, but the problem with evil doers is precisely their lack of conscience.

Another omission on Levinas's part is the ability of evil doers to compartmentalize good and evil activities, so that they never have to explicitly confront a bad conscience as such but may instead relegate their evil actions to moral or practical necessity while converting their bad conscience "pangs" to physical symptoms. Jonathan Bennett, for instance, discusses Heinrich Himmler, head of the Nazi S.S., an architect of "the final solution," who was in charge of the entire concentration camp system. Bennett argues that Himmler viewed Nazism as a morally good imperative, quoting the following lines:

> I also want to talk to you quite frankly on a very grave matter . . . I mean . . . the extermination of the Jewish race. . . . Most of you must know what it means when 100 corpses are lying side by side, or 500, or 1,000. To have stuck it out and at the same time—apart from exceptions caused by human weakness—to have remained decent fellows, that is what has made us hard. This is a page of glory in our history which has never been written and is never to be written.[15]

According to Bennett, Himmler followed what he believed was a path to glory, at the expense of what would have been promptings from his bad conscience or by ignoring these promptings. Himmler apparently suffered from a variety of nervous and physical ailments, which his physician attributed to the contradictions he lived with.[16]

It may be that Levinas's imputation to evil actors of a passive state receptive to bad conscience is an attempt to humanize them. However, such humanization may not be just, and if it is just, how will it prevent further occurrences? Loopholes for escaping bad conscience may remain open for many: They could confess and refresh and go on with their same destructive intentionality. They may never relax in this way, which apparently Himmler never did. Or they may relax into the nonintentional state without experiencing the vulnerability of the Other as their responsibility; they may forego intentionality for a natural or chemically induced stupor that bypasses nonintentionality. Levinas has not established the inevitability of the nonintentional state of fear for the Other for those who are or will be guilty. Without such inevitability, there is nothing to prevent further harm and murder of the Other.

But perhaps prevention was not Levinas's priority. Perhaps he did not think future evils could be prevented, so that diagnosing and understanding was all that philosophers could do. There is nothing inherently wrong with such philosophical passivity—it could be a scholarly virtue—but in the years since Levinas thought, philosophy itself has become more activist, prompted not only by an urgency to understand its contemporary world but also by the need to say "what should be done." And, as we shall see with regard to Hannah Arendt, philosophers may give up philosophy in order to address political issues. However, in 1946, Jean-Paul Sartre in *Anti-Semite and Jew*, although more directly relevant to the Nazis of the Holocaust than Levinas (because he was explicitly writing about anti-Semites), neither addressed this subject of prescription directly nor went beyond an abstract diagnosis.

Sartre

In *Anti-Semite and Jew*, Sartre applies to anti-Semites his earlier analyses of consciousness as necessarily free and bad faith as a refusal to recognize and act upon such freedom in one's own case. Consciousness is a nothingness that "secretes" itself between any immediate moment of subjective human existence and everything else, including the subject's past external conditions and states of consciousness. Absolute responsibility for the creation of oneself as the person one is, and the impossibility of determinism, means that someone who treats their past as determining, or their present self as an object, is making a kind of category mistake, a metaphysical error that has the implications of *bad faith*. Because someone chooses this error, they are not innocent of its bad effects; indeed, some may will the bad effects. Sartre developed this theory of consciousness and freedom as the fulcrum for a worldview holding that human beings, in all of the senses that are socially and psychologically important, have no predetermined nature.[17]

> Man simply is. Not that he is simply what he conceives himself to be, but he is what he wills, and as he conceives himself after already existing—as he wills to be after that leap towards existence. Man is nothing else but that which he makes of himself. That is the first principle of existentialism.[18]

According to Sartre, the French anti-Semite falsely believes that he is imbued with certain qualities as the result of his ancestry on French soil. He lives as though these qualities pre-form him as a being who is inherently superior to those who lack them, especially Jews. That his material inheritance is also unearned only adds to the anti-Semite's self-esteem, through a magical form of belief:

> The true Frenchman, rooted in his province, in his country, borne along by a tradition twenty centuries old, benefiting from ancestral wisdom, guided by tried customs, does not *need* intelligence. His virtue depends upon the assimilation of the qualities which the work of a hundred generations has lent to the objects which surround him: it depends on property. It goes without saying that this is a matter of inherited property, not property one buys.[19] . . . To put it another way, the principle underlying anti-Semitism is that the concrete possession of a particular object gives as if by magic the meaning of the object.[20]

In considering the Jew, Sartre disavows belief in races in favor of shared situations. The itinerant condition of the Jew is a contrast to the Anti-Semite's illusion of rootedness. Finding little shared religion and history among Jews, he concludes that it is the designation "Jew" and acceptance by other Jews, which both unites Jews and constitutes their shared identity as Jews. "The Jew is in the situation of a Jew because he lives in the midst of a society that takes him for a Jew."[21] But there is an interesting asymmetry in Sartre's treatment of Jew and anti-Semite. The location of the French anti-Semite, as well as the object of his hatred, is contingent.[22] The object of hate could be other minorities and others can hate in the same way. The anti-Semite is thus something of a universal type. But for the Jew, Sartre expressly limits himself to the Jews in France, asserting enigmatically, "for it is the problem of the French Jew that is *our* problem."[23]

Writing in 1944, Sartre was aware of a silence about anti-Semitism and scant mention of the gas chambers of Lublin,[24] because French society was still generally anti-Semitic or reluctant to condemn anti-Semites. As a result, Jews themselves often chose to avoid special notice when they returned home as survivors from Lublin: "The less we are noticed the better."[25] Sartre's impression in this regard may have expressed a widespread opinion of Jewish thinkers that to be noticed by anti-Semites was dangerous. Twenty-five years after *Anti-Semite and Jew*, Karl Popper hesitated to accept an offer of assistance in obtaining a position at the University of Salzburg, disclosing in his 1969 letter to Friedrich Hayek that he did not want to appear to be requesting the position. Popper recognized that anti-Semitism in Austria was ongoing and his reason was a strategic assessment that it was better for Jews "to keep away, in order to allow the feeling to die down."[26]

On Sartre's account, the self-cyphering of Jews, combined with an identity caused by external views of them, would seem to hollow out Jewish subjectivity. And given Sartre's theory of consciousness as a nothingness, it deepens the question of why he did not view the Jews as a universal type, on his metaphysical level where absolute freedom was posited. Because the Jews lacked positive qualities based on continuous family histories in the same places, Sartre seems to have surmised they had no psychic traits apart from those projected onto them by anti-Semites. This would have made them ideal candidates for the good faith of recognizing their own freedom.

However, despite this imputed emptiness, isolation, and/or anonymity, Sartre has no qualms about applying his notion of bad faith to [French?] Jews. He reasoned that because Jews have historically been confined to or chosen certain service occupations and professions in which they deal with the public, their identity is inseparable from their interactions in society and reputation is of the greatest importance to them. But all of their occupations and achievements are contaminated by negative stereotypes about them and real French culture is held off-limits from them. For example, they might buy land, but there is no way that they can create a history of their ancestors' relations with the ancestors of their neighbors.[27] Nevertheless, Sartre insists that, like members of other groups, Jews are obligated to be authentic, which means that they cannot deny or try to escape from their condition of being Jews. Running away, denying their individual responsibility for their circumstances, or retreating into isolation only gives rise to or reinforces stereotypes held by anti-Semites. And this situation in turn results in extreme reflection, anxiety, and "over-determination from the inside," as well as masochism, all of which strengthens those stereotypes.[28] For Sartre, the situational aspects of good faith require recognition of one's circumstances, so it seems that all he had to say about "authentic" Jews was that they would acknowledge the anti-Semitic barriers to their assimilation:

> Thus the authentic Jew who thinks of himself as a Jew because the anti-Semite has put him in the situation of a Jew is not opposed to assimilation any more than the class-conscious worker is opposed to the liquidation of classes.... The authentic Jew simply renounces for himself an assimilation that is today impossible; he awaits the radical liquidation of anti-Semitism for his sons.[29]

In *Anti-Semite and Jew*, Sartre does fill a gap left by Levinas, through his focus on the victims of political evil. But his analysis of the consciousness of French Jews is profoundly unsatisfactory. He first argues that their identity is ascribed, a result of hatred and discrimination. Then he assumes that because this identity is ascribed, there are no positive Jewish traits apart from anti-Semitic stereotypes. In other words, the ascribed identity of Jews is presented by Sartre as their only identity.

The ascribed nature of subaltern identities is not limited to Jews. African Americans, for instance, have always had ascribed identities of race that were invented by their oppressors. But this has not meant that they lack shared histories or distinctive cultures, much less common aspirations or rich subjectivities, despite their racial identity formation that has been at least in part reactions to external oppression. Still, something like the resignation Sartre assigns to Jews was evident in

Frantz Fanon's claim that "Negroes" had no "ontological resistance" to how whites saw them:

> The black man has no ontological resistance in the eyes of the white man. From one day to the next, the Blacks have had to deal with two systems of reference. Their metaphysics, or less pretentiously their customs and the agencies to which they refer, were abolished because they were in contradiction with a new civilization that imposed its own.[30]

There is a parallel here to the situation of Jews. Blacks have been denied their cultures, while Jews are denied what would be their cultures. But, unlike Sartre, Fanon was willing to stop short of a metaphysics of the black situation and describe it ("less pretentiously") as the loss of custom and agency.

Overall, the metaphysical error of bad faith by anti-Semites is easier to digest than the bad faith raised as a likely path for French Jews. This may be because despite his denial of engagement in an ethical project, Sartre's notion of bad faith has bad moral connotations. When we attribute bad faith to those oppressed, it may seem as though we are judging them to be morally bad. It is as though Sartre believed that anti-Semitism and the Nazi Holocaust really did succeed in its genocidal aims, which he interprets as psychic as well as physical. In Sartre's analysis of Jews, there are no recognized possibilities for taking up the freedom of consciousness and therefore, no real resources for resistance in the here and now, but only hope for future generations "after the revolution."

Perhaps Sartre simply could not imagine the subjectivity of French Jews in any positive way, because he did not know enough about it. The situation was different for Hannah Arendt, who as a Jew directly experienced the rise of Nazism during the 1930s and was profoundly shocked by the indisputable revelation of the concentration camps in 1943.

Arendt

Arendt is very well known for her historical analysis of the conditions enabling the Third Reich in her *The Origins of Totalitarianism*.[31] But it is in her particular experience and analysis of the Eichmann trial that a focus on the Jewish victims of the Holocaust might be sought. Arendt was galvanized by the burning of the Reichstag in 1933 and although she was not a Zionist, she helped Zionists put together a list of anti-Semitic statements in ordinary professional and social life at that time. She was found out and arrested by the S.S. Her arresting officer, who remained in charge during her confinement, was a former policeman who advised her and enabled her to get out after eight days. She then emigrated and later on considered her own experiences with the Nazis as something of an adventure.[32] At the time, Arendt noticed the "coordination" of intellectuals she knew, who managed to rearrange their lives and opinions in accord with Nazism. While she cut these people off, she was more disappointed than angry. Nor did Arendt condemn those intellectuals, presumably philosophers such as her professor, Martin Heidegger (with whom she had fallen in love at the age of nineteen[33]), who became Nazis.[34] She attributed their involvement with Nazism as a kind of entrapment by their own silly ideas and what they fabricated about Hitler.[35]

Arendt was also somewhat cavalier about her account of Eichmann as stupid and banal instead of evil. While she denied blaming Jewish organizations for the Holocaust, claiming it was the prosecutor of the Eichmann trial who voiced that sentiment, she did admit to an ironic tone in her famously controversial account of the Eichmann trial.[36] Nevertheless, despite such disengagements, Arendt did take up her Jewish identity for a serious pronouncement against Nazi murderers, which was evident in her comment referring to what one of the Eichmann trial judges, quoting Grotius, had said:

> He said that it is part of the honor and dignity of the person harmed or wounded that the perpetrator be punished. This has nothing to do with the suffering endured, it has nothing to do with putting something right. It's really a question of honor and dignity. Look, for us Jews, it's a crucial question when we're in Germany. If the German people think they can carry on living quite undisturbed with the murderers in their midst, this goes against the honor and dignity of the Jewish person.[37]

Here, Arendt makes a practical claim, which, while it might valorize revenge, seems to go beyond that into the subjectivity of Jews after the Holocaust. And we do have a focus on the victims, which for Arendt may have been possible, because she had early in life rejected philosophy as a vocation, in favor of political theory. She said:

> There is a vital tension between philosophy and politics. That is between man as a thinking being and man as an acting being, there is a tension that does not exist in natural philosophy, for example. Like everyone else, the philosopher can be objective with regard to nature, and when he says what he thinks about it he speaks in the name of all mankind. But he cannot be objective or neutral with regard to politics. Not since Plato![38]

Arendt's idealization and valorization of philosophy as universal can be read in contrast to Sartre's willingness to philosophically analyze political types. She knew more about the experience of Jews than Sartre, but set that apart from philosophy.

One wonders how Arendt and Sartre might have conversed. Before the war, and later on throughout her academic career in the United States, Arendt was a successful assimilated Jew, with a genuine subjectivity and intellectual life. So Arendt's existential example would have negated substantial claims in *Anti-Semite and Jew*. Arendt's insistence that philosophy attend to universals, exclusively, might have been tempered by the universal existential structures posited by Sartre and other points of comparison pertaining to the distance of philosophy from life. Sartre did not hesitate to delve into both Marxist theory and contemporary politics in his later years, and it is not clear that he believed he was taking on these projects through an alienation from philosophy. We can say now that it is possible for philosophers to philosophize the unphilosophical. Of course, there is no reason to expect that such projects would have occurred to Arendt under that description and she may have strongly resisted it, out of deference for philosophy. Arendt also had a traditional deference for men, saying, "It is entirely possible that a woman will one day be a philosopher."[39] This traditional gender exclusion was buttressed by her support of traditional female roles:[40]

> I have always thought that there are certain occupations that are improper for women, that do not become them, if I may put it that way. It just doesn't look good when a woman gives orders. She should try not to get into such a situation if she wants to remain feminine.[41]

Yet, just as some political philosophers have claimed Hannah Arendt, so have some feminist philosophers.[42]

Historically, from a progressive perspective, it would be anachronistic to criticize Arendt's neglect of feminism as a practical subject in political theory. During the World War II era, it was not only women who had not yet been theorized in ways that could ground mass liberation. The Nazis murdered at least 11 million people, of which 6 million were Jews. Additional groups included ethnic Poles, Soviet citizens and prisoners of war, the Roma, the "incurably sick," political and religious dissidents, and gay men;[43] there was no widespread genocide against blacks, although they were killed, imprisoned, and sterilized.[44] All of these groups, and many others, only came to mass enlightened public consciousness and special scholarly awareness after World War II. The United Nations Universal Declaration of Human Rights (UDHR) was an historical turning point. Before that document, lip service was paid to universal human rights and dignity, but no great thinker made a point of it or accepted it as an axiomatic principle of justice until after World War II and the UDHR, when it was then just quietly assumed.

The history of philosophy itself is a long story of proclamations of rights, dignity, and happiness for "all"—usually phrased as "all men"—where "all" meant the privileged group that the philosopher in question represented. However, the history of the UN has proved that even the UDHR was not sufficient to bring the claim of universality home.[45] Since its inception in 1948, the UN has had to proclaim the rights of scores of specific groups to get humanitarian attention paid to them, even though their rights are logically implied by its own inaugural UDHR.[46] (That is, if all have rights, then so do, or should, women, children, Roma, people with disabilities, racial and ethnic minorities, and so forth.)

Returning now more specifically to Arendt, what can we make of her claim in the epigraph to this chapter that Nazism could happen again? Does this mean there is a substantial, practical probability that it will happen again? It does if she was not voicing a mere logical possibility, which her abandonment of philosophy, as a discipline removed from real life, would suggest. Does this mean that people who are members of groups likely to form the constituencies of new Third Reichs, as well as their victims, should just resign themselves to inevitable political evil, so long as it is not immediate? (Although once it were immediate, it would probably be too late to effectively resist it.)

This problem exceeds tyranny. There could be a benevolent or good-enough tyrannical system. If we are helpless to change the present system, then that system is already a form of tyranny. The problem is bad government that entraps its citizens and residents, with the power and will to destroy some of them. There are two options or stages in response to such bad government: How can it be prevented? How can it be abolished once in effect?

IDENTITY POLITICS

The neglect of the subjectivity of victims in the analyses of Levinas and Sartre considered above, and Arendt's apparent equanimity in the face of the "it could happen again" assessment of the Third Reich, can be viewed as part of the intellectual void that was filled by identity politics. This neglect also establishes the intellectual and cultural necessity for identity politics. Identity politics has been disparate projects to include diverse groups in exactly that human rights and dignity universality that the United Nations proclaimed. But I will argue in the remaining chapters of this book against the entry of identity politics into government—because subaltern identities will face too much backlash and dominant identities will use government power to crush subaltern identities, resulting in governmental instability, gridlock when two identitarian parties make up government, and dysfunction concerning the primary obligation of government to benefit all of those governed. But here I want to emphasize the importance of identity politics in society, short of government, with influence over government. Indeed, identity politics flourished in democratic societies, especially within the academy and in government, with the passage of the civil rights legislation of the 1960s. This was followed by feminism, mainly in the academy, and calls for immigration reform through activism, as well as Native American and disability rights advocacy. The Occupy movement touched off a national conversation about income inequality, although it remains to be seen whether poverty can ground an effective identity. As a critique of identity politics, my intention in this book is to limit the governmental political power of identity politics, but that does not affect its social or societal power.

After World War II, the lack of "what is to be done" discourse and neglect of consideration of victims constituted a stasis with two ways to move forward. The first path involved identity politics' valorization of subalterns, and I will be rejecting that as a part or parts of government. The second path, which is now an exit from identity politics, in terms of the intellectual progress or history of progressivism, leads to evidence-based government for anonymous subjects. Within the diagnostic projects in the aftermath of World War II, Karl Popper's political philosophy provided groundwork for attention to evidence-based government that is relevant to present times.

Popper

Popper's political philosophy had the same general structure as his philosophy of science. Both subverted traditional views of progress. In philosophy of science, he rejected prevailing empirical standards that scientific theories could be derived from factual evidence and that factual evidence could confirm theories. Instead, according to Popper, the hallmark of a scientific theory, what made it science in contrast to pseudoscience or ideology, was its *ability to be falsified*. Marxism, the prevailing progressive theory of his day, could not be falsified. Marxists were not prepared to describe evidence that would motivate them to abandon their theories. Marxism was therefore not a science. Science, for Popper, consisted of theories and hypotheses that could predict or explain evidence in ways that would motivate the retention or rejection of those theories and hypotheses. Evidence for theories could never confirm them to the point of truth but merely *corroborate* them if they could be falsified and had over time withstood various tests of falsification.[47]

In his approach to government, Popper had pragmatic, humanitarian goals, claiming that "human misery is the most urgent problem of a rational public policy," but he approached the topic of government indirectly, as a cognitive matter, through a focus on the methodology for developing political theory.[48] Popper assumed that his task as political theorist was to provide standards for the right ideas that would lead to the formation or correction of government, which in turn seems to have been based on the deeper assumption that the correct ideas had direct causal power for setting up or changing government. That he had World War II in mind is evident in the dedication of his *The Poverty of Historicism* that was first developed in 1919–1920 and published in book form in 1957:

> In memory of the countless men, women and children of all creeds or nations or races who fell victims to the fascist and communist belief in Inexorable Laws of Historical Destiny.[49]

Popper critiqued what he called "historicism," mainly Marxism, on two grounds: its holistic view of society and claims that political and historical predictions were possible. For Popper, society had no existence as a whole and historical prediction was impossible because the cause of any state of civilization was its collective knowledge and a future condition of knowledge could not be predicted from within any present knowledge framework.[50] It is highly debatable that the cause of a state of civilization is its *collective* knowledge, because what counts as knowledge has a large range from what is known by experts in the sciences to what is known by uneducated or ignorant people. Popper's idealism on this point further assumes that "collective knowledge" will be acted upon in ways that shape a state of civilization. If collective knowledge means the best approximation to truth, analyzed according to good moral principles of government, there is no guarantee that it will prevail under any form of government. But if collective knowledge means a combination of the best approximation to truth and ignorance, plus self-service, then Popper was correct. (The political struggle over response to COVID-19 over the early months of 2020 was a prime example of that concept.)

Popper's criticism of Marxism is part of the diagnosis of oppression discussed earlier. However, Popper did more than diagnose oppression—he had a positive empirical account of democratic government, which can set the stage for evidence-based government, as will be discussed in chapters 5 and 6. But before moving on from this chapter, the diagnostic focus on oppressors that followed World War II, while incomplete in light of identity politics, remains relevant for considering oppression within democratic societies. The oppression considered by progressives after World War II was state oppression under a totalitarian government. Within democratic societies, while there might not be explicit state oppression of citizens, social systems such as male dominance, white supremacy, and ableism are oppressive to members of the groups active in identity politics. Oppression in such systems does require diagnosis, which may require nuanced distinctions between those who explicitly express oppressive intent and those, the majority, who have not been sufficiently motivated to oppose them. It is also important that civil society remain civil and respectful through disagreement from the two sides of explicit and implicit oppressors and the oppressed and their advocates. I will take up the distinction between explicit and implicit oppression in terms of white supremacy in chapter 4. Before then, having given identity politics its due in terms of what is historically and theoretically required, chapter 2 will provide a critique of the ideas of social groups and identities, which theoretically underlie identity politics, and chapter 3 will provide a positive account of universalism.

2

FROM SOCIETY TO GOVERNMENT: PROBLEMS WITH IDENTITY POLITICS

> We the People of the United States, in Order to form a more perfect Union, establish Justice, insure domestic Tranquility, provide for the common defence, promote the general Welfare, and secure the Blessings of Liberty to ourselves and our Posterity, do ordain and establish this Constitution for the United States of America.
>
> —Preamble, Constitution of the United States
>
> Identity politics is when people of a particular race, ethnicity, gender, or religion form alliances and organize politically to defend their group's interests. . . . So long as some people are marginalized, victimized, or oppressed because of their identities, we will need identity politics.
>
> —Laura Maguire, "Identity Politics," Philosophy Talk, July 14, 2016[1]

Many progressive theorists focus on those who are unjustly treated and share identities, as political groups or potential political groups. These groups are socially recognized, posited, or imagined as identity groups. Often, there seems to be a seamless theoretical progression from identities, to identity groups, to group rights. As imagined and named, members of an identity group need not be fully complex and real individuals, but are rather abstractions, often posited without regard to differences among them. To some extent, this is the old problem of abstract general terms insofar as any person designated by only their identity group name has had a label ascribed to them, not an accurate description. And if we start with an abstract term (e.g., black person), no such person exists who is only and fully that. We should therefore call the members of identity groups thus posited or imagined "entities." If an entity has a right, then others are obligated not to act in certain ways toward that entity or obligated to provide certain resources to that entity.[2] Not everything posited can or should be a factor in government, so we need to carefully examine whether identity groups are or should be political in that governmental sense, as so many now assume. The method of this chapter is to interrogate the notion of identity, since identities would be the anchor for political group rights recognized by government. That is, to speak of group rights is to assume that groups should be political entities directly connected to government. This assumption bypasses argument for the political nature of identities and that they are best viewed in units of groups. Like individuals with identities, groups made up of individuals also have dubious concrete existence as "entities." But, like everyone else, I will still talk about identities and groups as real things, because their abstract status is not the main problem addressed here. The chapter begins with clarifications of key concepts and their historical backgrounds, followed by discussions of problems with identities for identity politics and problems with identity groups and group rights. A shift from identity groups to their interests is then proposed, and there is a final note on reparations.

KEY CONCEPTS AND THEIR HISTORY

In the preamble to the United States Constitution, "The People" are proclaimed as the authority for the founding document. But who were they? Were the people all citizens or residents, taken severally as individuals, or the whole group of citizens or residents? We know that women, slaves, indentured servants, indigenous people, and the poor were not considered stakeholders for the formation of the US government, so these questions would apply only to the white male property owners who were stakeholders. Nonstakeholders who had no say in founding government could not serve within government. It is progressive, but anachronistic, to point out such inequalities in colonial times. Today, objections about the exclusion from government of contemporary identity groups can be made without anachronism, given their present legal or formal equality. Yet, even today, because identity groups do not have access to government as groups, they are not (yet) political groups. Still, from a social standpoint, within society, outside of government, we can ask who they are and whether the groups themselves should be taken severally, as individuals, or collectively, as groups that have identities that transcend their membership.

The contemporary counterparts of those excluded from founding or serving within government are members of "The People," outside of government, in society. Some of the people are dominant over others and hierarchical differences in status, wealth, and power all tend to be translated into who is elected or appointed and who benefits from government policy. In a society dominated by whites, the rich, and men, even a democratic government is likely to be populated disproportionately by white, rich, male officials, who tend to be most attentive to those who share their demographics. Political candidates devise messages for target populations who they think will vote for them and members of those target groups also share their demographics, usually gender and race.[3] The nonmale, poor, and nonwhite part of the people is not as numerous within government, and candidates from these populations need to garner support from potential voters who do not share their gender, race, or economic disadvantages. Their campaign financing is often very difficult, especially when black female candidates seek contributions from large donors.[4]

Nevertheless, at this time, some elected officials are women or people of color and those who share their demographics can say that an official or candidate "looks like me." Such diverse "optics" may reassure the people that government access is fair and it may be necessary for government access to be fair. But many now talk as though optical diversity of race, ethnicity, and gender within government—that is, a "looks like me" factor—is sufficient to solve pressing social problems. However, apparent or even real diversity in access to government service is only one aspect of the democratic nature of government. Another aspect requires that officials have the skills and commitment to carry on the normal functioning of government and inclusively address the problems in society that it is the job of government to address, which is an aspect of public service. Democratic government also requires adherence to democratic procedures and legal structures—it is commonly called "government by laws," in contrast to "government by men." (This tradition dates back to King John's signing of the Magna Carta in 1215 and before then jurisprudence in Ancient Rome.[5])

Proponents of identity politics often fail to pay enough attention to what should happen after members of identity groups in society are elected or appointed to government positions. They want to ensure both diversity in representation within government and better response from government to the needs and demands of identity groups in society, as described by members of the groups. But, although identity politics is intended by its proponents to be politically progressive, consideration of the nature of government as inclusive and beneficial, is often lacking. In other words, identity politics is at this time under-theorized as a form of politics—if it is, or can, or should be, a form of politics in ways directly pertaining to government. Part of the reason more analysis is needed is that given the coercive power of government—that is, its ultimate support through legitimate force—government is not merely one factor among many *within* society. Government stands *apart* from society because of its force. For that reason, it should be contextualized as an institution that will benefit all of those governed and solve problems that entities and organizations within society cannot solve as efficiently, or at all, without government.

As noted, the US Constitution was authored by persons outside of government, because the government did not yet exist. But even after a government is founded, "The People" can be imagined as retaining the power they have, apart from government. The modern social contract tradition about the separation of government from society dates back to Thomas Hobbes and John Locke. Hobbes is explicit that the social contract is an agreement among the people to transfer their rights to a ruler.[6] Locke, the founder of American social contract theory, did not use the term "social contract" but relied on the concept of a social compact (which I will soon explain). Historian Mark Hulliung writes:

> Locke explicitly disallowed the notion of a contract between government and people. The sovereign people owe nothing to the rulers; the rulers owe everything to the governed. . . . There is a social contract by which the people bind themselves to one another, but no subsequent political contract. The rulers hold power temporarily, as mere "trustees" of the people. A second contract [between the people and the government] must be disallowed on the grounds that it contradicts the sovereignty of the people. What the people give they

can take away whenever they please, because they are bound by no contract between governors and governed.

However, even Locke was not overly concerned with such abstract rights. Locke's chief purpose of government was the protection of private property: "So the great and chief purpose of men's uniting into commonwealths and putting themselves under government is the preservation of their property."[7]

In the United States since the Civil War, the relation between government and governed is referred to as "the social contract," taken to be an implicit agreement between citizens and government. For examples: After the inadequate government response to Hurricane Katrina, in 2005, the social contract was invoked as a basis for criticism;[8] Bill Clinton and Newt Gingrich presented Locke's social contract as a contract between the people and their government.[9] The social contract has also been expressed as economic expectations that citizens have about their employment opportunities, job security, and purchasing power.[10] Federal government assistance to those unemployed and furloughed as a result of social distancing measures to curtail COVID-19 contagion implicitly draw on a social contract idea that the government is obligated to benefit those governed (in this case, help sustain their lives). These formulations are present in neither Hobbes's nor Locke's political philosophy, but they reflect widespread beliefs about the obligations of government.

The basic idea of social contract theory is that government is a utility that benefits those governed—their lives are better with it than without it, so they choose it or consent to it. But that does not address an important aspect of the origin of government. The origin of any government in the so-called social contract tradition is its creation and consent by those governed—hence, the "We the People" authorship of the US Constitution. When failures of government are protested, mention of these conditions of its origin are rare, because the US Constitution is accepted as the origin of the US government. But the conditions of government origin are important, because they do not dissolve after government is founded, and can be invoked among the people.

The conditions of the origin of government involve a *social compact*, which is an agreement among those governed, who retain ultimate political power and authority, even after government is formed. It is this power that enables the people to demand changes in government that extend civil liberties to minority and marginal groups, to call for popular support of a "Green New Deal," or to demand economic justice. Basic rights may be stated as universal in the US Constitution, but if the US government does not specify that they be applied universally, especially if the US Supreme Court does not rule for their enforcement for disadvantaged identity groups, then the people, as an ongoing highest political authority, retain the power to make further demands of government. Such demands take a variety of forms: protests and demonstrations, petitions, attempts to get new constitutional amendments, and voting. Changes within government may also sometimes implicitly invoke the social compact, although it is against political norms for government officials who are bound by the US Constitution to engage in actions on the premise that they are carrying out the will of the people for an unconstitutional policy.

The idea of the social compact comes down to us only implicitly and inchoately, but it is evident whenever the people exercise their First Amendment right to criticize existing government. There is nothing in social compact theory that either precludes the existence of identity groups or claims that they be recognized by government. However, incoherence in the ideas of identities and political identity groups are cause for concern about their recognition by government or inclusion within government.

PROBLEMS WITH IDENTITIES FOR IDENTITY POLITICS

The ambiguities of identity and identification concern the natures of individuals' relationships to groups and the illusion of identification with group leaders. The social idea of identity politics is that members of identity groups are or should authentically *be* something. Contemporary ideas of group authenticity are often traced to Johann Gottfried Herder (1744–1803), who founded many aspects of modern linguistics (as well as cultural anthropology).[11] The tradition Herder founded incorporates culture into national identity and posits identity as both a matter of individual fulfillment and identification as a member of one's group.[12]

Charles Taylor has been an influential advocate for inherent authenticity in this sense—individuals can seek and find the reality of their specific identities. In his 1991 *The Ethics of Authenticity*, Taylor focuses on individualism, instrumental reasoning via technology, and overhanging bureaucracy as "malaises" of our modern age.[13] He examines the connection between individualism and relativism in salutary terms: "The moral ideal behind self-fulfilment is that of being true to oneself, in a specifically modern understanding of that term."[14] According to Taylor, self-fulfillment is a moral ideal, achieved through (and culminating in) *authenticity*. Authenticity is a moral project, so that we can ask, "What are the conditions in human life of realizing an ideal of this kind? And what does the ideal properly understood call for?"[15]

Theo de Wit observes that Taylor draws on Herder to develop his idea that particular identities can be based on group membership, as well as individual striving.[16] As Janne Mende emphasizes, for Taylor, the locus of group identity is shared language and from that expressive and constitutive starting point, group rights are posited for a given linguistic community. The individual demands recognition as a unique individual, but also as a member of a group. And something analogous holds for identity groups, in that they are equal to other groups but also different from them.

Taylor's emphasis on the relation of language to identity is an important abstract insight about language in general. But people express and make their realities using specific languages (e.g., French, German, Spanish, Swahili), and it is those languages that are often imagined to characterize identity groups. As a locus of group identity, any specific language is problematic for diasporic groups (for example, Mexican Americans who do not speak Spanish or bilingual Chinese Americans). These exceptions may obstruct unified political action for the posited identity group, because the group worthy of recognition ought to be inclusive. But such exceptions divide or destabilize group membership, as well as create obstacles to communication and understanding.

Continuing with Taylor, the relationship between the individual as a member of a group and authenticity is developmental or dialogic. The achievement of authenticity requires dialogue with significant others. Beyond that, recognition of the dignity of one's identity, especially from members of dominant groups who deny recognition, is required.[17] Taylor wrote, "Not only contemporary feminism but also race relations and discussions of multiculturalism are under girded by the premise that denied recognition can be a form of oppression."[18]

Thus, a widely accepted theoretical foundation of identity politics in our time is that individuals yearn and strive for authenticity, in dialogue with others. The results are identities related to group membership and a felt need for dignity and recognition for that group connection. Yet, although authenticity and recognition sound like worthy expectations or goals, some may not be able to achieve secure group membership and this condition may become part of their identities. For instance, people with mixed-race parentage may not have stable identity group membership, and that instability may be claimed as a right.[19] Transsexual people may choose to belong to the identity group of their gender, but members of their birth group and others in a binary system may require them to identify as a member of their birth gender group.[20] (For example, a male-to-female trans person may be categorized as male by cis men and women and pointedly rejected as female by cis females.) Groups may also express or claim to express a collective will about who can become members of them. For example, at the turn of the twentieth century, white Americans were fearful of and indignant about black people joining them if their appearance allowed them to pass for white. And in the early twenty-first century, black Americans have expressed fear and indignation when white people identify as black.[21] Social politics within Native America has also been rife with intense questions about who is or can be Indian.[22]

Authenticity in a general sense turns on the tension between identities that are culturally constructed to serve oppressors (by means of false generalizations and distorting stereotypes) and identities based on free or core selves.[23] For instance, Nigrescence theory was a psychological model of black identity development that was widely influential toward the end of the 1960s Black Power movement. In 1971, William E. Cross Jr. posited stages of black identity development, which prescribed withdrawal from the white world and its devaluation, toward internal grounding for self-esteem after saturation by the black world. Cross's main goal was to incorporate distinctively African American psychological processes into mainstream clinical psychology.[24]

Cross's models were broadly considered and have progressed through quantitative scalar dimensions and revisions.[25] The fundamental premise of Nigrescence theory is that white antiblack racism is a homogeneous absolute to which black people must adjust by creating racially self-centered identities. This premise does not allow for the active, ongoing psychological resistance to antiblack white racism in progressive thought and action. To make adjusting to such racism an important individual project may be a path to one kind of constructed authenticity, but it comes with pessimism and resignation (as well as overgeneralizations about whites). Moreover, because racial identities may have no foundation apart from racism and its histories, self-esteem created through Nigrescence stages may reinscribe or posit false biological ideas of racial difference. It is questionable whether self-esteem based on false ideas is valid self-esteem. This is not a matter of intellectual validity alone, because false ideas of race accompanied by insult or assault usually or often mask motives that have nothing to do with race. Incorporating such false ideas into one's sense of self may create a blindness for identifying the masked motives in social reality. That is, when racism is an excuse or justification for material exploitation and the real motives are acquisition or greed (for example), persons adjusted to racism may fail to recognize other injustices against them if they succeed in adjusting to stereotypes by moving through the stages proposed by Nigrescence theory.

The search for identity may also take the form of emulation or imitation of group leaders or same-group celebrities, through the inspirational example of their success. But fans or followers may not have the talents and resources to fulfill such aspirations. In other words, a search for identity or authenticity can lead a person outside of their self, away from the resources they already do have, which paradoxically results in inauthenticity or failure. The popularity of celebrities themselves seems unlimited in the second decade of the twenty-first century. Emulating those who are famous for the reason that they are famous seems to be an illusory foundation for authenticity. Not everyone can be famous, to begin with, and fame based on fame may do no more than mirror flimsy reasons for fame in the first place.

Recognition of an individual as a member of a group requires recognition of the group. Frantz Fanon, in *Les damnés de la terre*, claimed that for the colonized or former colonized, recognition is a primary need, even worth dying for.[26] But Fanon was also deeply skeptical that real recognition could be achieved, because of the false view dominant groups have of subordinate groups, which they project onto them in almost all interactions.²⁷ A more abstract tension between oppressive individual identities and ideas of equality promulgated by white elites was evident in Fanon's quarrel with Jean-Paul Sartre. Fanon rejected Sartre's assumption that Africans would ideally and eventually shed their African identities in favor of universal human identification in Marxist and existentialist terms.

To require that identity groups be both the same as and different from dominant groups—albeit in different respects—does create an obligation to describe or define universal humanity. This may not be impossible, or even difficult to do, but it requires a theoretical and perhaps even utopian description of humanity as an ideal. If members of dominant groups are unwilling or unable to undertake this project, it then falls to members of subordinate groups to do the work. Many have been doing exactly that for a very long time. But how can these members of subordinate groups rely on dominant group agreement with their descriptions or definitions of common humanity? Fanon wrote of reaching for the universal:

> One can understand why Sartre views the adoption of a Marxist position by black poets as the logical conclusion of Negrohood. In effect, what happens is this: As I begin to recognize that the Negro is the symbol of sin, I catch myself hating the Negro. But then I recognize that I am a Negro. There are two ways out of this conflict. Either I ask others to pay no attention to my skin, or else I want them to be aware of it. I try then to find value for what is bad—since I have unthinkingly conceded that the black man is the color of evil. In order to terminate this neurotic situation, in which I am compelled to choose an unhealthy, conflictual solution, fed on fantasies, hostile, inhuman in short, I have only one solution: to rise above this absurd drama that others have staged round me, to reject the two terms that are equally unacceptable, and, through one human being, to reach out for the universal.²⁸

There is a precipice here. In protesting and resisting an identity imposed by colonizers, while at the same time refusing to identify with the former colonizers, a subject might fall into an emptiness of having no identity. The problem is that the former colonizers also have identities and their identities are presumed repugnant to the former colonized. Black Americans may demand the same recognition as human accorded

FROM SOCIETY TO GOVERNMENT

to white Americans, but that does not mean they want other aspects of white identities, particularly not a tolerance of white supremacy or racial privilege in comparison to other identities. Many explicitly or implicitly racist whites may be unaware of their humanity as distinct from their taking the advantages of being racially white for granted, or more offensively positing or being complicit with posits of white superiority. Their humanity would need to be constructed or reconstructed, before a trans-racial humanity could be posited. But Fanon immediately makes it clear that he is seeking the universal as a Negro:

> Today let us hail the turn of history that will make it possible for the black men to utter "the great Negro cry with a force that will shake the pillars of the world" . . . And so it is not I who make a meaning for myself, but it is the meaning that was already there, pre-existing, waiting for me.[29]

Logically, this point takes Fanon full circle, because he did not say what a universal Negro identity would be.

To sum up the problems with authenticity and recognition, the ambiguity of group membership, and thereby group identity, is a challenge for the development of individual authenticity. The lack of recognition of identity groups from more dominant groups means that recognition may be impossible to achieve at different times. In addition to these problems, there are ambiguities about identity on individual psychological levels, involving aspirations and the nature of the self who identifies with others. As a practical matter, an attempt to identify with universal humanity by members of subordinate identity groups may be rejected by dominant groups, who need to reconstruct their own humanity. Indeed, the idea of recognition seems to rely on the imagination of theorists, which can be quite unbounded. Francis Fukuyama, who approaches these issues with an historical sweep—in contrast to Taylor's social-political approach and Fanon's existentialism—posits the lack of recognition as motivation for both individual and group protest, all the way to international aggression and war. He writes:

> Russian president Vladimir Putin has talked about the tragedy of the collapse of the former Soviet Union, and how Europe and the United States had taken advantage of Russia's weakness during the 1990s to drive NATO up to its borders. He despises the attitude of moral

superiority of Western politicians and wants to see Russia treated not, as President Obama once said, as a weak regional player, but as a great power. Viktor Orbán, the Hungarian prime minister, stated in 2017 that his return to power in 2010 marked the point when "we Hungarians also decided that we wanted to regain our country, we wanted to regain our self-esteem, and we wanted to regain our future." The Chinese government of Xi Jinping has talked at length about China's "one hundred years of humiliation," and how the United States, Japan, and other countries were trying to prevent its return to the great power status it had enjoyed through the past millennia of history.[30]

Also, Fukuyama refers to Jean-Jacques Rousseau's idea that society, as the mass of rules and customs external to the individual, blocks the fulfillment of individual potential and happiness. Fukuyama then claims that such restriction "is evident in the complaints of a Vladimir Putin who feels the American-led international order wrongly disrespects Russia, and who then seeks to overturn it."[31]

Fukuyama takes a lot of theoretical license in deploying his notion of a politics of resentment. His justification for projecting individual psychological motives onto world events and the motives of world leaders is not evident. We do not know what Putin, the man, feels. Insofar as recognition and its lack now has wide coinage, it should be assumed that a wily ruler's appeal to the lack of recognition of his country is a rhetorical device to justify aggressive policies that are simply grabs for more power. That is, Fukuyama is simply assuming that the rhetoric of Putin, Orbán, and Xi expresses what they themselves believe when it is likely carefully crafted propaganda.

PROBLEMS WITH IDENTITY GROUPS AND GROUP RIGHTS

Identity groups have labels or identities and it is assumed that their interests remain unfulfilled because they conflict with the interests of dominant groups or because members of dominant groups are biased against them and won't even consider their interests. Public expression can direct attention toward groups, so that demonstration becomes a dimension of identity. But such recognition through media coverage may take the place of effective formulation of the group's interest. For instance, the Women's March in Washington, DC, after the 2017 presidential inauguration, #Black Lives Matter after Michael Brown's killing, Occupy Wall Street, and the encampments at Standing Rock were ephemeral and merely expressive, insofar as no coherent political changes ensued from them. This is not to say that they were without indirect influence and inspiration, and we should not overlook the value of gratification during collective expressive action. But if demonstration is considered political action when it is not so in practical terms, the question arises of how energies expended may have been better directed and whether the freedom allowed for such expression is sometimes no more than a safety valve to expel discontent (into the ethers of the internet). If recognition is intrinsically valuable, such displays are immediately successful. But if recognition is instrumental, they are ineffective.

Recognition of mass expression is part of a progression of events that can culminate in political change, but this is always after the fact, in hindsight. Not all movements or expressions do result in progressive change. It cannot be predicted which are likely to be successful, insofar as their path to real government is vague.

Individual identities pertain to who or what people in a certain category *are* and in that sense they require an imagined essentialism that need not be related to human needs that government can and should fulfill. When people think that they *are* something that importantly defines them, everything about that trait or essence becomes important and fraught if they also believe they are treated unjustly on the basis of it. Opposition and resistance to oppression can seem to be a fight for existence itself (and many times it is just that). The essential trait can be an imagined, deep, spiritual quality, a moral essence, or even superficial physical appearance, such as skin color. Such essentialism distorts the nature of identity (if there is such a thing) because it is based on the idea that something in "me" causes me to be what I am, as a member of an identity group. For both Taylor's idea of dialogic identity formation and Nigrescence theory, an identity is constructed or achieved, and then, presumably, one has it and thereby is it. This idea limits identities to those who bear them and leaves out interactions with others and existence in the social environment that constructs or co-constructs those identities.

In reality, people enact, re-create, develop, innovate, and *perform* what constitutes their identities. Judith Butler famously showed how this works for gender and the same dynamic is in process for most marginalized group identities—as well as central ones.[32] This is not as much a matter of choice as in "How will I be this something?/What should I do?" but rather what it means to have an identity with others who also have identities. We have to interact with others and respond to the systems that already place us, by behaving in specific ways in specific contexts, not only in the formation of our identities but also in what it means to "have" them (i.e., in demonstrations of authenticity or even revealing what our identities are). Identities are thus ongoing interactions, in contrast to the windup-toy model of static essentialism. Only when a person stops interacting, can we say what their identity *was*.

The real political question for identity politics is whether government can respond to such real flux. The answer is no if government is supposed to intercede progressively, because the flux is fast and government is clumsy and should not be that involved in social processes. The identity flux is oppositional, a real stream of actual and potential dislocations and the task of government is to unite identities, not take sides. But, of course, when identity opposition in society becomes violent or oppressive, government does need to intervene in order to protect those treated unjustly.

As noted, racial identities are often encapsulated for voters by the "looks like me" factor. But in having achieved the status of a political candidate, racial appearance may not reflect economic and social status. Perhaps a similar racial appearance endears voters to a given candidate, but that similarity is no rational presumption, much less a guarantee, that the candidate understands and will serve the interests of voters with the same racial appearance. Similarly, although greater numbers of women in government are likely to change political agendas to serve the interests of women, no one knows what that critical mass of female officials is. This may be more than a question of numbers, because if one-tenth of the members of an organization are women, these women may conform to the misogynistic system created by men. But why should it be any different if women are one-half? Numerical gender equality may lead to more substantive gender equality, but that will require systemic changes beyond the gender of a number of members.

Politicians of color and women always need more than their individual identities of race and gender to effectively serve the interests of the people of color and women who have voted for them. By the same token, both progressives and conservatives find the progressivism of certain leftish white males reliable, year after year. If candidates need to get out the votes of minorities and women, then, if government is to be more than a spectacle, they should focus on issues that further interests rather than optics. Such interests follow from group rights and group rights, as will be explained soon, imply that others have duties to respect those rights.[33] But first more needs to be said about whether identities alone are politically sufficient within government.

If the sole political issues were white supremacy versus racial egalitarianism and/or male dominance versus gender equality, then "looks like me" politics could be all that was needed. But even in an age of extreme spectacle, everyone knows that the problems associated with race and gender cannot be addressed through race and gender alone. Such problems require economic, political, and social solutions, which, if framed correctly and executed in accordance with law, need not directly take up either race or gender as individual identities. For example, the problems attending nonwhite race involve violations of nondiscrimination laws and unequal protection from police violence. The problems of gender concern unequal pay for equal work and inadequate child care, as well as inadequate enforcement of laws and policies against abuse and battery. In the initial response to COVID-19, it was reported in early April 2020 that minorities, especially African Americans, were disproportionately dying. Posited causes included higher rates of preexisting disease (comorbidities), poverty with cramped living conditions, and greater exposure through "essential worker" jobs. Another factor was misinformation that African Americans were immune to COVID-19.

None of these problems are the effects of causes tied to racial or gendered identities per se. These causes involve constitutional rights violations, the security of persons, economic ethics, and public health resources, which all go beyond race and gender as identities. When a disease disproportionately affects people of color, justified outrage may obscure the real causes of these effects when outrage settles on racial identities and attendant structural or institutional racisms. Legislative and public policy remedies will not likely target minority groups by their racial identities, but rather provide support and relief for all who suffer from the causes, because of the high public intolerance for race-based affirmative action.

Group Rights

There is a comprehensive literature in philosophy alone, regarding the United States, the United Nations, and international relations, which advocates political recognition of group rights.[34] This literature criticizes official wording that grants rights to individuals only, thereby withholding recognition, as well as rights, from groups. The general progressive motivation for gaining political recognition of groups is twofold: individual rights, when recognized, tend to be the rights of members of dominant groups in a jurisdiction; groups can be experienced as organic wholes. These claims merit closer consideration.

In nonegalitarian societies, individual rights become the rights of some individuals only. Individuals who are socially disadvantaged based on their nondominant or low-status social identities are not granted the same individual rights in practice, despite official neutrality about all relevant identities. Catharine MacKinnon's classic argument against the goal of gender neutrality in a misogynistic society that privileges men has an analogue in arguments against official racial neutrality in a society that privileges whites. MacKinnon claims that male dominance, exerted through violence, is the key factor in a hierarchal gender system that is based on falsely constructed identities for women.[35] The same can be said about a white-dominant racial system that is based on falsely constructed identities for nonwhites, especially blacks. However, in both cases, the problem is neither race or gender, but rather dominance. Not "How are women not to be dominated by men?" or "How are nonwhites not to be dominated by whites?" but "How is dominance to be stopped?" It is true that dominance is exerted in both gender-specific and race-specific ways, but in both cases there are common elements of what it means for one person or one group of persons to be dominant over others—through arrogant and entitled personality traits, corruption in power structures, cronyism, violence, bullying, disrespect, and other morally bad behaviors, many of which are also illegal.

In most cases, the dominant behaviors seem to be tied to group-based identities that are socially privileged in present society and, in the past, in law (e.g., post-Reconstruction and Jim Crow laws). If the problem is not with the gendered or racial identities of dominant groups, but rather with their dominance, then the problem cannot be thoroughly solved without addressing dominance. However, the problem of group-based dominance seems to be viewed as tractable, given the goal of group-based equality. But this misses the point. There cannot be group-based egalitarianism so long as dominance is a "free-floating variable" that can range over any group identity. There can only be group-based equality if dominance is eliminated beforehand.

So far, the advocacy for political group rights has not been effective but maybe it could be. There are two kinds of progressive calls for group rights when the subject is racial and ethnic minority, nontraditional gender, cis women, disabled people, or indigenous people: Either individual identity is tied to membership in a group or whole groups are held to be deserving of political recognition and inclusion. If a group is understood to be no more than its members—that is, the group is taken severally—then recognition of group rights is not as crucial because group membership can be described as an attribute of individuals against which discrimination cannot be practiced or for whom certain entitlements are available. But if the meaning of group rights is literally the rights of a group or a collective that can be defined in terms of its preexistence in society and the group is held to have moral importance on that basis, then recognition of group rights would override individual identities. This difference is somewhat metaphysical, but its settlement is political.

If disadvantaged groups were to be recognized by government, then so would advantaged groups and a new struggle would ensue, within government, for group equality or the maintenance of preexisting dominance. Group conflict, especially ethnic group conflict or (in the United States) racial group conflict, is not ameliorated by strong group identities, but rather made more bitter by them. Thus, the liberatory revolution that began in the 1960s has been met with an alarming counter-revolution, complete with a resurgence in violent hate crimes committed by male white supremacists.[36] There is a long history throughout the world of mendacious and villainous leaders coming to power by exacerbating preexisting group conflicts, up to and through war. Efforts toward proactive peace making and peace enforcement have been recently developed on international levels, but it remains for Americans to apply such measures within the United States.[37] Returning to Taylor and Fukuyama, recognition and respect should be important limits to public discourse, but it is not clear how they can be enforced by government beyond expansion of the definition of hate crimes to include hate speech. Recognition and respect are moral virtues, not formal political rules. It does not matter which side is morally right, because the assertion of identities and demands made by identity groups attract counter identities in ways that escalate ideological conflict into violence. It should be of primary importance for US disadvantaged identity groups to avoid situations of violent strife that they cannot win, because they are outnumbered (as well as less likely to be armed). Moreover, such conflict should not be brought into government, because when the "wrong side" wins control of government, they will also have control of coercive state force.

THE SHIFT FROM IDENTITIES TO INTERESTS

The basic political idea of identity politics has been that people should organize in groups to articulate and further their shared interests. The subjects for this progressive idea have been disadvantaged and subordinate members of the total population. The goal is to move from the informal or unofficial identities that subordinate groups have in society to influence in, and through, government. However, political power for identity groups is obstructed insofar as individuals are the subject of rights in United States and international law.[38] This is a Gordian knot that can be untied simply by government recognition of identity groups and their subsequent inclusion within government. But given intractable identity group conflict, as well as the problems with identities themselves, identity group recognition should not be a progressive goal.

The existing identity neutrality in formal political language and thought renders identity groups unsuitable for political projects involving government. The real cultural and political racial and ethnic strife among white and nonwhite identity groups at the present time also makes it important that individuals and groups leave their identities at the door before entering formal politics. Because identities have become political weapons, they now obstruct progressive accomplishments and even basic government functioning, which requires the cooperation of all relevant identities. If society and government were truly egalitarian, it would not matter whether individuals or groups were the ultimate recognized rights-bearing units. And if society and government are structured by inequalities, the inequalities of groups as recognized by government would not lessen, and could even increase, because disadvantaged and subordinate people imagined as groups might be easier to oppress en masse. Redescription in terms of the rights of much larger groups of generic individuals therefore seems the more viable methodological course, not only to conform to existing ideas of neutrality (which do not accurately describe reality) but also to restore or create an inclusive focus on the common good. Todd Gitlin, in 1995, called for a "vocabulary for the common good," which it is not too late to reiterate.[39]

In place of politicized identity groups with aggrieved membership but also historical lineages and individual narratives, we should consider redescription of the interests associated with contemporary identities, toward inclusivity that neutralizes strife. The focus of a group rights theorist can shift from identities to interests. It is possible to state what the present interests of a preexisting group are, without reference to those traits of individuals which ultimately define identity groups. Such "reverse engineering" would depersonalize much of contemporary political opposition and emphasize the problem-solving role of government. Questions posed would be of the form *"What would the equality of X group in regard to Y groups require in terms that can be proposed for all groups?"* For example, disabled people do not have special needs that would translate into special interests, but rather needs like everyone else for mobility and physical and social environments that fit them as human beings and into which they can fit.[40]

This shift for the advocates of identity group recognition and rights is already part of democratic government rhetoric and practice. Although progressive politicians are responsive to specific identity groups by name, their official policy proposals are usually constructed with identity-neutral language (for example, "a living wage," "guaranteed income," "college for all," "universal health care," "voting rights"). This verbal anonymity as to who gets these goods reflects a deep underlying accommodation to traditional and prevailing democratic political principles and norms. It is understood that some identity groups will immediately benefit from certain progressive policies or programs, but that acceptability for the majority of voters requires that those likely to immediately benefit should not be named in terms of their disadvantaged identities. This is not merely a matter of language. In the United States, implemented focus on a specific group for help or remediation by government is not well received. But if the same program is constructed in ways that benefit everyone and all groups with common interests, it can be received as inclusive, even by those who don't really need the program. For example, wealthy Americans may not need Social Security, but they get it anyway and have not mounted strong political opposition to it.

The "Green New Deal" is a strong example of presentation of inclusive change that is spearheaded by what could be called an identity group of environmental preservationists. However, this evolving proposal includes policies for jobs and programs that speak to much wider constituencies than that group. Those who would immediately benefit most from a Green New Deal or be gratified by its environmental protections are not named as primary beneficiaries and indeed, they would not be the sole beneficiaries of such a program. For another example: Those with low verbal and numerical literacy are not equal in education, employment, wealth, or health to those with high literacy. Policies to raise literacy would be available to those with any degree of literacy. Those with high literacy would probably not need those benefits, although they would benefit from others getting them through lower collective costs of compensating for existing low literacy, as well as better communication throughout society.[41] Common benefits need not always be material. An indigenous group could request noninterference with a feature of the land that it possesses, when interference would increase the wealth of the nation. But justice would require noninterference if respect for any group's right to choose to live in a traditional environment is a shared democratic value.[42]

A NOTE ON REPARATIONS

The idea of reparations is attractive as a means for correcting past harms that either persist into the present or are remembered across generations as a form of assault on present dignity. However, in practice there are several problems with the idea of reparations as generally applicable to identity groups: not all members of identity groups have genealogical histories of the harms at issue; while those who pay now may benefit from privileges resulting from harms committed in the past against others, they are not directly responsible for the actions of their forebears; and insofar as the United States became a wealthy power through the seizure of indigenous lands and the unpaid labor of black slaves, full restitution would destabilize existing wealth and ownership to a degree that would harm those receiving reparation, as well as those paying for it.[43]

However, these problems with general governmental reparations and restitution do not preclude practices of public national apology[44] and symbolic restitution, for example, the $20,000 per capita paid to survivors and their heirs of Japanese internment during World War II.[45] Also, the absence of general governmental restitution to identity groups does not preclude contextualized reparations undertaken within society. For example, in 1838, the Jesuit founders of Georgetown University sold 272 people to pay off college debts. In April 2019, two-thirds of the undergraduate student body voted to pay reparations to identified descendants of those slaves, by increases in school fees. While the student vote was nonbinding, the university administration expressed ongoing commitment to this and other proposals to reconcile such past practices with present values.[46] Notice that in this case, reparations would be voluntary and private and not coerced by government. Precisely specific private reparation is a sound moral idea and exact specificity, as in the Georgetown University case, need concern only parties directly involved. But broad governmentally imposed reparations would ignite identity group strife in their generality.

CONCLUSION

The multiplicity of contemporary social identities, as well as differences within them, supports diversity, cosmopolitanism, or communitarianism, in ways that are highly compatible with happy and vital social interactions, as well as healthy disagreement (except for hate crimes and other forms of gratuitous violence). Besides their popularity in popular discourse, many progressive scholars focus on identities and identity groups exclusively. Individual or imagined shared-trait identities in social, literary, and intellectual life outside of government are gratifying to define, create, and cultivate. However, there is no direct path from identity groups to egalitarian political life. This does not mean that the interests of such groups cannot be captured and furthered through inclusive language that proposes government programs that include these interests and those of other groups. Also to be kept in mind are large and vague groups that are "pop-ups" which center contemporary concerns and interests. Government is supposed to serve common interests and the common interests of one decade or even one year may change. Adaptation to climate change, for instance, is an intense interest of many environmentalists but not yet an urgent common interest, although sooner or later it will be an intensely urgent common interest.

The trajectory of this book moves toward evidence-based government without identities. However, the recrudescence of White Supremacy in present times, along with the complacency of white supremacy, has been a shocking attack on ideas of human equality that many assumed were beyond challenge. Therefore, the critique of identities and identity politics developed in this chapter is not theoretically sufficient as a foundation for government without identity politics. We need first to consider ideas of universalism and the nature of white supremacy in our time. These two subjects will occupy chapters 3 and 4.

Finally, throughout this chapter, I have discussed identities as personal attributes, known to the self and communicated to and by others. Identities are also social machines or mechanisms that enable people to call on shared conceptual schemes and plans of action, once they acquire them. The ultimate political identities in our time are political party affiliations, and there is already broad awareness of how and when these identities are brought into government. Republicans versus Democrats and Democrats versus Republicans politicize government actions in all branches. Such politicization can create a stasis in government function, leading to dysfunction. And it serves as a barrier for elected officials to consider issues and make decisions on their own merits, even blocking agreement on facts and scientific evidence that are necessary for decision making. In the United States, the acceptance of the COVID-19 threat and responses to it during the early months of 2020 were politicized in exactly this way. The responses of the Republican administration were slow and weak, coming short of its capabilities in a federal system. These delays had apparent political motives, and in some cases the Democratic reaction may have exaggerated dangers for their own political motives. Of particular constitutional legal interest is how that partisan response has changed the nature of the federal system.

Traditionally, the federal system has been based on an assumption that states would resist federal rule as a general tendency—hence, doctrines of "states' rights." But in the early months of 2020, states have been demanding and even begging for stronger, more centralized federal action under the Defense Production Act. So far, as of this writing, the states have taken almost federal roles upon themselves, often competing for scarce medical equipment that could have been centrally produced and allocated under active deployment of the Defense Production Act, or else through forming mutual aid associations. As of this writing (in early April 2020), it remains to be seen whether future federal action results in policies that medical experts deem unsafe, or whether states will go the other way and resist central rule according to the traditional form of federalism.

3

UNIVERSALISM OR FORCE: INCLUSION OR DOMINATION

How is universality compatible with racism? The answer—to be found in the logic of what first inspires racism—involves a basic modification of the very idea of universality. Universality must give way to the idea of expansion, for the expansion of a force presents a structure that is completely different from the propagation of an idea.

—Emmanuel Levinas[1]

Governmental universalism or an ideal of one-size-fits-all government with the same functions and benefits for all citizens is viewed with suspicion by many contemporary progressive scholars. Political universalism, such as liberal democracy, as an intellectual by-product of the Enlightenment, was accompanied by colonialism and state racism in social environments of unbridled mercantilism and capitalism. The result has been the oppression and exploitation of the very people the Enlightenment should have liberated and supported. However, the architects of the Enlightenment never had these people in mind and that makes the "should" anachronistic. But pointing this out may seem frivolous given the gravity of contemporary progressive concerns. The point often made is that the idea of universalism is not a useful tool for helping oppressed and vulnerable people, who have never been included in its official ontology. Also, universalism that would or should include the oppressed and vulnerable is not appealing to those who have overriding wealth or power; their grip on these goods is generally not loosened by moral argument.

Perhaps the idea of citizen equality and political sameness is fundamentally out of reach, a regulative ideal for naïve progressives. People are not equal in society, mainly because of their differences in wealth, race, gender, ethnicity, ableism, age, and so forth. Government, especially democratic liberal government that is subject to influence and electoral manipulation by the powerful, cannot help but reflect and duplicate social inequalities. We should not be surprised by present realities, because the "We the People" of the United States who founded the Constitution were slave owners. Moreover, the 1948 Universal Declaration of Human Rights launched a United Nations that seventy-odd years later has done no more than reiterate ideals in a world where nonwhite and poor peoples continue to struggle in what Kant so cruelly and precisely called "glittering misery."

Nevertheless, the belief in equality, especially racial equality, persists. In the United States, racial inequality due to overt discrimination has been addressed through formal legal equality, rather than by measures to ensure distributive justice or material equality. The civil rights legislation of the 1960s prohibits discrimination based on race or ethnicity in employment, education, voting, and immigration. But real institutional progress toward racial equality has stopped with ideas of racial equality of opportunity for individuals—for jobs, education, and access to public office—rather than going on to economic equality, the provision of universal minima, or enduring social safety nets. Those who point to equal opportunity may avoid looking too closely at what it means, insofar as a universal right to attempt something does not ensure that all are able to attempt it with equal prospects of success. Within other affluent states, minority ethnic and racial groups also experience comparative inequality, and, among autocratic states, inequalities associated with race may be greater than within democratic states. In addition, inequalities between the inhabitants of the first and third worlds run counter to Enlightenment ideals even though, or because, they are referred to as differences in "development" or technological and economic advance.

Experts on race believe that institutional or structural racism against nonwhites in the United States causes disproportionate poverty and other social ills such as higher mortality and incarceration rates. These ills are understood to be connected to educational underachievement, but many scholars in the humanities view racism as the primary ill—if there were racial equality, the other ills would not disproportionately befall nonwhites. Nonwhite intergenerational poverty and educational underachievement is understood to be the result of unchallenged white privilege, or the benefits of being white, rather than simple cycles of poverty alone. But much of white privilege itself exists because of racial inequality, because what counts as privilege may only stand out as such in comparison to the unjust treatment of nonwhites.[2] Still, the residue of absolute, rather than comparative, white privilege is thought to be the result of benefits accrued to whites as "profits" from their exploitation and oppression of nonwhites.

Force is required to expand inequality and force is necessary to oppose or correct it. The term "force" here means not only physical force—although it importantly includes physical force—but also energy or action that breaks through some status quo, some habitual or inertial default practice. Emmanuel Levinas believed that force was present in the foundation of racist inequality (as the chapter epigraph states). We can add that even if those who benefit from a racist society did not create it, the racism that is already present in structures of inequality can require force to enforce and re-create them. Force is also required to maintain structures of inequality if those who suffer from them put up resistance and the use of force against subordinate groups may be an ordinary part of the structures of inequality themselves. This last offers a contrast between new forms of force and force that is already "baked in"—that is, force for enforcement is not the same as force as a general, habitual practice. In sum, within racist societies, new force creates them, new force expands them, habitual force protects them, and force may be part of their normal functioning. On the other side, force is required to resist them. This is a lot of force.

Force, especially physical force or violence, is an historical aspect of racist (and other hierarchical) societies and can be described in structural terms, according to race, such as de jure segregation, unequal education, disproportional incarceration, unequal employment opportunities, and unequal wealth accumulation. Since force, which includes enforcement, may be resisted or lack compliance, using the very terms "force" or "violent force" in societal contexts suggests that those to whom the force is applied would not otherwise do what they are being forced to do. Force "makes" people do things they do not choose to do. Thus, if we are going to talk about racist societies, it is necessary to talk about resistance and opposing wills, as well as force and oppressing wills.

This chapter is a theoretical exploration of why universalism should still serve as a standard for government. The strongest alternative to universalism is pluralism, and I will first examine W. E. B. Du Bois's vision of democratic pluralism as an instrument of liberation for African Americans. This will bring us to the elephant in the room with this kind of identity politics. A discussion follows of the surprisingly contemporary interpretation of true and degenerate universalisms that was set forth by Emmanuel Levinas in 1935. Next is a consideration of universalism without race. After that, universalism and justice are related by drawing on Levinas's idea of Enlightenment universalism, through an application of Gottlob Frege's treatment of thoughts.

DU BOISIAN PLURALISM

In recent philosophy, much has been written about Du Bois's 1897 address to the American Negro Academy, "The Conservation of the Races." The focus has been on the shaky metaphysical and biological foundation of his apparently essentialist defense of the idea of race. In the early 1990s, the "Race Debates" ignited by the question of the biological foundation of race actually launched philosophy of race as a broader subfield that was more abstract and inclusive of all races than African American philosophy had been until that time. The main question raised in these "Race Debates" was whether scientific skepticism about the existence of human races meant that race was unreal.[3] This question did not always have the precise framing of "If people think that race has a foundation according to the biological sciences, and it does not, then is the idea of biological race a false idea?" Instead, the suggestion that race is a false idea led some to immediately conclude that those who exposed its biological falsity were "racial eliminativists"—that is, that these theorists (myself included) were saying that race should be eliminated. But to this day, it is not clear what that means. Does "eliminativism" imply that nonwhite people should be eliminated? Obviously not, coming from progressive scholars. Does it imply that educated people should not use the language of race? It can't be that, because race talk is unavoidable in a society structured by racial differences—especially given free speech. At most, "racial eliminativism," given full recognition of the facts of racism, means it should be acknowledged both that biological race is a false idea and that it is widely retained. That is, educated people should be aware that biological race is an ongoing societal condition, as well as an outdated scientific construction.

If race is viewed as a purely social construct based on false biological ideas now revised in the sciences, but deeply embedded in custom and tradition, the presence or absence of its metaphysical or biological foundation is beside the point of its social importance. The falseness of the idea may make it even more recalcitrant, because it may be retained for emotional reasons that cannot be argued away based on evidence—the case for the falsity of biological race is a purely intellectual or cognitive one that is simply too dry for the kind of rhetoric needed to dislodge the tenacity of belief in it. Indeed, for Du Bois, race had an aspirational and, through that, emotional and even spiritual dimension. He rejected the science of his day for having dispensed with such social, in contrast to physical, metaphysics.[4] However, Du Bois rejected the biological racial science of his day because it said too little about the cultural aspects of race, not too much (as progressive critics, even in his time, claimed). Du Bois was engaged in a project of *transmogrification*, taking up disparaging ascriptions to make them valorizing. Different versions of this rhetorical tool have been repeatedly crafted: for instance, "Black is beautiful" and "We're here, we're queer."

We can understand Du Bois's "Conservation" as referring to "race" in terms of what his audience already understood by the word as well as an ideal to be striven for. Both the understanding and the ideal were on the side of conservation or what we would now call "retention." When Du Bois delivered "Conservation," Frederick Douglass had recently died and Booker T. Washington had become the foremost Negro spokesperson. Unlike Douglass, who was an integrationist, Washington was an *accommodationist*, willing to appease white supremacists. He had catapulted into global renown after his 1895 address to the Cotton States and International Atlanta Exposition.[5] Washington did not seek full civil or political rights for African Americans, but he exhorted the business-oriented white assembly to provide them (in preference to recent immigrants) jobs for manual labor, with the reassurance that "in all things that are purely social we can be as separate as the fingers, yet one as the hand in all things essential to mutual progress."[6]

Wilson Moses relates how the American Negro Academy (as addressed by Du Bois) would have been opposed by Douglass, who objected to racial separatism and race-exclusive organizations of all kinds. The "uplift" spirit of the Academy, as officially founded by Alexander Crummell, soon after Douglass died, was more elevated than Washington's focus on material gain through manual labor and his opposition to higher education for African Americans. Du Bois agreed with Crummell, against Douglass, first by valorizing the idea of race in proclaiming, "There can be no doubt first as to the widespread, nay, universal prevalence of the race idea, the race spirit, the race ideal, and as to its efficiency as the vastest and most ingenious invention for human progress." He decried the "immorality, crime, and laziness amongst American blacks, as a legacy from slavery." This scolding was in apparent ignorance of the fact that his own study begun in 1896, *The Philadelphia Negro*, would block such historical-moralistic judgment, because it would relate contemporary black problems to contemporary social structures that oppressed and exploited blacks.[7]

Crummell's inaugural presidential address, "Civilization, the Primary Need of the Race," had called for leadership to uplift the "crude masses" of African-descended people, an idea Du Bois echoed through his posit of "the talented tenth" (i.e., the high-achieving, successful top 10 percent of African Americans). Du Bois also followed Crummell into high-flown, aspirational ideas about race, so that for each race, "its particular message, its particular ideal, would help to guide the world nearer that perfection of human life for which we all long, that one far off Divine event."[8] And finally, the black race, which extended globally, still needed to fulfill its divine destiny. Du Bois's aspirational culmination draws on subtle differences among races, not "mere" physical differences, so that

> [the] advance guard of the Negro people—the 8,000,000 people of Negro blood in the United States of America—must soon come to realize that if they are to take their just place in the van of Pan-Negroism, then their destiny is *not* absorption by the white Americans. That if in America it is to be proven for the first time in the modern world that not only Negroes are capable of evolving

individual men like Toussaint, the Saviour, but are a nation stored with wonderful possibilities of culture, then their destiny is not a servile imitation of Anglo-Saxon culture, but a stalwart originality which shall unswervingly follow Negro ideals.[9]

Du Bois was here arguing for inspired separatism, not on the basis of biology, but rather on the basis of the unique destiny of Negroes in the grand scheme of world events. Du Bois's separatism as racial conservation was not framed to sooth or appease white people, so it was doubly defiant—against Booker T. Washington, as well as whites. Such defiance is insurrectionist—it goes against the general framework of beliefs and norms behind specific oppressions.[10]

Putting the religious and idealist metaphysical aspects of Du Bois's vision to one side, the secular and empirical interpretation of his idea of Negro identity is that it rests on the distinct culture and experience of African Americans. Late twentieth-century philosophers have emphasized black life in exactly this way. Lucius Outlaw, for instance, emphasizes Du Boisian interpretation based on black social experience;[11] Chike Jeffers takes up distinctive black culture.[12] The upshot of these interpretations is that they can support an idea of political racial pluralism. While that idea has not been realized within government, it already has considerable traction for elections leading up to government. It is now commonplace for pundits to refer to "the black vote" or "the Latinx vote."[13]

There is theoretical justification for a political view of society as organized into different racial and ethnic groups. If a group has a distinct culture within itself and its experience in the wider society is different from that of other groups, because its members are treated unjustly based on their perceived or ascribed membership in the group, then it seems reasonable that this group would want political representation in government. It seems reasonable, because only the ultimate authority and force of government could correct the injustice, a constitutional statement of universal egalitarianism (e.g., "All men are created equal") entails that members of the group are entitled to such correction, and the government of a democratic society with freedom of speech and belief should protect the group's rights to its distinctive culture and aspirations.

However, the contemporary philosophical "Race Debates" mentioned earlier, as focused on the metaphysics and science of race, as well as a Du Boisian racially inward view of black identity, may fail to take into account issues of contention between the oppressed racial group and other racial groups. I will argue in the next section of this chapter and throughout chapter 4 that these issues may portend defeat of the aspirational goals of an oppressed identity group should it gain full entry into the political arena as that group. Here, before leaving Du Bois and turning to those more practical general considerations, it is very important to note that his 1897 aspirational defiance of white Americans, could not have been voiced in ignorance of the violence of white supremacy in his time, which included lynching. (Later he would found and edit *Crisis Magazine* from 1910 to 1923, and lynching was explicitly described and condemned in those pages.[14]) Thus, although Du Bois was aware of the dangers to black Americans, through the force in normal use and for special enforcement, he called for them to resist by exerting moral force for their unique historical racial destiny. Both the force in effect and the force of resistance grew out of racial identities, normal and special force applied by whites against blacks, and moral and spiritual force by blacks against whites, because of their racial identities.

LEVINAS ON HITLERISM

In "Reflections on the Philosophy of Hitlerism," Levinas distinguishes between Enlightenment universalism, which is about expanding or sharing an idea, as opposed to racist universalism which comes from a perspective rooted in a particular racial identity that can only realize its destiny through force and the concrete expansion of real power, real geographical territory, and real, particular culture. This is the elephant in the room concerning Du Bois's vision of the destiny of the black race: White Supremacists have and continue to believe their race has a special destiny. In Du Bois's example, universalism among blacks can only fulfill black destiny through objection, protest, and real contest against the injustices of White Supremacy. While his words were inspirational in their rhetorical context, he was, throughout his life, well aware of the energy, disruption, and struggle—that is, the force—required to achieve what he saw as black destiny. We are safe to assume, given his dedicated career, that Du Bois did not think black struggle was limited

to black projects of self-help and "racial uplift." Du Bois knew and experienced the ways in which black Americans had to forcefully struggle against white Americans, if only by speaking out and accepting the consequences. While Du Bois's struggle was more of a moral struggle of righteousness against injustice, the struggle of the white racists—Hitler's opus was, after all, titled *Mein Kampf* or "My Struggle"—may also begin with high-flown racial self-glorification before becoming a justification for the use of violent force. It's one thing to pursue progressive aspiration and advocacy in a more or less democratic period when oppression is on the decline, but quite another undertaking when oppression is on the ascent. Not the least of a test of progressive acumen is to assess which of the two periods one is in.

If the ground of struggle is racial identity and racial destiny, and one side is restricted to moral weapons and the other side, which is already dominant, has no qualms about using physical weapons, who is likely to win? Not, who should win, but who will likely win, in practical reality? The tradition of inciting a "race war" in the United States has already motivated generations of white racists and White Supremacists.[15] In such a war, fought physically, and not morally, the white racists would win, because they are armed, have a taste for violence, and are already socially, economically, and politically dominant—their dominance means that many other whites would at a certain point support them and later accept their victory (i.e., might makes right). So one has to wonder what Du Bois was thinking if he was serious about the fulfillment of black racial destiny. Did he think it would be fulfilled without violent force in opposition from those who believed in white racial destiny? It is unlikely he would have believed that blacks could win by fighting back with violent physical force. But he is likely to have believed that the moral force of being in the right could bring victory for them.

Also, Du Bois may have been confidant that he could persuade others to join him in moral force so that the eventual moral force would ultimately win. This kind of belief in moral force not only has a long historical tradition, especially when a righteous God is invoked, but also continues to be reiterated in our own time, in secular terms that rely on reason. History has shown that God so invoked has not interceded and reason against racism opposes emotion that is impervious to reason or intellectual arguments and facts. My general argument is that while Du

Boisian spiritual racial aspirations, and many other progressive ideals, may be worth pressing in society and culture, they should be kept out of government, which has the ultimate preponderance of violent force. The principle and process of racial aspirations being fulfilled by government for minorities can be taken over by racial oppressors should their power in government increase. Racial aspiration is a double-edged weapon that is too dangerous to be placed in the hands of government.

Let's now return to Levinas on Hitlerism. His insights clear the way for incisive criticism of the metaphysics of white supremacy, which also applies to the ascendancy of nonwhite races, even righteously understood. Levinas claims that Nazi racism is linked to universalism in a degenerate way. Unlike proper Enlightenment universalism that involves the spread of ideas, racism is a twisted form of universalism that can only spread through force. Levinas describes this deviation somewhat contrastively, beginning with "Christian universalism," against which he reflects upon racist particularism. It is important, here, that Levinas does not begin with political freedom in the Enlightenment democratic ideas of government, but with a deeper, moral humanism:

> Political freedoms do not exhaust the content of the spirit of freedom, a spirit that, in Western civilization, signifies a conception of human destiny. This conception is a feeling that man is absolutely free in his relations with the world and the possibilities that solicit action from him. Man is renewed eternally in the face of the Universe. Speaking absolutely, he has no history.[16]

Levinas goes on to explain that history itself is a limitation that irreparably weighs on human destiny, because the past cannot be changed. But through the freedom proclaimed by Christianity, "time loses its very irreversibility" so that "Not only is the choice of destiny a free one," but "Once the choice is made, it does not form a chain." The soul is detached through its power to become detached and abstract, so that

> the equal dignity of each and every soul, which is independent of the material or social conditions of people, does not flow from a theory that affirms, beneath individual differences, an analogy based on a "psychological constitutions." It is due to the power given to the soul to free itself from *what has been*, from everything that linked it to

something or engaged it with something [*engage*], so it can regain its first virginity.[17]

Levinas is aware that the modern history of liberalism has "evaded" this kind of freedom, but he claims that the freedom has been retained in "the form of the sovereign freedom of reason." Reason has provided an alternative to the "blind" and "brutal" world of common sense and the "implacable history of concrete existence." The result is that all possibilities are not limited to individual choice, but include mere logical possibilities open to dispassionate choices by reason, while reason is "forever keeping its distance."[18]

Levinas claims that Marxism, in holding that material being determines consciousness, ruptures this tradition, although resistance to one's material situation represents an opposition to it, which can bring the freedom of reason back in.[19] However, a greater disruption is caused by insights that the self is fundamentally connected to its physical body (especially through pain), and some insist that the spirit's essence is this bodily connection. This feeling of connection to the body becomes a kind of bondage, determined by history and one result is a society based on consanguinity.

The idea of a society based on consanguinity was indeed part of the Nazi party platform as designed by Alfred Rosenberg.[20] Thus, Levinas could write, "And then, if race does not exist, one has to invent it!"[21] And, concerning Hitlerism, Levinas writes of Germany:

> Such a society loses living contact with its true ideal of freedom and accepts degenerate forms of the ideal. It does not see that the true ideal requires effort and instead enjoys those aspects of the ideal that make life easier. It is to a society in such a condition that the Germanic ideal of man seems to promise sincerity and authenticity. Man no longer finds himself confronted by a world of ideas in which he can choose his own truth on the basis of a sovereign decision made by his free reason. He is already linked to a certain number of these ideas, just as he is linked by birth to all those who are of his blood. He can no longer play with the idea [*jouer avec l'idée*], for coming from his concrete being, anchored in his flesh and blood, the idea remains serious.[22]

According to Levinas, this new truth, based on common blood, still seeks to be universal, so that it can create a new world. But racism modifies the idea of universality: "*Universality must give way to the idea of expansion. For the expansion of a force presents a structure that is completely different from the propagation of an idea.*"[23] Levinas offers a fascinating account of the propagation of an idea, which I will consider in the next section. Now, it is necessary to delve a little deeper into how racist force expands. Such force is part of the personality or society exerting it, "enlarging that person or society while subordinating the rest." Through war and conquest, there is a new universal unity of "masters and slaves."

Howard Caygill takes up Levinas's universal interpretation of Hitlerism by relating it to a theory of history as an account of racial struggle. Caygill argues that the interpretation of Hitlerism as particularist and not part of basic ideas of "the political" is incorrect, given this world historical race-struggle interpretation.[24] We should note that there are two different ideas of race involved here, as well as the two different ideas of universalism identified by Levinas and Caygill. A universal thought or idea is about everyone and anyone, everywhere. But a universal history of racial struggle is about the spatial world, in real time. Logically, the first is abstract, while the second has existential import. These two different ideas of universalism are universal thought versus universal dominance as international or global political order. The two different ideas of race are similarly genealogical and abstract. The genealogical idea of race pertains to the inheritance and geographical location and movement of specific, concrete peoples. Its main mechanism for transmission is intergenerational heredity or lineage and it concerns the actual history of peoples or groups, such as Germans under Hitler (but also Jews, French, Roma, and other peoples). Even if racial group struggle explains major events in common human history, it can only do that part by part, by putting together components that are empirically studied. It is particular and existential, through and through. By contrast, the abstract idea of race applies to the whole of humanity. The seventeenth-century French physician and world traveler François Bernier introduced the modern universal, abstract idea of race in his "Nouvelle Division de la Terre." Bernier divided all humans into races or species based on skin color, hair type, and bodily shape. The result was four categories: Europeans, North Africans, Middle Easterners, and occupants of India and part of South Asia; African Negroes; East and Northeast Asians; and Lapps. According to this system, racial identity did not depend on genealogy or geographical origin, but simply observable traits.[25] Although the traits are identified by means of geographical origin, if people of different races move around, they fully remain members of their race and continue to resemble other members of that race.

The relation of race to world history varies, depending on whether a genealogical or abstract idea of race is at stake. Du Bois, who focused on the history and contemporary reality of African Americans, thought in terms of genealogical ideas of race. German ideology during the time of Hitler also focused on the "blood and soil" of the actual German people. It is only from a genealogical idea of race that a particular people who self-identify by their race can either expand their power or strive toward what they envision as their destiny. In both cases, there is an expansion through force, either physical or moral (or both). Even if they have a view of all human history as motivated and constituted by struggles such as their own, it is difficult to see how this is or can be a universal idea, beyond an idea or ideal of constant strife between different genealogical groups. Genealogy undermines universality, because relations between genealogical groups form history and events in history not only are unique but also affect subsequent events. The abstract idea of race as ascribed identities or human taxonomy has better claims to universality, since it has as its subject the whole of humanity. However, its application to, or identification with, specific historical people would require genealogical accounts of such people. And again, race fails as a universal idea because it does not apply to everyone in the same way, except for the general abstract factor of having racial membership. Both belonging to a historical group and having racial membership fail to achieve universality either because of the false and changing idea of racial identity or because they are historical ideas.

It is understandable that Bernier would want to posit a human typology that was independent of geographical origins, because if such an idea has existential import—that is, if there are races into which all human beings "fit"—the result is a grand system of human classification. And this system, not coincidentally in Bernier's scheme, glorified Europeans. But, as noted, the universal theory of human races turned out not to be empirically supported in the sciences whose job it was to find evidence for their existence. So racial universalism in Bernier's sense is false. Genealogical racialism, or belief in the existence of race, may at first seem plausible as a theory of history, but, like any theory, it requires evidence. And while there is plenty of evidence that groups or populations made up of family lines do exist, they cannot be divided into anything as simple as Bernier's four races, or even Du Bois's eight.[26] Since so much of what is thought to be racial identity changes over time, the history of human conflict viewed as racial conflict would involve a great deal of anachronism. And since race is a social construct that often appears after the fact of exploitation and oppression, there is no primary meaning of race that can be objectified as a primary causal factor in all inter-group conflict.

UNIVERSALISM WITHOUT RACE

For history, as well as biology, there is nothing universal about the idea of human races, which has existential import. Without existential import, the idea of race is an abstract idea of human difference, whereas universalism, in both moral and political senses, rests on human sameness. The 1948 United Nations Declaration of Universal Human Rights (UDHR) is an example of an aspirational universal human claim that rests on human sameness. It begins vaguely, without defined terms—"inherent dignity," "equal and inalienable rights," "the human family," "freedoms":

> Preamble
> Whereas recognition of the inherent dignity and of the equal and inalienable rights of all members of the human family is the foundation of freedom, justice and peace in the world . . .
>
> Article 1.
> All human beings are born free and equal in dignity and rights. They are endowed with reason and conscience and should act towards one another in a spirit of brotherhood.
>
> Article 2.
> Everyone is entitled to all the rights and freedoms set forth in this Declaration, without distinction of any kind, such as race, colour, sex, language, religion, political or other opinion, national or social origin, property, birth or other status. Furthermore, no distinction shall be

made on the basis of the political, jurisdictional or international status of the country or territory to which a person belongs, whether it be independent, trust, non-self-governing or under any other limitation of sovereignty.[27]

We can see from this that UDHR is a universal statement—viz: "all members of the human family"; "all human beings"; "everyone." However, the United Nations has not been effective in defining or applying these rights, except for issuing thousands of subsequent declarations concerning their logical implications, such as declarations of the rights of women, children, and refugees, as well best practices for democratic and humanitarian procedural issues.[28] In this regard, the UN's universal declarations are perfect examples of universal ideals that pull away from crude and brutal reality in the way that Levinas described the universalism of the Enlightenment. These declarations are derived from and by reason and they soothe people and remind them of better standards for human interaction, than those they encounter in real life.

The question is whether there can be human universalism that does not mention race, but nonetheless addresses racial injustice by presenting an ideal view of justice, something akin to Rawls's ideal theory of justice, but claiming even less existential import than that.[29] Given the problems and inconsistences with universal statements that do mention race and the practical dangers of righteous expressions of racial injustice, it may be time to reconsider or recraft inclusive universal humanistic liberalism in a way that allows for progress toward racial equality without attracting hatred and violence from those who are interested in promoting the interests of their already-dominant race. So much has been written about human dignity and rights with a subtext that it applies to whites only, or white men only, that it should be possible to create new concepts that just as implicitly promise egalitarian progress for nonwhites and other minorities. In the beginning, there need to be ideas that are both new and aspirational, as well as egalitarian and inclusive of both dominant and subordinate groups in society. With those ideas would come new words, new vocabularies, and new conceptual schemes that are in turn inclusive. A rising tide could float all boats in this sense.

UNIVERSALISM AND JUSTICE

Let's return to Levinas's comparison of what we can now say is blood-and-soil pseudo-universalism with his view of the universalism of the Enlightenment. According to Levinas, Enlightenment universalism has been a universalism of ideas. Thus:

> The idea propagated detaches itself essentially from its point of departure. In spite of the unique accent communicated to it by its creator, it becomes a common heritage. It is fundamentally anonymous. The person who accepts it becomes its master, as does the person who proposes it. The propagation of an idea thus creates a community of "masters"; it is a process of equalization. To convert or persuade is to create peers. The universality of an order in Western society always reflects this universality of truth.[30]

Levinas is here insisting not only that ideas about human equality have spread and can continue to do so but also that the spread of ideas itself has an egalitarian nature, because ideas are impersonal. Clearly, many would argue against this claim, by insisting that this model of human cognitive communication is limited, because there is more to communication than cognition. The communication of truths about particular bodily selves or groups of kinds of bodily selves is not universal in its content. We have seen how Levinas focuses on the self-superiority claims of racists who seek to expand their domination, but there is another side to that coin—namely, the self-oppressed claims of those treated unjustly and, as with Du Bois, self-potential claims of those who contest their inferior racial status. But that is no more than the other side of Hitlerism, because it is the resistance by force, mainly moral, against those who are willing to use violent physical force unjustly, on the same grounds of race, although the races are of course different. However, suppose we suspend disbelief and seriously entertain Levinas's analysis, which requires remaining on the level of ideas.

The metaphysics or ontology or reality of ideas is not a subject that can generally be settled here (if it can be settled anywhere). But what we can do is consider the kinds of ideas that might be at issue here and, if not determine their ontological status, perhaps describe how they are experienced. The primary idea in political life, including society as well as government, is justice. As John Rawls pronounced, justice is a general concept that admits of conceptions or particular contextualized versions of it, and his conception of justice was fairness. In describing an institutional structure for fairness, Rawls explained that he was presenting ideal theory. Rawls did not dwell on what he meant by "ideal" except to specify that ideal theory would pertain to well-ordered societies, only, societies with shared understanding of their constitutional foundations and consisting of law-abiding citizens. His followers and critics have generally paid attention to this normative aspect of "ideal," without too much concern about its metaphysics.

If one is interested in practical politics and social change and observes activism, it is obvious that people are not all that concerned with justice in this normative sense of an ideal, but with specific injustices that they want corrected.[31] A Rawlsian might insist that in order to identify injustice and work for its correction, some idea of justice itself must be in mind. However, the history of complaint about injustice predates Rawls's theory for probably all of recorded Western history. So whatever people have had in mind as a positive concept or conception of justice, it is not likely to approach the elaborateness of Rawls's theory.

The idea of justice is general and vague and highly variable, depending on historical context. Those with ideas of justice as something that is absent in what they consider injustice may have very different ideas of justice, depending on their circumstances. Levinas talks about the anonymous universality of shared Enlightenment ideas. Justice would be a candidate for such an idea, but given this variation, particular ideas of justice are unlikely to be universally shared. This is where Frege is relevant for further clarification. Frege distinguishes between ideas that individuals possess, and thoughts, expressed by indicative sentences, which are grasped. We could say that people have their own particular ideas of justice but that they share the common thought of justice, which they grasp.[32] The universal, anonymous idea of justice is more of a vague, but not less fervently grasped, idea—that is, a term or concept rather than an indicative sentence. It doesn't qualify as a thought in Frege's sense, but more as a public "something" that can be called upon or referred to as validation for particular ideas of justice. This vagueness of the anonymous idea of justice loses its universality when it is defined. We could say that all definitions of justice are conceptions of justice.

Even Rawls accepted this idea implicitly when he wrote at the beginning of *A Theory of Justice*:

> Justice is the first virtue of social institutions, as truth is of systems of thought. A theory however elegant and economical must be rejected or revised if it is untrue; likewise, laws and institutions no matter how efficient and well-arranged must be reformed or abolished if they are unjust.

However, in providing a deontological description of justice immediately following, he was moving to his conception of justice—that is, his (Rawls's) idea of justice—because not everyone who calls upon justice need agree with what he then wrote, viz:

> Each person possesses an inviolability founded on justice that even the welfare of society as a whole cannot override. For this reason justice denies that the loss of freedom for some is made right by a greater good shared by others. It does not allow that the sacrifices imposed on a few are outweighed by the larger sum of advantages enjoyed by many. Therefore, in a just society the liberties of equal citizenship are taken as settled; the rights secured by justice are not subject to political bargaining or to the calculus of social interests.[33]

Utilitarians would not agree with Rawls, and neither would those expressing the values of some traditional societies.

To tie this together, race-based strivings for justice, as well as power, are strivings for ideals that are conceptions of justice. Justice, as a universal idea that everyone can grasp, is necessarily vague and indefinable.

CONCLUSION

The factor of force, both physical and moral, is important to keep in mind for considering practical issues of justice. The "Race Debates" in philosophy have been about the metaphysical foundations of race, in cognitive terms. They leave undisturbed the emotional and spiritual aspects of race in society. Du Bois created a foundation for black racial destiny in this sense, though seemingly oblivious to the dangers of violent White Supremacy. Still, his conception of black identity endures as motivation for a possible political identity. Levinas offers a vision of racial conflict as expanding force, in contrast to universal Enlightenment ideas. The need for such universalism is at this time prudent as well as aspirational, given those dangers of violent White Supremacy. We are now ready for the closer look at the nature of white supremacy in chapter 4.

4

WHITE SUPREMACY AND STATUS: THE RACISM OF RACE

> But even a stellar résumé wasn't always enough to secure a booking. Over time, complaints began trickling in from minorities who felt they'd been discriminated against by hosts who declined to accept booking requests from them. By 2016, that trickle had turned into a tsunami as black users took to Twitter, Facebook, and other social media sites to share their stories. Their experiences requesting [Airbnb] accommodations—whether in small-town Idaho or cosmopolitan Philadelphia—were remarkably similar: They'd tried to book a place and were told by the owner that it wasn't available. Some had white friends try to book the same place for the same time period, and it suddenly became available. Some users even tried posing as white, changing their photograph and name, and, when they did, found that they could easily book places that were unavailable to them as black. . . . A rigorous field experiment found that blacks were 16 percent less likely to be accepted as guests than whites.
>
> —Jennifer Eberhardt, "Can Airbnb Train Hosts Not to Be Racists?" *The Daily Beast*, June 12, 2019[1]

The discussion of Du Bois in chapter 3 highlighted the role of identity groups for oppressed and exploited minorities, specifically African Americans, in their progress toward justice and self-elevation. But Du Bois and his heirs have always been inward facing, and although they may be morally righteous and justified in their aims, they have failed to take the full measure of those who oppose them, both by directly attacking them and by not disrupting a racist status quo to help them. The result is that racial progress is followed by regress, such as Jim Crow after Reconstruction, what Michelle Alexander has called "The New Jim Crow" after the civil rights legislation of the 1960s, and the Tea Party and recrudescent White Nationalism before and after Barack Obama became president. Following Obama's presidency, but related to white objection to the fact of an African American president, White Nationalism became more open and explicit during the Trump administration.

Something is wrong with a movement or system of progress that cannot anticipate and avoid regress. It does not help to fatalistically accept a cyclical theory of ebb and flow or two steps forward and one step back. To accept that is to abandon expectation that it is even possible to steadily move ahead toward racial equality or the absence of inequality based on race. Needed are mechanisms and perspectives that can make progress permanent. The resulting progressivism by and on behalf of racial minorities needs to be inclusive in ways that will forestall regress, so that those who want to go back will be deterred by having too much lose.

From the Third Reich in Hitler's Germany to the years of Trump in the United States, the opposition to nonwhite racial minority group efforts to achieve equality or even to manage to survive have been variants of White Supremacy and white supremacy. White Supremacists (capitalized) are explicit white anti-nonwhite racists who want to expand the power of whites over nonwhites, sometimes with the use of force; white supremacists (lowercase) are a large number of racially nonviolent white people who accept the status quo of racial inequality and do not strongly or effectively oppose White Supremacists. Part of this inertia can be captured by a description of political party affiliation groups that includes the majorities of Democrats and Republicans. According to a 2018 report, "Hidden Tribes," conducted through surveys over a year by More in Common, the majority of Democratic and Republican voters have more in common with their majority counterparts in the other party than with radicals or extremists in their own parties.[2] That is, the political majorities within each party have a broad range of agreement about what citizens need government to do for them. If we assume that whites who tolerate but do not strongly or effectively oppose White Supremacists are part of this group among Republicans, this result suggests that the nonwhite and white liberal majority of Democrats may not urgently object to White Supremacists either, although for reasons with a different emphasis. Some of the Republican white supremacists may be tacitly racist but focused on practical issues, while the Democratic majority, although not tacitly racist, may think that practical problems involving health care, education, and employment are the most urgent political concerns. Thus, it may be that in pragmatic empirical terms, the mass of traditional or conservative whites (i.e., Republican whites who have not crushed White Supremacists) and liberals and people of color (i.e., Democrat whites and people of color, who raise stronger voices against White Supremacy) have more in common than either group does with extremists in their own political parties.

The point is that both majorities in the dominant American political parties are focused on what government should do to make life better for large numbers of Americans. Here, the matter of priorities can be added to the likelihood of defeat for progressives who explicitly concentrate on racial identities and conflicts. However, if and when the primary concerns of both political groups are emphasized and addressed, there would still remain live issues of racism and racists, which it falls to theorists to cogently explain. This chapter begins with a brief discussion of that racist residue and moves on to the nature of white supremacy (lowercase). A closer examination reveals that white supremacy is a status system of race. The intellectual history of the idea of race in the modern period shows that it has always been racist. If race is viewed as a status, several puzzles can be solved and the discussion shifts from concrete racisms to the general intractability of white racial status.

THE RACIST RESIDUE

Doesn't a focus on middle-of-the-road majorities simply ignore the heart of anti-nonwhite racism?[3] Racism should not be ignored, but, like landmines, there is nothing wrong, either practically or morally, with avoiding direct contact with its dangerous aspects before removing it—if it can be removed. Institutional racism that results from outdated systems favoring whites is impersonal, and it can, in principle, be corrected in a top-down way by changing policies. Rights that are supposed to be egalitarian can be protected across racial groups, or throughout them. However, not only are these big goals that are difficult to achieve, but, even if achieved, there would still be a residue of aversion to nonwhites by whites. This aversion is often emotional, visceral, and intimate, and it plays out in complexes involving bodily reactions and social and physical distance between whites and members of other racial groups.[4] Should progressives passively or fatalistically accept that white supremacist residue? Of course not, because the racist residue is a waste of collective energy, which harms people of color, distracts whites from real problems, and creates cumulative stress for nonwhites.[5] It should not be accepted as a moral matter, because it is unjust and its irrationality damages the psychological health of shared society. The residue has to be dissolved, a multivarious project that probably comes down to individual hearts and minds and one-on-one interactions, after the structural issues are solved or resolved for instance by programs for reparation, enforcement of nondiscrimination laws, or more inclusive systems for the distribution of justice and material goods. Rules and behavioral expectations in nongovernment institutions are also extremely relevant.

The United States remains socially segregated in K–12 education, residential neighborhoods, and churches, which are important sources of individual values at all stages of life. But given this private and social segregation, workplaces (including business, government, the military, entertainment and media studios, professional offices, and institutions of higher education) are all continuous sites of interracial interaction that do allow for attitudinal change on individual levels. Indeed, such extragovernmental institutions and organizations have been in the process of becoming more racially egalitarian and inclusive since the civil rights movements of the 1960s. This has been a slow and unsteady process. But government cannot directly intervene into society concerning the residue of aversive white dominance, without exacerbating white racist resentment and hatred. So governmental efforts toward racial egalitarianism need to be framed and implemented in ways that bypass such aversion while it remains undissolved.

History teaches us about the dangers of the use of government force against specific forms of social racism in violent reactions to civil rights activists[6] and the formation of new White Supremacist groups when nonwhites appear to receive special treatment.[7] Backlash and regress against progress toward racial equality have come to seem almost inevitable, and they are often "philosophically" accepted. But this view is incomplete. If progress were thorough, if the work of racist dissolution were accomplished, progress could continue without interruption and stalling. Required is a critical mass of whites behind such progress, with the force of moral imperative, or, if that cannot be mustered, collective advocacy for groups that include both whites and nonwhites, such as poor people, children, the elderly, LBGTQ+ communities, those who are disabled, very poor people who are homeless, and disaster victims. This could be brought about by more cross-racial egalitarian framing and implementation of programs and policies that benefit nonwhites—but there has to be something in it for whites as well. In other words, given backlash and regress, the inclusivity sought by nonwhites has to be matched by inclusivity *for* whites.

The logic of this situation of exclusion and inclusion as practical matters, depends on the *existential standpoint* or where people are, and what they accept as knowledge or think that they know. Little can be accomplished by insisting that whites are willfully ignorant, because people do not have access to that of which they are ignorant and they will act only on what they accept as knowledge. From the standpoint of nonwhites, inclusivity for them means that they will be included where they are presently excluded, *in practice*. But from the standpoint of many whites, new efforts by nonwhites for inclusion would be changes in a status quo, appearing to them to be special treatment for nonwhites, which they will reject, because it leaves them out. Many whites claim that nonwhites are already included, either because whites are ignorant of practical exclusions of nonwhites or because whites believe that inclusion is no more than the formal rights extended to nonwhites by law as a result of the civil rights legislation of the 1960s. From the standpoint of membership in the whole unit that includes whites and nonwhites, any change in the status quo will be accepted, and thereby acceptable, only if it clearly benefits both whites and nonwhites, on the basis of what whites, as well as nonwhites, accept as knowledge. Such epistemological multiracial inclusion is necessary for progress because whites are dominant in society and generally more powerful than nonwhites.

To spell this idea out further, if whites believe that racial equality already exists and are ignorant of practical inequalities and do not actively seek to correct or undo their ignorance, then they will only accept change that is a clear benefit to them, given their ignorance. At any given time, the project of making change acceptable is a different project from that of dispelling ignorance. In practical terms, the whole unit of whites and nonwhites will accept progress only if it is progress for the majority of the whole unit. As a practical matter, and especially as a political matter, progress has to be devised in ways that will be perceived to benefit all who are affected by it, taking into account what some members of the whole may not know and may refuse to learn. Concealed practices of discrimination that work against minority groups indirectly by targeting proxies for their racial identities, instead of those racial identities themselves, need to be bypassed. The new racism of the post–civil rights era often has "plausible deniability." Bias against culture is deemed acceptable after bias against physical race no longer is. For example, those Airbnb hosts who reject black guests (as described in the chapter epigraph) may claim that it is not black people per se who they are rejecting, but rather people who may watch television programs or play music that they would find disruptive. To understand the practical need for such indirect strategy, it is necessary to take a closer look at white supremacy and take its measure.

THE NATURE AND MEASURE OF WHITE SUPREMACY

Institutional racism continues through its own inertia that consists in mechanisms for reproducing itself. White privilege in comparison to the violation of rights of nonwhites remains in place. And there is a residue of racism that would remain, even after institutional racism and comparative white privilege (that is, by comparison to violation of the rights of nonwhites) were curtailed. Much of this residue is the result of a *racial status system*. Whites have higher status than nonwhites. Even if all things such as class are held constant, whites still have higher status based on race. In Brazil, money is said to override the social disadvantages of race.[8] But in the United States, while middle- and upper-class blacks are better off than lower-class blacks, they are not as well off as whites in the same socioeconomic class. While lower-class whites may not be better off than middle- or upper-class blacks, they are better off than blacks in their same socioeconomic class. That is, if class is constant, differences in measures of other forms of well-being, such as upward mobility, vary with race.[9]

Overt racial resentment, insult, and assault have long been considered more prevalent among lower-class whites, even though it may be just as salient in covert ways among middle- and upper-class whites. US progressives have for a long time—it is now an obstructive tradition based on stereotyping—assumed that poor whites are more likely to be racist than middle- and upper-class whites, out of resentment, induced competition for economic resources, and/or capitalistic propaganda that splits the working class along racial lines. The thesis is that workers in general are divided into whites and nonwhites. Whites are made more tractable in exchange for having racial whiteness ascribed to them ("the wages of whiteness") and nonwhites can be exploited and discriminated against by white workers, as well as owners and managers.[10] However, during the 2016 presidential election, in which Republicans campaigned with racist innuendo, the average Donald Trump supporter had a higher income than the average Hillary Clinton supporter.[11] Also, at this time, poor whites may be more concerned with the educational, achievement, wealth, and income gaps, which apply to them, than with racial inequality from which they benefit.[12]

Recent studies have indicated that increasing numbers of blacks, as well as whites, are more likely to posit character traits as the cause of racial wealth and achievement gaps, than institutional factors or racial discrimination.[13] That is, many blacks agree with the majority of whites that individuals are responsible for how well they do in life. Nonwhites thereby have come to join whites in not taking seriously the very idea of institutional racism as an overriding determining factor of the disadvantages of being nonwhite, especially black. Whether this is shared ignorance or a consensus on which progressives can build is an open question, but it does increase the need to focus on how the majority of Americans probably still define racism as a matter of hearts and minds, as well as feelings and attitudes.

The foregoing subtleties about how class is not related to racist attitudes in simple ways, together with reluctance of the public to join academics in emphasizing institutional racism, does not diminish the reality of race in society. As socially real, race is connected to an absolute status system. What exactly does that mean? One thing it means is that the United States is a white supremacist society. But the United

States is not a White Supremacist society in the early twenty-first century, because the legal structure is formally egalitarian regarding race and most powerful elites do not promulgate racist ideologies. The recent movement in academia and the media concerning white privilege is an attempt to put the spotlight on the advantages of being white, usually toward the goal of making whites aware of their own racism. But does the concept of racism provide a comprehensive analysis of persistent racial inequality? All or most whites benefit from being white. Some of these benefits are institutional, such as having close relatives who were able to accumulate wealth through home ownership or attending good schools in all-white neighborhoods. All of the benefits add up to most of white privilege, with the rest belonging to a residue of aversive racism or simply being white. Not all whites are aversive racists. Many whites continue to believe that racism means individual heart-and-mind aversion to and hatred of people of color. So it is not inconsistent of them to claim that they are not racists, even though they accept and enjoy white privilege. Thus, someone may be a white supremacist but not be a racist in the hearts-and-minds sense. They may perpetrate nonwhite suffering through *microaggressions* (i.e., small insults and slights) that they do not recognize are racist.[14] They may indignantly and even angrily deny that they are racist. How is this possible?

Let's reword and complicate this question. People of color in US society experience anti-nonwhite racism in many or all aspects of their lives, on a daily basis, but there are relatively few self-acknowledged white racists. And yet millions of white people benefit from being white, either in comparison to nonwhites or in some absolute sense that they do not believe entails they are racist. Much of white ignorance of the suffering of nonwhites inflicted by whites and their exploitation by whites is closed. This ignorance is closed because many whites who are ignorant of the experiences of nonwhites could become knowledgeable about them. But they will likely not take the trouble to expand their knowledge, because they believe their knowledge to be adequate or complete concerning race. The questions are: What keeps this expanse of white supremacy in place? Why does it endure, generation after generation? Why do so many white people not want to discuss their own racism and become angry and defensive when they are accused of being racists? What keeps white ignorance closed?

One explanation given by Robin DiAngelo in *White Fragility* is that racism is morally bad and many white racists want and need and otherwise have reason to believe they are morally good.[15] This explanation would be plausible if moral goodness were broadly understood in US culture and most Americans were continually interested in cultivating their virtues. In reality, virtues tend to be related to religion and moral goodness in ordinary life reduces to being nice, polite, or respectable. Even on a deeper moral level, most white people who are ignorant about race and racism are not evil monsters but probably good enough.

A more likely explanation of the impermeability of white attitudes and behavior concerning nonwhites is that whiteness is a racial status and racial identities are master identities in public and private life, because of that status. A positive status is an ongoing claim and a positive racial status is a lifelong ongoing claim (because racial identities are lifelong). White racial status is not a set of beliefs, attitudes, or actions, such as racism, but a static condition. We now need to take a closer look at the nature of status generally and racial status in particular.

STATUS AND RACIAL STATUS

Status and status systems are distinct from socioeconomic class and class systems, although in reality, the two are interrelated or "intersect." Max Weber's distinction is useful here. A class is defined by its situation, which is the likelihood of being provided with goods, certain external conditions of life, and subjective satisfaction of frustrations. A class is a group of people in the same class situation. The main types of classes are determined by property holdings, opportunities for the exploitation of services on the market, and a structure consisting of interactions with individuals in the same class and the transmission of the class situation over generations. In contrast to class, a *status* is a claim to positive or negative privilege in terms of social prestige that rests on a mode of living, education and training, and its modes of life, or the prestige of birth. Status may be based on class situation (for example, the poor have negative status), or status may determine class situation (for example, the status of a student as poor but nonetheless middle class). In sum: "A status group is a plurality of individuals who, within a larger group, enjoy a particular kind and level of prestige by virtue of their position and possibly also claim certain special monopolies." The most important sources of status group development are a distinct style of life, including occupation, hereditary charisma from a successful claim to prestige by virtue of birth, or the appropriation of political or hierocratic authority as a monopoly.[16]

In much of contemporary social science, studies of social goods, including income, wealth, and education, are further broken down by racial identities, according to which minorities fare worse than whites on almost all measures. These disparities are further complicated when blacks from the same socioeconomic class as whites do not equal whites in those class-related goods of life. Such racial inequalities are usually explained in terms of either institutional or structural racism or else interpersonal racial discrimination. However, we have seen that the disparities persist even though structural equality was formally secured with the legislation of the 1960s civil rights movement and even though few, except for White Supremacists, are willing to self-report as racists. Structural or institutional racism may account for differences in socioeconomic class, but it cannot account for differences within the same class. Interpersonal racial discrimination is a plausible posit, but it is difficult to prove when most whites claim that they are not racist in the hearts-and-minds sense. The soul-searching among whites who examine their own race privilege is supererogatory, because these whites are not deliberately racist or even otherwise aware of their racism in the normal course of events. And yet it makes sense to understand that these whites are white supremacists insofar as they benefit from what is overall a white-dominant system. Racism is thus attributed to the white-dominant or white supremacist "system" by progressives who emphasize institutional racism, while the majority of both traditionalists and conservatives, as well as political liberals, do not believe that "the system" really is responsible for racial disparities in life success.

Adding to overall opacity concerning varied racial gaps, reluctance to discuss their own racisms by possibly a majority of white people is widely reported in discussions of microaggression.[17] This reluctance, in combination with the other discrepancies, suggests that something is being left out of the typical progressive analysis that searches for concealed, subtle, and inexorable racisms as the primary cause of disparities in white and nonwhite human well-being. What has been left out in discussions of American (and, indeed, world) racism thus far is that race is not a biological kind, or even a stable social kind, but a *status*. Race is not a biological kind because there is no independent foundation for human racial taxonomy in the biological sciences. As a social kind, racial identities—that is, who is considered black or white or whether Latinx peoples are a race—vary from place to place and over history; the US Census that identifies respondents in terms of their self-reported races has continually changed official racial categories since its inception in 1790.[18] The concept of status is an important methodological mediating term and it is necessary, because it allows for analyses in which race is on the same conceptual level as class, instead of a kind of mysterious, random wild card that intervenes with class situations at different times.[19]

An account of race as status would proceed something like this. Racial identity is a location in a social status hierarchy of race. Racial status is a positive or negative charisma based on family descent and physical appearance. At this time, physical appearance, specifically skin color, is the leading racial identifier, although at other times (for example, when passing for white was considered a major social transgression in the United States) ancestry had more importance.[20] The "one-drop rule," or strong *hypodescent*, which was in effect during that time, preserved ideas of white racial purity by relegating those who had mixed black and white ancestry to the black race.[21] Many who were considered black under the one-drop rule in late nineteenth- and early twentieth-century America were mixed race, including both Booker T. Washington and W. E. B. Du Bois.

This one-drop rule for black descent has persisted into the twenty-first century. President Barack Obama, of widely known mixed-race descent, was classified as the first black president of the United States when he was elected in 2008.[22] That the highest political status of the president of the United States was not sufficient to cancel out this "one-drop rule" attests to the overriding power of the racial status system. Race is a "master identity," exactly because of this reality of the racial status system. As a master identity, the top status of white racial identity is presumed to be more closely associated with other important identities and status markers, such as ownership, wealth, and civic prestige. It is well known that many whites have historically claimed ownership of the United States as a nation. Contemporary white nationalism is an expression of such ownership and prestige in ways that complicate both racism and racial status. A strong part of the reaction against Obama's presidency rested on "birther" claims that he was not a legitimate US citizen, as required for holding that office. His racial blackness brought with it the idea that he could not have the highest civic prestige.[23] For many white racists, Obama's presidency was a contradiction, something impossible that had become actual.

The entire paradigm of antiracism, including hearts-and-minds racism in individuals, institutional or structural racism, and microaggression, rests on a justified assumption that there should be racial equality. Because there *should* be racial equality, thought, speech, actions, and social institutions that proceed as though races are unequal or nonwhites are less than human, or that contemns nonwhites in comparison to whites, is an evil that often has an element of surprise when it is identified in particular cases. However, if we think in terms of the racial status system, there is nothing surprising about racism(s), except their ability to manifest in new forms in changing times. White racial status is a lifelong claim to racial superiority that whites are born with, possess over their natural lives, and pass on to their children if they do not have nonwhite coparents. This racial status system that places whites first in terms of social prestige is already an overriding racist system that precludes real human equality across race. If equality across race is not assumed to be inherent in racial differences—that is, if racial differences are fully understood to be socially constructed and socially variable—then such equality cannot be grounded in race itself. Indeed, racial differences themselves, apart from what is identified as racism, are already unequal. This is because racial difference has never been a case of mere variety that in principle even allows for racial equality. To see how this is so, we need to consider the origins of the modern system of race and we need to understand that race as we have all come to know it, is fundamentally a hierarchical system of races. This conceptual claim cannot be fully understood apart from the intellectual history in which the modern system of races was invented.

THE INVENTION OF THE MODERN SYSTEM OF RACES[24]

As discussed in chapter 3, racial divisions were introduced by François Bernier, who posited a universal system of races, ranging over all humankind, to supplant existing ideas of peoples as historical groups. There is no limit in principle to the number of historical groups. But races in Bernier's universal sense have always entailed some specified, limited taxonomy. Bernier first published his "Nouvelle Division de la Terre" ("New Division of the Earth") anonymously but prestigiously in 1684 in the *Journal des Scavans*, the first academic journal in Europe. This pedigree is important because it set the stage for racial science—that is, the science of races—as issuing from premier publications and institutions of European and, later, American knowledge.

Bernier's new universal system of race had extensive and well-anointed influence, including from philosophers. Bernier divided humankind into races or species (he used these terms interchangeably), based solely on physical traits. He presented skin color, hair type, and bodily shape as more fundamental criteria for human classification than geographical origin or location, and he claimed that there were four or five species or races, according to those criteria: (1) the "first race," made up of people from Europe, North Africa, the Middle East, India, part of Southeast Asia, and the native population of the Americas; (2) the African negroes; (3) the East and Northeast Asian race; (4) the Lapps.[25] Bernier posited the greatest differences between 1 and 2, and he referred to 1, the "first race," as "we" throughout his text.

In 1735, Carolus (Carl) Linnaeus (1707–1788), a highly acclaimed Swedish botanist, physician, and zoologist, published *Systema Naturae*, in which humans were first classified as primates and then given their own category: *Homo sapiens*. Homo sapiens had four varieties (types within species) according to skin color and geography: *Europæus albus* (white European), *Americanus rubescens* (red American), *Asiaticus fuscus* (brown/yellow Asian), and *Africanus niger* (black African). Linnaeus later associated each variety with a humor or temperament: Europeans—sanguine; Americans—choleric; Asians—melancholy; Black—phlegmatic.[26] Linnaeus's racial posits were neutral, except for the humor posits—who would not prefer being sanguine, or associating with those who were sanguine, in preference to choleric, melancholy, or phlegmatic?

Johann Friedrich Blumenbach (1752–1840), who followed Linnaeus, added more explicit valuation to Linnaeus's racial distinctions, as well as a fifth race: the Malay variety among Asians. In *De Generis Humani Varietate Nativa* (*On the Natural Variety of Mankind*), Blumenbach invented the term "Caucasian" after the mountain range in Russia and Georgia. He described Caucasians as very beautiful and the likely origin of all human races. As Stephen Jay Gould pointed out, the five-race system enabled Blumenbach to center Caucasians in visual models. Blumenbach also designated nonwhite groups as "degenerations" from Caucasians. He believed that such degeneration was the result of environmental factors and that it could be reversed, with restoration to Caucasian racial identity.[27]

In 1749, French Naturalist and mathematician George-Louis Leclerc, Comte de Buffon (1707–1788) published the thirty-six-volume *Histoire Naturelle, générale et particulière, avec la description du Cabinet du Roi* (translated as *Natural History*), and his colleagues added eight posthumous volumes. Buffon took up Blumenbach's idea of degeneration and described racial differences as the effects of differences in climate, which he considered heritable. He emphasized gradations of difference between races, rather than abrupt species-type discontinuities. While such differences were inherited, Buffon also considered them changeable, even in single lifetime.[28] Buffon's enthusiasm about breeding projects to improve races anticipated eugenics (although eugenics did not aim for "improving" nonwhite races, but rather keeping them out of the white race).[29] Altogether, Buffon's contributions to early race science were not intrinsically hierarchical, but that was to come.

Not only did nineteenth-century racial science support the eugenics movement of the early twentieth century, but hierarchical racial taxonomy was also established through the writings of Georges Cuvier, Louis Agassiz, and Joseph Arthur de Gobineau, as well as the research of Samuel Morton. French naturalist and zoologist Georges Cuvier (1769–1832) departed from Blumenbach's five-race taxonomy by positing three distinct races—Caucasian, Mongoloid, and Ethiopian. He agreed with Blumenbach's ideas about Caucasian beauty and went beyond it to hold the white race to be "superior to others by its genius, courage and activity." He described the black race in ways that definitively set the stage for racial hierarchy:

> [M]arked by black complexion, crisped or woolly hair, compressed cranium and a flat nose. The projection of the lower parts of the face, and the thick lips, evidently approximate it to the monkey tribe: the

hordes of which it consists have always remained in the most complete state of barbarism.[30]

Attempts made to reinforce popular ideas of racial hierarchy, especially in mid-nineteenth-century America, built on work such as Cuvier's, moving into speculations about differences in mental endowment that were based on unreliable empirical data. It was assumed that brain size is directly related to intelligence. Stephen Jay Gould chronicles some of this work in his 1981 *The Mismeasure of Man*, including the craniometric or skull measurement studies conducted by physician Samuel George Morton (1799–1851). Based on skull size, Morton, who believed that human races were different species, rather than varieties (greater differences were posited between species than between varieties), claimed in *Crania Americana* that whites had the biggest skulls and blacks the smallest. Gould casts doubt on the accuracy of Morton's measurements that included substituting bird seed for birdshot (shotgun pellets) in measuring the volumes of black skulls, which resulted in less volume.[31]

Gould also discusses the career of Swiss naturalist Louis Agassiz (1807–1873), who became a professor at Harvard in 1848 and in 1859 founded the University's Museum of Comparative Zoology, directing it for the rest of his life. Agassiz was and still is highly honored on the campus of Harvard University,[32] but today he would be considered a virulent racist. Although he opposed slavery, he believed that African Americans were a distinct species. In the great nineteenth century debate about monogeny (one human origin) versus polygeny (multiple human origins), Agassiz began as a monogenist in Europe but was persuaded to polygenism by American colleagues and his experiences with black Americans who waited on him in a hotel. Besides his polygenism, Agassiz believed that races should be ranked in human worth:

> There are upon earth different races of men, inhabiting different parts of its surface, which have different physical characters; and this fact presses upon us the obligation to settle the relative rank among these races, the relative value of the characters peculiar to each, in a scientific point of view. As philosophers it is our duty to look it in the face.

Of Africa, he wrote:

> There has never been a regulated society of black men developed on that continent. Does not this indicate in this race a peculiar apathy, a peculiar indifference to the advantages afforded by civilized society?[33]

Agassiz believed that after the Civil War, blacks would remain in the South and that they should be educated only in manual labor; he was an adamant segregationist, as well as a great admirer of Morton, whom he visited in Philadelphia when Morton had collected six hundred of his eventual total collection of over one thousand skulls.[34]

Mention of French avowed elitist Joseph Arthur de Gobineau (1816–1882) completes this very brief account. Gobineau responded to the French Revolution of 1848 by publishing *An Essay on the Inequality of the Human Races* (the same year Harvard hired Agassiz). Gobineau's ideas were well received by white supremacists and anti-Semites in the United States, although the extirpated form of his 1,200-word tome that circulated left out his claims that most Americans were not racially pure (Gobineau believed that the downfall of all great civilizations was the result of race mixing).[35]

Racist science in the twentieth century supported the eugenics movement restricting inclusion and reproduction of members of groups considered inferior to others. British scholar Francis Galton (1822–1911), a relative of Darwin, is considered the founder of the eugenics movement, although his efforts were not as effective in England as in the United States (or especially Nazi Germany). Charles Davenport (1866–1944), who was educated in zoology at Harvard University, founded and was director of the US Eugenics Records Office. He was influenced by Galton's work and involved with the journal *Biometrika*. Davenport's influence extended to congressional passage of the Johnson-Reed Immigration Act of 1924, which limited immigration to 2 percent of nationalities then residing in the United States and restricted entry from Southern and Eastern Europe.[36]

And now for the philosophers, beginning with David Hume, followed by Kant and Hegel. Hume first referred to racial differences in the 1754 edition of his *Essays* during a public intellectual debate about whether the human species had one origin (monogenism) or several corresponding to each race (polygenism). Eighteenth-century monogenists believed that differences in climate, geography, and food caused racial differences, which they did not think were permanent but could change over a few generations, when people changed environments. The polygenists believed that Africans, Asians, and Indians were permanently inferior to whites, because their inferiority was part of their original, unchanging racial identities. As a doctrine, polygenism posited strong racial differences, and in keeping with this practice, in the first version of Hume's infamous footnote, he referred not to different human races but to species, a more general taxonomic division than race, which does not allow for interbreeding:

> I am apt to suspect the negroes and in general all the other species of men (for there are four or five different kinds) to be naturally inferior to the whites. There never was a civilized nation of any other complexion than white, nor even any individual eminent either in action or speculation.[37]

Hume developed a general thesis that differences in human groups or "national characters" were moral—that is, the result of history, custom, and psychology, rather than physical, environmental factors. According to Hume, cultural differences had cultural causes, because of the strong human tendency toward imitation of those nearby and a near-universal sentiment of sympathy. However, this moral/cultural nature of causes of human difference apparently did not apply to groups living under extremes of temperature—particularly the inhabitants of Africa—and it is when Hume is discussing exceptions to moral causes of difference in temperate climates that his footnote appears. It is puzzling that Hume draws such strong differences based on race, because in his essay "Of the Populousness of Ancient Peoples," written before 1754, when the harshest version of the infamous footnote first appeared, Hume also refers to the uniformity of the human species:

> Stature and force of body, length of life, even courage and extent of genius, seem hitherto to have been naturally, in all ages, pretty much the same. The arts and sciences, indeed, have flourished in one period, and have decayed in another . . . . As far, therefore, as observation reaches, there is no universal difference discernible in the human species.[38]

Immanuel Kant, unlike Hume, was a monogenicist, believing that all humanity was descended from the same *stem*. But, like Hume, he assumed that there are races: "The reason for assuming the Negroes and Whites to be fundamental races is self-evident."[39] Overall, Kant put forth and advanced ethnological Eurocentric theses about differences in human reason, morality, and taste—for example, his often-quoted "The white race possesses all motivating forces and talents in itself"[40] and "This fellow was quite black from head to foot, a clear proof that what he said was stupid."[41] Kant wrote about differences among the anthropological "national characters" of the French, Spanish, and English, but he exalted Germans, referring to their "distinctive feeling of the beautiful and the sublime." In considering Africans, however, his discourse changed from anthropology to race in a geographical sense, with acknowledgment of Hume:

> The Negroes of Africa have by nature no feeling that rises above the trifling. Mr. Hume challenges anyone to cite a single example in which a Negro has shown talents, and asserts that among the hundreds of thousands of blacks who are transported elsewhere from their countries, although many of whom have even been set free, still not a single one was ever found who presented anything great in art or science or any other praise-worthy quality, even though among the whites some continually rise aloft from the lowest rabble, and through superior gifts earn respect in the world. So fundamental is the difference between these two races of man, and it appears to be as great in regard to mental capacities as in color.[42]

Robert Bernasconi observes that Kant was the first to define "race" as a term for large groups of people with heritable difference in his 1775 essay, "On the Different Races of Human Beings."[43] Bernasconi compares Kant's discussions of the Khoikhoi (also known as the Hottentots) with that of Jean-Jacques Rousseau. Rousseau discussed the culture and perspectives of the Hottentots, whereas Kant simply treated them as objects without subjectivity. This was damaging to any attempt to include nonwhites in the moral universe, because Kant was the preeminent theorist of moral dignity who based intrinsic human worth on the fact that a person's life was subjectively valuable to that person.[44] Kant's racialism, or belief in the existence of human races, was thus indistinguishable from his racism or weighted comparison of races in terms of superior and inferior human worth.

In contrast to Kant, Hegel's reliance on geography was directly tied to Western history, insofar as nonwhite racial categories were imposed on people in Africa, Asia, and the Americas during the so-called "Age of Discovery." By the time Hegel addressed race in the early nineteenth century, the effects of colonialism had concretely changed ways of life in many non-European parts of the world: lands were taken, cultures disrupted, and inhabitants brutalized, tortured, killed, enslaved, or subjected to hostile foreign rule. But more than that, geography for Hegel was an expression of abstract spirit, and he wrote African people out of human history on that basis:

> Africa Proper is the characteristic part of the whole continent as such. We have chosen to examine this continent first, because it can well be taken as antecedent to our main enquiry. It has no historical interest of its own, for we find its inhabitants living in barbarism and slavery in a land which has not furnished them with any integral ingredient of culture. From the earliest historical times, Africa has remained cut off from all contacts with the rest of the world; it is the land of gold, forever pressing in upon itself, and the land of childhood, removed from the light of self-conscious history and wrapped in the dark mantle of night. Its isolation is not just a result of its tropical nature, but an essential consequence of its geographical character.[45]

WHITE STATUS AND RACIAL TAXONOMY

Yes, we can now say that the scientists and philosophers responsible for the modern invention of race were racist. But not only is that anachronistic, because they had no concept of racism as they exercised their intellectual privileges to create hierarchical racial taxonomies, but it is also too quick a move. What is important to infer from that intellectual history is that the fact of racial hierarchy was historically coincident with the invention of race. Except for the Scottish clergy who castigated David Hume, there were few then-contemporary projects of substance to disprove those who posited racial hierarchy.[46] Now, the idea of racial hierarchy is presumed bogus in the face of self-evident universal human rights and moral equality. However, insofar as "race" originally meant "races in a hierarchy privileging whites," it became the theme of a racial status system that endures to this day. Status and race have remained coextensive and inseparable. The time for arguments with facts against founding claims of racial hierarchy was long past by the beginning of the twentieth century. Between Bernier and someone like W. E. B. Du Bois, there were two centuries of manifest racial inequality, caused by White Supremacism. All factual arguments that the so-called races always have been equal have been cast as what *should* be the case in terms of human worth, not what is and has been.

White people have white racial status, which is the best racial status. They have not earned this status and it is not justified by the facts of human nature and achievement, but there is scant reason to believe that expressions of racial equality or demands for it are sufficient to dislodge that status. White racial status is the racist residue that would remain after institutional racism were corrected and racial hatred and other forms of emotional racism were abolished. The only way that white racial status could be eliminated would be to eliminate all ideas of race itself. Racial distinctions and differences are not mere varieties, they never have been, and there is no reason to believe that they ever will be. (Of course, there are relatively "decent" and polite, as well as abusive, forms of white status, but that is not the point here.) White racial status has ranged from colonialism, slavery, and state-mandated second-class citizenship (Jim Crow) to post–civil rights movement backlash against remedies for racial inequality. It perhaps comes to rest in microaggressions in otherwise egalitarian liberal society.

Social scientists and humanistic scholars should discontinue analyses of racial inequality that rely exclusively on racism. The concept of white racial status can take over some of the work now done by the concept of racism. As noted, racism involves beliefs and actions, whereas status is a state. White people do not have to say or do or think anything to retain their white status within a system of races. White racial status generates advantages and privileges without conscious intent or awareness.

Returning to Du Bois's vision of the destiny of the Negro race, discussed in chapter 3, there can be no such thing. Modern races are not isolated groups that take their turn on some stage of civilization. Members of the different races are already co-mingled in places of work, major social institutions, and private life. Whenever whites and nonwhites come together, whites have higher racial status. Even if the black race were to produce new unimaginably important achievements, as the achievements of black people, which white people fully recognized, white people would retain their superior racial status. White racial status could only be eliminated with the elimination of race.

Now that really would be an eliminativist proposal! But it could not be fulfilled at this time because nonwhites have experienced too much as nonwhites to give up a shared identity based on those experiences, and whites or mixed-race people do not have the right to request they give that up.[47] Nor could government impose an elimination of race, and racial status with it, without another civil war. Race and racial status thus constitute an impasse for racially egalitarian society. But they do not preclude egalitarian government that inclusively delivers to members of all racial groups the goods that only government can deliver and to which they are equally entitled. This is the meaning of "progressive anonymity," and its fulfillment would require government without constituent identities, based on the best information available. This would be evidence-based government, to which chapters 5 and 6 are devoted.

CONCLUSION

Not all white people who benefit from a system that favors whites are White Supremacists. In the early twenty-first century, White Supremacy is no longer legally mandated and its violent expressions are still considered deviant. However, white supremacy (lowercase) is a different matter and it would be part of the racist residue if both institutional and hearts-and-minds racisms were corrected. For this reason, the idea of race as a status system should be added to progressive analyses, along with racism. This is because the meaning of race has always been a hierarchy of races, with whites having the most prestige. Those scientists and philosophers who posited the existence of human races in the modern period no sooner said there were races than they began to rank them. The idea of race is thus inherently racist and given white racial status as a static lifelong condition, egalitarian liberatory projects based on racial identities are not likely to succeed—white people have and will protect their racial status. For the same reason, it would be advantageous to people of color to forgo representation within government, based on their racial identities, in favor of racially anonymous government that aimed to solve the problems of all groups, based on evidence.

The last is not the kind of suggestion that would be welcome to most progressives. US history is replete with longings and actions in which government stepped in to restore justice and right wrongs. Such fulfillment may work when criminals are apprehended and punished, or in providing safety nets such as Medicaid, Medicare, Social Security, and broad relief and compensation in disasters, but it does not have a good record for instituting social progress or fulfilling aspirations. Thus, despite the legislation of the 1960s, discrimination against people of color remains evident internally and at our borders, and women continue to be lesser citizens than men. Although life has generally become more bearable for both domestic people of color and women, inequalities in wealth and income are well entrenched. Remedies for people of color, women, immigrants, and the poor—which are often "intersecting" (that is, overlapping) social categories or identities—are no sooner proposed in the names of these contingencies than they become intensely politicized. As a result, there is little progress from government, because government is itself intensely politicized, to the point of dysfunction about such issues. Race and racial distinctions have always been imbued with status. There is nothing transformative about the idea of racial equality. The history and continuing traditions of the racial status system have so far not yielded to moral argument, and beyond that, there has so far not been sufficient incentive for white supremacists to give up their status.

5

EVIDENCE-BASED GOVERNMENT AND ITS OBSTACLES

There is no longer any doubt that neither arts nor governments provide for their own interests; but, as we were before saying, they rule and provide for the interests of their subjects who are the weaker and not the stronger—to their good they attend and not to the good of the superior.

—Plato, *The Republic*[1]

I think God calls all of us to fill different roles at different times. And I think he wanted Donald Trump to become president and that's why he's there.

—Sarah Sanders, White House press secretary[2]

And more important even than opening the political debate may be a proper attitude towards the political Day of Judgment.

—Karl Popper, "Democracy in America"[3]

It may be that one of the reasons philosophers continue to canonize Plato is that he said philosophers would rule in the ideal state, although his own attempts at statecraft in Syracuse notoriously failed.[4] Indeed, practical failure has not proved incompatible with philosophical acceptance of theories of government, because the theorists simply move to higher ground. The result may be ideal theory, refinements of ideal theory, so-called nonideal theory, or concentration on the terminology and methodologies of analysis in detailed areas of political philosophy.

All of this is nice enough for philosophers who have secure sinecures and delightful private or semiprivate gardens while the world catches fire, floods, or unravels during a pandemic under corrupt and incompetent government. Government is exactly an invention with the capability of addressing, ameliorating, and sometimes solving big problems that cannot be tackled within society. Unfortunately, the history of government as an institution has been rife with extreme social inequalities and dissipation of resources through military confrontations over issues that only rarely affect those governed in constructive or progressive ways. I don't think that philosophers in general or this philosopher in particular are capable of solving our species' collective Big Problems, because even if we came up the right ideas, we neither know how nor have the ability to implement them. But we could at least aim our efforts in that general direction. So in this chapter and the next, I will examine some of the promise and problems that would attend evidence-based government policy.

We are not done with Plato, because he did not seek political power for philosophers purely for the sake of power or because their superiority merited such a high position. As the first epigraph to this chapter shows, Plato's idea of rule by philosophers was connected to a presumption that their education and talents would result in wisdom, specifically political wisdom that would benefit those they ruled.[5] Sometimes overlooked is his argument in *The Republic* that governing is a craft, so that rulers need to be specialists.[6] Such specialization can be interpreted today as past work experience and education or previously held elected office and knowledge, real factual knowledge of history, peoples, government, society, culture, and science. It strikes some as remarkable when celebrities or others with no apparently relevant education or experience are occasionally elected to high office.[7] And it is also against traditional norms in a country that is not a theocracy to connect holding high office with the preferences of deities (e.g., the second chapter epigraph).

Disruption of norms for governmental electability and legitimacy occur, because the rationality of the norms can be by-passed by emotional qualities of popularity, charisma, and whether voters identify with candidates. The doctrine of the divine right of kings was written out of the US Constitution, but increases in the power of the US presidency have been largely unchecked in the early twenty-first century.[8] Another disruptive factor is provided by a prominent theory of how human language evolved, which suggests that public speaking—that is, speech making, as well as gossip—developed out of primate grooming habits.[9] Many more people can be groomed via a microphone and electronic broadcast than would be the case if bugs and skin crusts were individually removed, one by one, one on one, by any given speaker. The modern political scandal is a form of gossip, writ large, and when it is vulgar and salacious, it may be a symbolic return to the physical intimacy of one-on-one primate grooming. Neither modern political speeches nor gossip are intellectual or factual discourse, so if this theory is correct, effective critical responses to them cannot rely on cognitive content, alone. For many recipients of contemporary political messages, cognitive evaluation is by-passed by emotional reactions that are faster than conscious thought and originate in different parts of the brain. Moreover, there may be no conscious awareness of the processing of emotional reactions, as there is with thinking.[10] It therefore requires effort to sort out the cognitive and emotional content of modern political messaging, before evaluation is even possible, and many people are neither aware of the effort required nor motivated to expend it. It also requires effort for otherwise informed observers to understand this emotional dimension of political life and action, and many have still failed to recognize contexts in which rational, cognitive persuasion that is presented logically, with factual evidence, will not change people's minds.

The moral and political philosopher whose insights are most relevant to this issue of reason in (or for) government was, of course, David Hume. He wrote in the *Treatise*:

> On this method of thinking the greatest part of moral philosophy, ancient and modern, seems to be founded; nor is there an ampler field, as well for metaphysical arguments, as popular declamations, than this suppos'd pre-eminence of reason above passion. The eternity, invariableness, and divine origin of the former have been display'd to the best advantage: The blindness, unconstancy, and deceitfulness of the latter have been as strongly insisted on. In order to shew the fallacy of all this philosophy, I shall endeavour to prove first, that reason alone can never be a motive to any action of the will; and secondly, that it can never oppose passion in the direction of the will.[11]

If David Hume was correct that "reason" is a "slave of the passions," some of those who agree with him might be content not to bother sorting out the emotional-cognitive mix. But those who take a cognitive approach to emotions as expressive of beliefs that are matters of cognition would reject Hume on this description and go further to disagree with Hume's additional claim that reason *ought* to be the slave of the passions.[12] Moreover, even if one thoroughly agreed with Hume that reason is and ought to be a slave of the passions, there is still a place for reason in figuring out how any particular passion can be served. Even very powerful passions, such as greed, require instrumental reasoning to be fulfilled.

To propose *evidence-based* government is to propose a cognitive ideal, which at this time is impractical. While some political leaders continue to present ideals of educated citizenry, education is required to comprehend and appreciate such ideals.[13] But here and there, political candidates and government officials do discuss practical issues, rather than ideals, based on evidence, so the impracticality is not an absolute impossibility, and incremental change can lead to more incremental change and eventually paradigm change. (During the first half of 2020, a number of otherwise anti-scientific governmental officials slowly yielded to the efficacy of social distancing and widespread business closures to mitigate COVID-19 contagion.)

If relevant education and past experience were widely required for election and appointment, then both would be evidence-based. More frequently referred to is evidence-based public policy, which is about as unpopular among administrators as evidence-based elections and appointments would be among voters, political candidates, and those who appoint others to political office, as well as their lucky appointees. It is unpopular because officials use public office to serve themselves or those who support their careers—that is, because public service remains an ever-receding mirage of an ideal. But evidence-based public policy can be understood, it has been practiced, and lessons learned can be applied to elections and appointments.

The cognitive ideal of evidence-based government pertains to the purpose and functioning of government, not to the scope and aim of that purpose. It is a form of instrumental reasoning, based on agreed-upon goals or desirable effects. However, the whole of government itself, or any particular government, can also be viewed as evidence-based in terms of whether it is making life better for those governed. That view of government was developed in modern social contract theory—benefit to those governed is both a founding goal and an ongoing test of any government in existence. In this sense, government itself is always falsifiable—it might not live up to its founding purpose, and the people therefore (in principle) have the right to abolish or change it. From this chapter to the end of the book, evidence-based public policy is considered as an empirical approach to governing. The first section about Popper's empirical approach to government leads into the difference between ideological and evidence-based government. Next comes a discussion of several obstacles to evidence-based government, from the perspective of public policy studies. The last section is a discussion of the Nudge movement.

POPPER'S EMPIRICAL APPROACH TO GOVERNMENT

There were two parts to Popper's empirical approach to government—diagnostic and prescriptive (as discussed in chapter 1). His use of the falsifiability principle from philosophy of science to criticize Marxism was part of the overall diagnostic project undertaken by a progressive cohort in the aftermath of World War II. It is the prescriptive or positive part of Popper's political theory that is of interest now. In his 1988 article for *The Economist*, he identified the primary problem in the history of political philosophy, from Plato to Karl Marx and beyond, as "Who should rule?" He claimed that this framing led to endless battles over the legitimacy of government in general or particular governments, as based on the people, God, the workers, capitalists, the US electoral college, and so forth. Popper's innovative theory, which he had developed in *The Open Society and Its Enemies*, was that there should be a new problem: "How is the state to be constituted so that bad rulers can be got rid of without bloodshed, without violence?" Popper assumed that this practical problem had been solved in modern democracies that hold the principle that "the government can be dismissed by a majority vote" that he called "the political Day of Judgment" (see the third epigraph to this chapter).

According to Popper, democracy is not rule by the people as commonly thought, because the people never directly rule. It is rule by law.

Thus, "we do not base our choice on the goodness of democracy, which may be doubtful, but solely on the evilness of a dictatorship, which is certain."[14] Popper thus posed a pessimistic problem, which, if taken seriously, requires acceptance of political criticism and dissent as a democratic process that both precedes the "Political Day of Judgment" and continues after it, until the next one. Principles or claims made within the democratic process, like scientific theories, are falsifiable on this view. But Popper's claim about getting rid of bad government is confusing. Can the bad government to be got rid of arise in a democracy? The answer is yes (for instance, the Third Reich).[15] And can bad government—that is, totalitarian government—be eliminated by the rule of law? Insofar as bad government overrides the rule of law, the answer is generally no, because it required a world war to topple bad governments such as the Third Reich. Without the rule of law associated with democracy, there can be no political day of judgment through majority-rule free elections. What remains from Popper's thesis is something like this: Between periods of violence and bloodshed, the rule of law in democracies makes it possible to get rid of bad government. And only so long as the rule of law is in effect can bad governments be voted out.

However, there is rarely a consensus over the entire electorate about what constitutes bad government. There may also be different views of what the rule of laws is, for example, during presidential impeachment proceedings in the US Senate.[16] In times of intense political division in a two-party system, both sides might proclaim endorsement of the rule of law but mean different things by it (i.e., provide different instantiations of this idea). So perhaps the rule of law has to be understood to hold in only a very broad sense that requires the absence of violence and bloodshed by or against the government, during an administration or regime, periods of election, and changes in administration.

THE DIFFERENCE BETWEEN IDEOLOGICAL AND EVIDENCE-BASED GOVERNMENT

Popper's empiricism concentrated on his demand that political theories be empirical—that is, falsifiable—and that government practice consist of piecemeal policies that could be revised if they did not produce expected results—that is, if they did not work. However, because political theories do not themselves cause the structure and workings of government, the empiricism/falsifiability of political theories is not as important as he thought. No political theory automatically becomes a government through the strength of ideas alone. Ideas have to be accepted and then applied in concrete historical circumstances and rulers have to be selected and certain policies created and applied. Popper consistently seems to have believed that ideas cause different forms of government. Ideas may inspire particular forms of government, but it is also possible that the practices of a government do not fulfill the ideas or ideology professed by its leaders and created by its theorists.

Like Jean-Paul Sartre in *Search for a Method*, Popper's quarrel with Marxism was not a quarrel with the ideology per se, but with the rigid thought processes of those who professed it. Both Popper and Sartre rejected Marxism as a description of real historical events and castigated Marxists for refusing to change the predictive nature of their theories when real historical events did not fulfill their predictions.[17] While Sartre's criticism of Marxism cleared the way for him to restate his philosophy of existentialism in political terms, Popper thought that the rejection of Marxism was the rejection of a certain kind of government.

At any rate, Popper abandoned Marxism for its nonempiricism and was criticized for doing so while most progressives were still Marxists. He responded to these critics, whose views he otherwise respected, by referring to a more general principle of humanitarianism, which he thought Marxists also sought. In 1943–1944 letters to Hyman Levy, Herbert Read, and Friedrich Hayek, he addressed his correspondents as members of "the humanitarian camp" or "the camp of the left." And he reiterated a goal of uniting liberals and socialists.[18] This move to a more abstract level for the sake of unity was logically coherent. But if Marxism or other ideologies are not automatically instantiated as forms of government, why should humanitarianism or any general principle of benevolence have that power? The issue here is not one of internal logic and overcoming disagreement, but rather the question of how empirically based government works, what it is. In reality, bad government is not so much the effect of bad ideas about government but of how the process of governing functions in specific historical, cultural, and economic contexts, with competing interests. Still, it remains important that although Popper sought to unify socialists and liberals on the ground of humanitarianism, he did not try to derive a utopian theory of government from such theoretical unity.

In the United States, governmental theories have at least these two levels: accounts of goals within elite groups according to general values that serve such elites, and interpretations of these goals and values in scholarly, legal, and popular political discourse and rhetoric. A government has two working parts in these terms: the permanent bureaucracy that allows it to function under different administrations or regimes with different ideologies and elected officials and those appointed by them. The permanent bureaucracy need not hold or interpret any particular political theory or ideology, because its job is to keep government working according to policies and specific directives with which elected officials and their appointees charge them. The elected officials and their appointees usually reiterate party platforms and their relationship to political theory has both an inner and an outer form—what they tell each other and what they tell the bureaucrats and the public.

The empiricism of political theories is probably of interest mainly to scholars, intellectuals, and only some of the activists who want change. This empiricism, while intellectually important and motivational, is not likely to have any direct effect on the actual functioning of government in normal times, although findings of dishonesty or hypocrisy (e.g., the workers in a communist regime are starving; the leaders in a democracy are lying to the people) may be used to inspire public dissent. The real empiricism of government pertains to policies or general rules for concrete practices, which are crafted in response to contemporary problems in concrete situations. While theorists and other intellectuals may speak and write as though their theories are life and death matters, in normal government, it is policies, loosely justified by shared values, with some shared general theory, which are empirical. Empirical policies need to have specific goals and there need to be ways of seeing whether their implementation has achieved those goals.

Political theories such as Marxism, capitalism, or socialism are ideological because of their normative dimensions, but policies can be purely practical, so that what is important about them is whether they accomplish their specific purposes—that is, whether they work (e.g., social distancing has worked as a public health policy that "flattens the curve" to decrease COVID-19 cases and prevent a collapse in healthcare systems). Political ideologies and evidence-based public policies that do things subject to empirical evaluation are like apples and oranges. Both are political fruit, but ideologies feed mainly intellectuals and sometimes politicians, whereas policies can feed the people. All that policies need for theory is the evident goal of promoting the well-being of all or some citizens or residents. For example, as policies, due process (as, in principle, applied to everyone) or preexisting-condition acceptance medical insurance do not require political theories or ideologies for causes or justification. (The same is true of social distancing to curtail COVID-19 contagion—it is based on epidemiological theory, not political theory, despite how it has been politicized.) The most successful policies for a populace with traditional democratic values that are shared in a general sense, will benefit everyone, for obvious reasons (e.g., child protection laws, because the state has an expressed interest in the well-being of children).

Very specific policies may be proposed and debated in practical terms, without any discussion of underlying or overriding ideologies. For example, in the fall of 2019, Democratic presidential contenders for nomination all agreed that health insurance is a social problem, because not everyone has it, premiums creep up, and treatment and drug costs continue to rise. There has been discussion of a "single-payer system" (in which the federal government would be that payer) and disagreement about whether existing private or employer-funded insurance plans will remain or be abolished in the solution of choice. The kinds of reasons and objections given for this or that proposed program do not draw on ideology but consist of issues of how it will be funded and whether union workers and others who are satisfied with their insurance are willing to risk giving that up for a new system. Apart from pundits who presented a spectrum of radically progressive to centrist candidate views on these issues, no well-developed ideology was aired by Democrats during the primaries. Everything was a matter of what would work, what would get votes, and which candidate's plan—assuming they could put it into effect—would help defeat the incumbent.[19]

What is read as ideology in contemporary politics is a lot lighter (more superficial) than normative theoretical formulations, including Marxism. Consider income inequality. According to the Urban Institute, between 1963 and 2016, the assets of the poorest 10 percent of Americans decreased from zero to a $1,000 debt. Middle-income households doubled their wealth, while the wealth of those in the top

10 percent increased fivefold, and those in the top 1 percent, sevenfold. These figures were reported without evaluation or further analysis in *Investopedia*, a free internet source of financial information for the public.[20] Of course, income is not the same as wealth. In 2014, Thomas Piketty, professor at the Paris School of Economics, published his highly acclaimed *Capital in the Twenty-First Century*. The English translation of this 685-page tome was an immediate best seller and for months the top-selling book on Amazon. Piketty's thesis was accessible to a range of general and multidisciplinary intellectual readers: Wealth inequality has been increasing because wealth, especially in the form of real estate, passively increases at a rate greater than economic growth, about 3–4 percent, compared to 1.5 percent. Not only do the rich get richer at a faster rate than workers can accumulate wealth, but this trend also suggests a return to *patrimony capitalism*, or the dominance of elites with inherited wealth. Piketty's proposed solution was a progressive annual tax on wealth.[21]

There is no consensus in the United States that income and wealth inequality are social ills in themselves. There is a general political sentiment, going back to the founding fathers, that such inequalities do not bode well for democracy.[22] The reasons are obvious: economic inequality stifles equal opportunity; the interests of those with great wealth can unfairly shape government policy; economic inequality results in differences in status that obstruct egalitarianism. However, the conventional wisdom has not reversed ever since the introduction of Ronald Reagan's idea of trickle-down prosperity, that increasing the after-tax income or wealth of rich people and after-tax profits of corporations will create more jobs for poor people.[23] And the idea of taxing the rich brings knee-jerk censure from the capitalistic establishment—for instance, a reaction to the success of *Capital* in *The Economist* called Piketty "a modern Marx" and pronounced that "as a guide to action, [it] is deeply flawed."[24] The 2011 Occupy Wall Street movement, which was initiated by the Canadian anti-consumerist and pro-environment group/magazine *Adbusters*, turned out to be primarily expressive.[25]

There is no viable public policy to tax the rich more in the United States; instead, they are now routinely awarded tax breaks during Republican administrations. While some report broad public support for taxing the rich at a higher rate, the media may redigest studies of such support, so that the broad public fails to see it mirrored or represented.²⁶ Good ideas with minimal ideology, such as in Piketty's *Capital*, have no efficacy on their own, which is to say that policies associated with them are also no more than ideas, unless they are accepted by the public, who then demand them from their representatives and others in power.

A policy has to be accepted before it can be put into practice. And then the important question about any policy as applied in any specific context is whether it will work there—that is, whether it will be *effective*.²⁷ It is not necessary for functioning government in democracies to have detailed political theories, which can become ideological sources of discord. All that is needed is a general goal of promoting well-being or not making citizens and residents worse off, both collectively and individually. If this goal is stated as a theory of government, all that it amounts to is that government should benefit those governed, a principle going back to social contract theory, from the ancient world and early modernity. This principle is no more falsifiable than Marxist or capitalist theories of what government should do, because it is a normative principle. And despite disagreement about what is a benefit from government, everyone seems to agree with it.

The main difference between ideological and evidence-based government does not lie in the empiricism or falsifiability of theories about government, but in whether policies that are adopted and implemented for well-being can be empirically evaluated, both in the evidence that predicts their effectiveness before application and after they are applied and in the evidence used to assess their effectiveness. The best policies may not be able to solve the worst problems. In addition to claiming that no more than "piecemeal engineering" (as opposed to "utopian engineering") is possible, Popper cautioned that what is undertaken on that basis may not be effective.²⁸

It is on the level of policy or public policy, where evidence is relevant to governing. However, the idea that ideological political theories are unnecessary is itself an empirical claim that could be—but has not yet—been tested. We know from historical examples that governments presenting themselves as ideological are likely to be resisted by those with competing ideologies. And that situation may lead to protest and contest that brings governments down or renders them dysfunctional. But we do not know whether governments that are not presented as issuing from ideology can generate policies that will be effective. (For example, would a progressive tax on the rich that was justified by a need to balance the budget be more acceptable than one justified by decreasing income and wealth inequality?) Nor do we know whether a policy's success in some places is sufficient to expect that it will be effective elsewhere, or whether different segments of the public will welcome the same rationale for any given policy. (For example, left-leaning Democrats might reject a progressive tax on the rich that is justified by balancing the budget, whereas some conservative Republicans might support it.)

Apart from how they are justified, some policies may have different successes or failures, according to where they are implemented. Unless we fully understand the causes of success "there," there is no highly probable way to predict success "here." Always, these questions require answers: Why did it work there? Are the causes to be manipulated, here, the same or similar to the causes in action there? What is the evidence for asserting the presence of relevant causes, both there and here? What is unknown?[29] Any overriding principle of empiricism for policy would be tentative or experimental, in this respect.

When the average citizen thinks about government, it is not likely to be in terms of general ideology, but rather specific policies that will have effects they will experience directly. So-called "single-issue voters" have been studied in poles of the electorate, but usually in terms of what the issues are, for any given election (instead of the traits of these voters). Voters may care about several issues that are more or less united in party platforms or candidate commitments, but this is not the same as consistent motivation by a single issue. Voters may decide during elections which mix of issues they prefer, but single-issue voters will approach elections in search of candidates who favor their issue. Their choices are predetermined. For examples: In a 2012 Gallup poll, one in six Americans voted based on the candidate who shared their views on abortion;[30] immigration was projected and confirmed as a single issue by Republican strategists in the 2016 presidential election.[31] If single-issue voters can be identified by candidates, and there are enough of them who vote, single issues can determine races in ways that float free of ideology or party platforms. As a single issue, immigration restrictions have at different times been promoted by both (or either) Democrats and Republicans.[32] The attachment of issues to parties and elections is determined not by ideology but by concrete historical circumstances.

The disconnection or irrelevance of ideologies for public policy, together with an experimental approach to political campaigning, mean that government remains a rational process for those who want to govern or are already in government. But this rational process is less a matter of appealing to ideals and more a question of how most effectively to manipulate public opinion. This is instrumental rationality. From seat belts to smoking bans, public policies have required presentations that scare people into ratifying and complying with disruption to their habits. Machiavelli was more broadly correct than he intended in his advice to rulers: It is more effective to scare people than try to activate their aspirations. This idea applies to public policies as well as getting or keeping political power. What Machiavelli did not think through is that the motivational factor of fear need not be fear of the incumbent or prospective ruler, which would not work in most democracies, but fear of something else, such as dying of lung cancer, or in fiery automobile crashes, for domestic policy; fear of invading and disease-ridden criminals for immigration policy; fear of terrorism for foreign policy; and, as mentioned, fear of contracting or spreading the COVID-19 virus for social distancing as a public health policy.

PUBLIC POLICY STUDIES AND OBSTACLES TO EVIDENCE-BASED PUBLIC POLICY

To start with evidence-based policy instead of ideology as the major factor in government would seem to be a bottom-up or horizontal approach, instead of a top-down one. However, strains of different ideologies cannot be fully separated out of policies. Although it is not top-down, policy-based government, which is what we now have de facto in the United States—political candidates routinely campaign on promised policies—is fraught with ideology and, of course, values. Either ideology is invoked in political disagreements over the adoption of policy or ideology is embedded in implementation of policies. An important, structured way of looking at this is through the lens of public policy studies.

Any description of policy that encompasses evidence, decision, implementation, and effects must somehow accommodate the fact that neither decision makers nor end consumers or participants are completely evidence-motivated actors. If decision makers and citizens were classically rational, delivering and expecting government actions and processes that matched what citizens correctly perceived as their self-interests, well, in that utopia, evidence-based policies would be a simple matter of doing the best thing, given the best evidence at any given time. The only problems would be real material or resource budgetary constraints and limited expertise because of a given state of knowledge. There would be no kickbacks, cronyism, ideological bias, or demographic bias (e.g., racism or sexism), and the best people would be doing the best jobs. When outcomes disappointed, plausible reasons would be forthcoming for why decisions made were the best decisions at the time they were made, and it would not be necessary to have accountability beyond the reconstruction of reasons for decisions. Reality is not like that, and obstacles plague not only actual policies and their adoption and implementation but also the field of policy studies itself.

It would help to have a definition of public policy. However, as Kevin Smith and Christopher Larimer write in their 2017 third edition of *The Public Policy Theory Primer*:

> What springs from our attempt to seriously engage and answer the question "What is the field of policy studies?" is what we believe to be a coherent and logically organized survey of the field itself.[33]

Thus, a definition of the field is not likely to be forthcoming from its experts and instead only different theoretical approaches to policies can be described. The policy studies field lacks a general framework for policy making, with identifiable causal relationships that can generally predict and explain. Smith and Larimer also note that the academic disciplines that study policy (for instance, political science, economics, public administration, and specific areas such as health and education) tend to compartmentalize policy studies as subfields in their disciplines.[34] Philosophically, the different theoretical approaches could be united through a meta "family resemblance" approach, but that may too speculative. More interesting here is that the variety affords freedom to focus on descriptions and models that seem closest to evidence-based public policy, given *bounded rationality*.

Bounded rationality is the real nature of rationality in contrast to substantive rationality. *Substantive rationality* is a posit in neoclassical economics, according to the theory of subjective expected utility (SEU): Choices are made from a fixed set of alternatives with known probable outcomes for each, so that the expected value of a given "utility" is maximized. When one or more of these SEU assumptions are not met, the result is bounded rationality, so that alternatives may be generated through a process, instead of fixed; there may be estimates of outcomes or strategies for dealing with uncertainties, instead of known probable outcomes; a utility may be *satisficed* (i.e., it is good enough) instead of maximized. Theories of bounded rationality do not posit irrationality but emphasize knowledge and computational limitations in human abilities. Decision makers are consistent in their preferences. (COVID-19 public policy has so far proceeded with exactly this kind of bounded rationality—it is unknown which policies will work beforehand, how they will be unwound, or what future medical research will produce, much less when.)

Some theorists have emphasized the incremental nature of decision making, hypothesizing that small changes in existing policies were preferred, as opposed to treating decisions as isolated events.[35] *Incrementalism* was first tested empirically in studies of federal budgetary decisions. Given the complexity of the federal budget, budgetary decisions are based on agency requests and congressional appropriations that can be predicted based on the prior year's appropriation—the alternative would be now-abandoned "zero-based" budgeting techniques, requiring completely new computations each year.[36]

The concept of bounded rationality has of necessity made policy studies itself an empirical, evidence-based field. This does not directly get us to evidentiary bases for policies themselves; rather, it shows the built-in difficulties for decision makers, in both their own limitations and the nature of the evidence they need to deal with, when it comes to making decisions based on evidence. Recently, there has been renewed interest in bounded rationality in terms of accommodating it through changes in "the task environment" or institutional norms and rules. According to the evolutionary perspective that humans have developed in ways that facilitate group interaction and cohesion, there has been an emphasis on "rationality in design," in comparison to "rationality in action." (It is easier to design or describe evidence-based policy than to implement it.) There have also been findings that perceptions of fairness and legitimacy are more important for building interpersonal trust than the success of past policy decisions.[37] (People trust other people more readily than records.)

Smith and Larimer apply this evolutionary perspective on policy making to criminal justice policy. They consider these three factors: (a) a tendency to seek retribution for unfair behavior; (b) the occurrence of criminal behavior; and (c) the inefficiency of jury trials. Smith and Larimer's evolutionary approach provides explanations: (a) People are very sensitive to injustice, neurologically and behaviorally, and they favor public punishment, deriving satisfaction from it. This accounts for the ongoing popularity of the death penalty, despite its ineffectiveness in deterrence. (b) It is posited that men commit more crimes than women because status seeking is more predominant among males than females. (c) Although juries are supposed to be impartial, they are likely to be more strongly motivated by social and biological pressures.[38]

To further complicate the nature of public policy in reality and in policy studies, the concept of public choice in democratic strains of public policy studies rejects the idea of "elitist technocrats" or "policy scientists" making public policy, in favor of participatory, bottom-up choices by citizens. On a market model, these citizens become customers or consumers, whose free choices determine outcomes. However, the results of such procedures can be disappointing to designers. For example, citizens who "voted with their feet" and moved to localities offering better utility services did not show increased knowledge of or satisfaction with different localities on account of services. Such "vote with their feet" models favor affluent and highly educated citizens who already enjoy good services and are knowledgeable shoppers for better ones. Also, mobility of this nature sacrifices the ideal of the commons for private, individual preference.[39] For another example, studies of policies allowing for school choice and vouchers have shown that although parents claim to be interested in academic quality, in reality they search for schools that have their preferred demographics, thereby increasing racial segregation in K–12 school systems.[40] What this situation amounts to is that if people are given freedom of choice in bottom-up policy making, the democracy of the process may not have democratic outcomes.

Two recent books have examined this dimension of public opinion and choice in relation to government policy, with similar pessimistic assessments: Bryan Caplan's *The Myth of the Rational Voter* and Ilya Somin's *Democracy and Political Ignorance*. Caplan attributes failures in democracy to the irrationality of voters in their xenophobia and unwarranted pessimism about the economy and free trade He ingeniously argues that since voters know their individual vote won't matter much, they are rational to vote in accord with their mistaken ideas, because it makes them feel good. But when many voters do this, there is an unintended consequence. Caplan recommends smaller government and better economic education. Somin is pessimistic that voter misinformation can be corrected through education. His main suggestion is to reduce the areas in which voters can choose by reducing the size of government and limiting voter autonomy to local issues.[41] Neither Caplan nor Somin are enthusiastic about democracy as it currently works, and in both cases there is a reliance on the "better" knowledge of experts concerning desirable outcomes, either by changing voters or by limiting the damage they can do. We should also consider that public policies are not chosen and implemented in isolation from other economic and political factors. The influence of interest groups such as large corporations, religious groups, and other social entities, including economic and cultural segments with robust lobbies and resources for campaign financing, may shape the field in which policy is designed. And even after policies are administratively authorized, their success depends on implementation and obedience to the law and new norms, which may be lacking. Examples of the latter include nondiscrimination laws, racial integration in public education, and meritocratic hiring and promotion practices within institutions.

Altogether, given the vagaries of human rectitude and fairness, the relegation and reduction of government to democratic public policy results in unpredictability and disappointment for idealists—and economists. This is the mess of social reality as it has ever existed. While it disappointingly falls short of ideals, nothing short of empirical, falsifiable public policies would have the ability to match it with the least amount of government enforcement that would likely be met by violent resistance. In the case of top-down ideological government, it is force and enforcement that leads to the totalitarianism so many have feared. It is not the ideas of this or that ideological government which make it totalitarian, but rather how it becomes obligated to implement and enforce those ideas, against the will of some of the people. The best form of government imaginable can become intolerable if there is no toleration for human limitations, irrationality, ignorance, noncompliance with institutional missions and rules, and some disobedience of law.

"NUDGE"

The upshot of the imperfections of evidence-based public policy is to accept these imperfections as evidence for new forms of policy. This is exactly what has been done in governmental uses of behavior economics in the Nudge movement, simply called "Nudge." Nudge is an application of principles of behavioural modification from social psychology, which were adopted by economists who increasingly realized that their models of reasonable, self-interested citizens did not match new information on how people were in reality motivated in noncognitive ways. Originally called "libertarian paternalism," nudge policies are designed to influence public response to existing policy, with no penalties for noncompliance and random controlled experiments for selecting the new policies that work. Governments throughout the world have been using forms of this technique since about 2005 and the results are usually very successful. The nudge approach manipulates responses by appealing to emotions and other extra-rational, noncognitive factors, such as sensitivity to group norms or laziness. For UK examples: A simple sentence that most people pay their taxes on time increased timely tax payments; a program to insulate attics got a boost when paid services were offered for removing the clutter in people's attics. Pension and organ donor programs, which are believed to be of great mass public benefit, have been nudged by changing "opt-in" models to "opt-out" ones—individuals are automatically enrolled in the programs and must "opt out" to cancel their enrollments, while previously individuals had to actively "opt in" and their failure to do so left them out.[42] The facsimile of a fly in men's urinals, now present throughout the world, is reported to reduce "spillage" by up to 80 percent, because men "naturally" aim at the fly.[43]

To be clear, the use of nudges is a policy decision, as is the choice of nudges for specific policy goals. Nudges facilitate compliance with existing policies which government or private-sector organizations want to work better. The language describing the existing policies is usually straightforward statements of rules, which are assumed not to evoke emotions. Punishing people for not obeying the rules can be costly and oppressive, whereas nudges are usually easy to administer and relatively inexpensive. But the nudges, in comparison to underlying policy, communicate by appealing to motivations that are not activated by the original language of the policy requiring compliance. Take the example of the fly facsimile in men's urinals. Institutions or organizations that maintain urinals want to decrease the cost to keep them clean and also keep them clean to please and protect consumers or customers. Assume that signage would not motivate most who use the urinal to take greater care not to "splash." But if they are given an opportunity to drown a fly while urinating, apparently this motivates them to more carefully aim their urine stream. It's easy to laugh at this example, because excrement is often a subject of humor in Anglo-Saxon culture, and the lives and well-being of flies are not taken seriously. But a policy that activates what is believed to be a built-in male desire to drown insects, while at the same time experiencing a sense of power through ordinary bodily functions, is based on a motive that making the effort to keep one's surroundings clean is not.

Returning to the earlier examples, is it desirable for citizens to fulfill their obligations to pay taxes on time, because they want to conform? Should environmentally constructive actions such as insulating dwellings depend on whether they are convenient? These examples are petty. But do we want such techniques to be used for compliance with a draft, military enlistment, behaving in accordance with professional ethics, or other virtuous or public-spirited acts that require voluntary effort? Should people who are too lazy to "opt in" to a pension plan, automatically benefit, assuming that the plan is beneficial for them? Should those who do not want their employer's pension plan (because they want to craft their own or do not intend to remain with their present employer long enough to become vested) be required to "opt out"? The substitution of "opting out" for "opting in" assumes that everyone should "opt in," but do employers have the right to make that decision for individual employees? In a more sinister vein, do we want it to be a foregone conclusion that everyone's organs will be harvested when they die as a default policy? Does this imply dismissal of the wishes of those who do not want their organs harvested or the effect on family members who have to deal with other aspects of an unexpected death?

In normal everyday life, new voluntary programs require consent and active participation. Substituting "opting out" for "opting in" might therefore be deceptive, because people may assume that programs to which they have automatically been "opted in" are mandatory; it may also foster an illusion that institutions take total care of participants, when in reality they take the care that benefits the institution. To the extent that nudges support the wrong reasons for doing the right things, then, depending on their context, they may violate basic norms of morality. And in the process of doing that, they reinforce weakness of character, vices, and insensitivity.

Because Nudge's behavioral approach to policy compliance is coercive, it is also potentially undemocratic. There is no added penalty for failing to comply with the policy that people are being "nudged" to comply with, so the lack of punishment for not taking any given "nudge" means that a policy of nudges avoids totalitarianism. However, the question is always how far "nudges" can go without seriously invading privacy or restricting freedom. As far as behaviorists are concerned, behavior, or observed and measurable action, is all that anyone need be concerned with in terms of ethics. Thus, for a behaviorist, the question may not arise of whether one kind of motivation for individual actions that benefit everyone is better than another kind of motivation. For economists who jettison their rational-actor model for a model of outcomes resulting from nudges, the question is how much that original rational model depended on what people thought and felt, as opposed to what they actually did.

Philosophically speaking, from a virtue ethics and duty ethics perspectives, plain evidence, taken cognitively, is still the most respectful and democratic approach to participatory public policy. However, a consequentialist approach might welcome nudge-related results if they would maximize happiness and well-being.[44] Can the public be nudged toward plain evidence, taken cognitively, so that the nudges strengthen virtues and fulfill duties? Is it morally acceptable to use nonrational means to get people to behave rationally? Presumably chemical means are acceptable because there are not widespread moral objections to chemical treatments for mental health, and mental health, generally, is closer to rationality than mental illness.

CONCLUSION

As Karl Popper insisted, the origins of government are less important than whether citizens are able to change or get rid of bad government by voting. That same pragmatic perspective shows how ideology is less important for government than what it actually does. In other words, the design and implementation of public policy is the main function of government. Ideally, public policy should be evidence-based, but both resistance to change and nonrational motivations are obstacles to evidence-based public policy. There are alternatives for getting citizen compliance, as the Nudge movement has shown. However, citizen rationality lies in complying with a policy or program that has benefits for the right kind of reasons—that is, its benefits to oneself and others, based on cognitive evidence. And freedom, privacy, and autonomy are best served if citizens comply based on cognitive or good evidence. Of course, this is to assume that evidence itself is a stable factor and that everyone knows what counts as good evidence. The problems with the idea of evidence are the subject of chapter 6.

6

THE PROBLEMS WITH EVIDENCE AND UNIVERSAL BASIC INCOME

Many forms of Government have been tried, and will be tried in this world of sin and woe. No one pretends that democracy is perfect or all-wise. Indeed, it has been said that democracy is the worst form of Government except all those other forms that have been tried from time to time.

—Winston Churchill[1]

It is not the critic who counts; not the man who points out how the strong man stumbles, or where the doer of deeds could have done them better. The credit belongs to the man who is actually in the arena, whose face is marred by dust and sweat and blood; who strives valiantly; who errs, who comes short again and again, because there is no effort without error and shortcoming; but who does actually strive to do the deeds; who knows great enthusiasms, the great devotions; who spends himself in a worthy cause; who at the best knows in the end the triumph of high achievement, and who at the worst, if he fails, at least fails while daring greatly, so that his place shall never be with those cold and timid souls who neither know victory nor defeat.

—Theodore Roosevelt[2]

Beliefs and conclusions in different spheres of life in society require different kinds of evidence and have different rules for acquiring it. For instance, within legal contexts, there are different standards of evidence for criminal trials for homicide and civil wrongful death suits for the same crime.[3] Legal evidence is a good example of how evidence is not self-evident, because the main task of juries is to "decide on the facts"—that is, to come to conclusions about the evidence presented to them.[4] Courtrooms are excellent examples of the closed nature of spheres of evidence, because not all facts relevant to a case are allowed to be admitted as evidence. Another closed sphere is science, or, rather, the specific sciences. Evidentiary standards vary across different fields and are generated by a combination of observation (including instrument data) and the application of theories. Indeed, competing theories may generate different kinds of evidence. But without some theoretical framework or worldview, evidence cannot even be collected.

The connection between evidence and conclusion, or the verification of a theory or hypothesis, is open ended. Rarely are all instances of relevant evidence collected before the theory or hypothesis is accepted.[5] In addition, theories can be used to both explain and predict data or events, with explanation pertaining to the past and prediction pertaining to the future. However, despite this abstract symmetry, there is a big difference between understanding what happened, after it happened, and making plans or contributing resources to what is predicted to happen. The difference is that the future remains unknown, even when it is believed to high degrees of probability that causes have been identified.

The fundamental problems with prediction and the identification of causes have not been philosophically resolved since David Hume first raised them. These are skeptical problems based on a general commitment to empiricism as the belief that knowledge derives from experience, in the sense of observation. First, there is a lack of proof that the future will resemble the past or that inductive reasoning can yield any real confidence. Second, what we think of as causes and causal interactions are opaque, because causes and causal interactions can never be directly observed; all that we can know is that events of a certain kind have always been followed by events of another kind, which is the *constant conjunction* theory of causation.[6]

We believe that causal connections consist of compelling connections between cause and effect, but all we can ever have are statistical regularities. If the problem with induction is combined with the constant conjunction theory of causation, we cannot know for certain that even events that have 100 percent correlations with other events will repeat the same pattern in the future. And statistical correlations rarely reach 100 percent. Instead, there are accepted measures of the likelihood that what correlations there are do not exist due to chance.[7]

That is the nature of scientific knowledge and prediction in a nutshell. What does it have to do with government and evidence-based government? Evidence is always imperfect, but it is the only basis for informed decisions. It seems reasonable to say that evidence-based public policy sounds, and often is, rational and prudent and that, in principle, it provides for accountability when things go wrong. The evidence for making a decision based on a policy can be demanded in the form of reasons where judgment has been exercised (e.g., what was the threat leading to a punitive action?) and before application, policy choice should be based on evidence (e.g., smoking bans). There already is a general expectation that policies will be based on evidence, or else that certain kinds of dispositive evidence would not be suppressed (e.g., government secrecy about epidemic deaths). Indeed, as wacky as any conspiracy theory may be, those who hold it can usually produce what they accept and proffer as evidence.

The inherent imperfection of evidence in cases when exact predictions cannot be made, may not be broadly understood. Officials and the public may expect more from available evidence than is possible and there may be ideological or political commitments blocking evidence or leading to disagreement about how to interpret it. The first two sections of this chapter provide examples of failures to understand evidence in the 2009 earthquake in L'Aquila, Italy, and errors in the received opinion about the connection between poverty and health care. Both cases illustrate the importance, not of evidence in itself, but of how evidence is viewed and what action is taken on that basis. Issues for which there is evidence for certain policies but the evidence is ignored or denied by numerous or powerful enough factions to block the policies are then very briefly discussed. The chapter ends with a discussion of universal basic income (UBI) as an example of a policy ideal that may be attractive and plausible, even though the evidence in its favor is scant.

THE RESPONSIBILITY OF SCIENTISTS FOR THE 2009 ITALIAN EARTHQUAKE

Just after 3:30 AM on April 6, 2009, a 6.3 magnitude earthquake struck the thirteenth-century city of L'Aquila, which is about 60 miles northeast of Rome. In L'Aquila and nearby towns, 309 people were killed, 1,500 were injured, and 65,000 were displaced. The earthquake was a surprise, given how scientific predictions had been relayed to the public. In July 2011, seven prominent scientists, including the president of Italy's National Institute of Geophysics and Volcanology, were put on trial for manslaughter, because they had not predicted the earthquake.

The scientific community in Italy and throughout the world claimed that predicting the location, time, and strength of an earthquake in the near future is technically impossible. But the indictments held, and the case was said to have a stunning and silencing effect on scientists who had so far shared their risk assessments with the public by communicating them to officials and journalists. However, the public prosecutor in L'Aquila, Fabio Picuti, insisted that although it was known that scientists could not predict earthquakes, these scientists had a special obligation as government employees. Commenting on his 242-page indictment, he said:

> I'm not crazy. I know they can't predict earthquakes. The basis of the charges is not that they didn't predict the earthquake. As functionaries of the state, they had certain duties imposed by law: to evaluate and characterize the risks that were present in L'Aquila. . . . They were obligated to evaluate the degree of risk given all these factors and they did not.

Part of that risk assessment, according to Picuti, should have included "the density of the urban population and the known fragility of many ancient buildings in the city center." The seven scientists were convicted on multiple counts of manslaughter and sentenced to six years in prison. These convictions were overturned on appeal in November 2014.[8]

If government employment required risk assessment, why didn't other officials provide it? It is understandable, given the loss of life and destruction, that political officials would recognize a need for a target for blame and try to exonerate themselves. It was known that had the earthquake been predicted, human casualties would not have been as great, because people would not have remained in buildings. (This suggests that risks were already broadly assessed and the scientists had in fact been convicted for failures in prediction, not risk assessment.) There had been months of small tremors and a 3.9-magnitude tremor at 11 PM, before the earthquake. Nevertheless, Prosecutor Picuti seemed to hold contradictory descriptions of what had happened. He acknowledged that earthquakes cannot be predicted, but he insisted that better information about the risks should have been forthcoming from the scientists. It's not clear whether he meant that a statement of a higher degree of risk than the one received would have been accepted by officials as a reason to order evacuation. He did not say that evacuation had not been ordered because officials did not believe that an earthquake would have killed a lot of people or destroyed many fragile buildings. That is, Picuti seems to have conflated the risk associated with the earthquake with the occurrence of the earthquake, and he may have been correct in doing that. But the occurrence of the earthquake could not have been predicted! So it is difficult to see how his distinction between occurrence and risk amounts to more than a justification for his offering the public people to blame other than government officials.

The people, even educated people, such as Vincenzo Vittorini, a surgeon who remembered a family tradition of staying outdoors after tremors, but lost his wife and daughter because he did not follow it on the night of April 6, blamed the scientists. Vittorini said at their trial that words of authorities, "Be calm, don't worry," plus the lack of specific advice, meant that he could not make an informed decision about what to do before the quake. Vittorini was party to a civil suit against the scientists and claimed that he felt "betrayed by science" and that "either they didn't know certain things, which is a problem, or they didn't know how to communicate what they did know, which is also a problem."[9] If the scientists didn't know certain things, they are not to blame for that. And it is not clear how, if they had communicated the nature of risk more precisely, officials would have responded, because the risk was an integral part of the earthquake after it happened.

Earthquakes cannot be predicted in the short term for a number of reasons: among the thousands of tremors that are constantly occurring, there is no way to identify tremors that will grow into big quakes; quakes are caused by the release of energy after rough edges of tectonic plates that are temporarily attached (caught) come apart; not enough is known about the geological conditions accompanying or causing quakes below the surface of the earth. Although specific earthquakes cannot be predicted, based on past seismic activity and what is known about geological fault lines (where the plates adjoin each other), earthquakes can be *forecast* in conclusions of the form: Area X is likely to experience an earthquake of magnitude Y sometime within the next Z years.[10] The 2009 L'Aquila quake occurred in the Abruzzo region, which had had similar events numerous times in the past, most destructively in 1315, 1349, 1452, 1461, 1498, 1501, 1646, 1703, 1706, 1791, 1809, 1848, and 1887. After 1984, buildings were rebuilt to presumed anti-seismic standards. But the building codes were uneven and enforcement was lax, especially with the use of concrete mixed with sand, so it turned out that newer structures were less earthquake resistant.[11]

It is difficult to consider the L'Aquila earthquake and trial without understanding it to be an example of the public's frustration with lack of knowledge by experts and the reluctance of officials to make unpopular decisions that may turn out not to have been necessary. It would have been more prudent of the L'Aquila officials to order everyone out of buildings after the 3.9 tremor on the night of the earthquake. This would not have been a scientific decision, but rather a moral or political one. What the public seems unable to fully understand in a case like this is that there is no magic in scientific assessments of risk, given the impossibility of prediction. It is not the job of scientists to tell us what to do, given their findings. Strictly speaking, this is not a problem with evidence; instead, it is a problem in decision making and disaster preparation.

The lesson from the L'Aquila earthquake is that evidence may be incomplete as a basis for prediction and the real risk may not be physical, but rather the moral and political risk of making or not making decisions and failing to prepare. Preparation is always possible based on available evidence, even though such evidence may not be complete.[12] Preparation can only be based on existing evidence, and inadequate preparation cannot be excused because such evidence is revealed to be imperfect after a disaster. The real issue is what preparations and decisions are made before the disaster occurs. The officials in L'Aquila had not ensured adequate preparation, and they did not take the risk of making decisions based on the (imperfect) evidence that they nonetheless had.

THE ROLES OF WEALTH AND EDUCATION IN HEALTH

In contrast to questions about the adequacy of evidence, sometimes there is nothing wrong with evidence, except that it has not been thoroughly or correctly interpreted. It is a truism for contemporary politicians that the public, including and especially, those who are poor, want affordable health care. As discussed in chapter 5, after the Affordable Care Act of the Obama administration was partly dismantled by removing penalties for not having health insurance, health care became a primary issue for candidates for the Democratic presidential nomination.[13] Another important issue was the accessibility of college education, but the education issue has not received as much attention as the health-care issue. The reasoning behind the importance of health care is that health care is necessary for health; health care requires money; the poor are at a disadvantage in accessing health care, because they cannot afford insurance premiums; and, most important, those who cannot afford health-care insurance have a right to access to health care, because everyone has a right to be healthy. But what if the evidence doesn't support the importance placed on health care compared to education?

Education is understood by social scientists to be a component of socioeconomic class, so that, over generations, education increases with income. It is also known that health also gets better with income. For both connections, it is assumed that money is the driving factor: more money equals more education and better health. However, recent studies by John Mirowsky and Catherine E. Ross suggest that education increases health as well as income. Their argument, based on studies of statistics that hold income constant, is that education drives both income and social status by improving health. The connection between education and health does not run through greater use of the medical system by the better educated, because higher use of the medical system is not positively correlated with better health. Rather, education creates the potential for getting more fulfilling and fulltime employment, making healthier lifestyle decisions, and being more in control of one's life, all of which are factors that decrease disease-causing stress and provide space for creativity. That is, education prevents ill health in the first place. The gains from education are life-changing skills that transfer from structured learning environments in secondary or higher education to further contexts in life. Moreover, the gains in income and life mastery by the better educated continue to increase over time.[14]

I would add to these authors' insights the fact that it isn't what students have learned, because most students poorly remember course content after their courses are complete.[15] Rather, the *practice* of learning course content is what transforms a life. Sticking it out through a program of structured study requires discipline, organization, and self-direction, which are meta-skills that can be continually applied after degrees are achieved. The same especially holds for critical meta-skills that throw students on their own resources, so that they can make what they learn their own. Often, students who are already burdened by life stressors find the demands of fulfilling a structured educational program too challenging or overwhelming, given their obligations outside of the classroom. But it may be exactly those students, in those situations where their lives are overwhelming, who need to make their educational obligations a priority—accept that it is their responsibility to make the bandwidth for it. Educators might need to emphasize that this is not a matter of learning practical skills, but rather one of going through the process of learning new material, thinking with it, and forming one's own well-reasoned opinions about it. In other words, the intellectual content of education, especially in the liberal arts, may add to one's cultural capital, but that content is less important than the skills gained from getting it in mind. Thus, after forgetting what has been learned, the process of learning itself may be indelible.

The study by Mirowsky and Ross suggests that the bottom line of a right to health cannot be directly reached through economic adjustments to health-care access. Rather, the health of the population appears to be more causally dependent on education than wealth or income. Left out of the political calculations is the importance of lifestyle decisions that are likely to be more beneficial as education increases. This means that what political leaders should focus on, based on evidence, is not a national health plan to better the health of poor people, but rather a national education plan! However, the need for health care is an immediate experience that furnishes indisputable evidence, but the need for more education concerns future benefits. So it is not surprising that politicians would seize health care as the more pressing issue. But insofar as the object of health care is health, and that is best achieved through education, education might be viewed as preparatory for good health or capable of preventing ill health. Like disaster preparation, increases in funding for education will need to compete with allocations for causes that seem more urgent.

BLOCKED EVIDENCE-BASED POLICIES

The popularity of capital punishment, despite evidence of its failure to deter, was mentioned in chapter 5. There are several other important policies with good evidence about their benefits that are blocked by worldviews enabling dismissal of that evidence: gun control, limiting fossil fuel extraction and consumption to mitigate climate change, universal child care, greater resources for mental health, universal vaccination—the list is quite long. As discussed chapter 5, evidence suggests that cognitive evidence in favor of those policies is not effective in persuading people to change their minds. Perhaps very strong "nudges" would work to shift opinion, but the question remains open regarding whether it is appropriate for the government in a democratic society to use coercive behavioral techniques of persuasion in order to achieve good results. In favor of such government usage would be consequentialist strains of argument. Against it is respect for the autonomy of all individuals and their right not to have their choices manipulated in ways that they do not understand or even know about. Such manipulation occurs all the time through advertising in the private sector and there are many ways to criticize and condemn that. However, manipulation by the government is especially pernicious because it smacks of that aspect of totalitarianism which involves "thought control." Ideally, cognitive approaches can still be applied, although they may require laborious, one-on-one projects undertaken by friends and relatives of those in denial. Or people and institutions can use coercive "nudges" on the societal side, outside of government. What many on the left and other progressives consistently fail to recognize is that a large segment of voters do not believe that they are obligated to consider the evidence for conclusions that motivate public policy. This denial of the existence of closed ignorance matches the kind of denial that accompanies closed ignorance.

UNIVERSAL BASIC INCOME (UBI) AS POLICY

In 2020, there is little reason to believe that even the most coercive government nudges can shift attitudes held by the more powerful and advantaged against those less well off. At least since the 1970s, government welfare programs have been tied to getting and keeping employment. There is an American ethos about the moral goodness of work, according to which those who are not employed are suspected of not trying hard enough to find employment. Laziness is a stereotype that has always been applied to minorities, especially African Americans. The laziness stereotype is even applied by volunteers with charitable attitudes toward those believed to be afflicted with it.[16]

Government assistance for nutrition has been grudging at best and justification of cuts to food programs usually include predictions that people will find employment after certain benefits are cut. However, such assumptions are not evidence based. There is no evidence that removing single adults, including those who are heads of households with children, from Supplemental Nutrition Assistance Program (SNAP) programs after three months increases their employment incentives. This is because many are already working as much as they can. About 11 percent of the population remained food insecure in 2018, despite record low unemployment. If cutting SNAP eligibility does not significantly increase employment among the food insecure or decrease food insecurity, then the evidence suggests that what such cuts mainly accomplish is keeping food insecurity in place. This means that in times of record low unemployment, over 33 million people do not have enough food. By government estimates, which many believe are undercounts, there are also about half a million unhoused people in the United States. If people are unhoused, there is little (if anything) to cut as an incentive for them to find jobs.

Most feel sorry for the food insecure and unhoused, but since the late 1970s, there has also been a public preference for the "deserving poor," which includes the elderly, two-parent families, and those with disabilities, over single adults and young people; those with mental health problems are also neglected. In addition, poor people who have assets and income are more likely to qualify for government assistance than those who are destitute.[17]

The idea of universal basic income (UBI) can separate work and employment from income. But in its history going back to the Tudor period, the link between employment and income has been difficult to cut. Thomas More is often credited with the idea of basic income in *Utopia* (1516), but his colleague Juan Luis Vives was more explicit, proposing full, paid employment for those who would now be considered the undeserving poor:

> Even those who have dissipated their fortunes in dissolute living—through gaming, harlots, excessive luxury, gluttony and gambling—should be given food, for no one should die of hunger. However, smaller rations and more irksome tasks should be assigned to them so that they may be an example to others. . . . They must not die of hunger, but they must feel its pangs. . . . [B]eing busy and engrossed in their work, they will abstain from those wicked thoughts and actions in which they would engage if they were idle.

Vives included those not capable of working who may have been innocent of the vices of the undeserving, but only on the premise that something could be found for them to do:

> Whatever the source of poverty, the poor are expected to work. . . . Even to the old and the stupid, it should be possible to give a job they can learn in a few days, such as digging holes, getting water or carrying something on their shoulders.[18]

More than two centuries later, Thomas Paine, in 1796, proposed a novel idea that came close to a basic income detached from employment, although not by that description. Paine posited a kind of universal property right. He claimed that the value of property was based on improvements made by owners and occupiers and that owners had not paid for the ground itself, as necessary as that was. He therefore proposed collecting ground rent and accumulating it in a public fund that could be owed to those who owned no property, because the system of private property had excluded them:

> There shall be paid to every person, when arrived at the age of twenty-one years, the sum of fifteen pounds sterling, as a compensation in part, for the loss of his or her natural inheritance, by the introduction of the system of landed property. And also, the sum of ten pounds per annum, during life, to every person now living, of the age of fifty years, and to all others as they shall arrive at that age.

There is some confusion here, because in the United States, land owners are presumed to have ground rights, as well as air rights. Paine may have derived his idea of ground rent from the British system in which all property belongs to the Crown and most land owners lease dwellings and ground separately.[19]

Paine also thought that insofar as no one had been compensated for the value of the ground, the money in the ground rent fund ought to be dispersed to property owners, as well as those who do not own property. This universal payment is "in lieu of the natural inheritance, which, as a right, belongs to every man, over and above the property he may have created, or inherited from those who did."[20]

No UBI policy has ever been implemented in a large Western nation. UBI has been advocated for moral, pragmatic economic reasons, and aspirational rights-based claims. Although the idea of UBI seems to belong to the left or liberal side of the political spectrum, with recent supporters who have included Martin Luther King, Hillary Clinton, and #Black Lives Matter,[21] it has also been promoted by Charles Murray, who is a conservative, and Milton Friedman, a libertarian.[22] Given its disparate support, UBI is not an ideology but an idea for a practical plan to address practical problems—that is, a possible public policy. Although UBI is not ideological, its proposals can be distinguished by their types of motivating ideas. There has been a moral impetus that can be described as charitable toward the deserving poor, as in Vives's perspective. Conservative economists such as Murray and Milton have advocated UBI for its cost saving potential compared to existing entitlements and the complexity of current welfare payments. These analysts may also have a commitment to shrinking government in favor of individual responsibility and autonomy, but for them the ultimate evidence would be whether UBI saved tax payer money in the long run.

Thomas Paine developed his idea based on a universal right to ground ownership and his position was quasi-ideological in that it was based on a critique of private property. However, as we shall soon see, the humanitarian idea of universal human rights is an interesting basis for UBI, exactly because it cannot be falsified and does not, strictly speaking, require evidence for its aspirational dimension. There is not yet a consensus in the United States or other Western democracies concerning human rights that encompass positive rights, such as entitlements, as well as long-accepted negative rights that call upon the government not to harm citizens and to protect them from overt harm.

From a philosophical perspective, I suggest that the morally judgmental approach be left to moralists and the cost-benefit analyses be left to economists. This leaves us with the rights-based and human well-being-based approach to UBI programs. UBI is an unusual possibility to consider in terms of evidence-based public policy, because there is no real evidence that it would succeed or fail in the United States or what would count as evidence of success or failure given different motivations for it. If UBI succeeded in aspirational-humanitarian terms but failed according to economic requirements or moral judgment, the fate of the policy would probably be decided democratically, which is to say, politically. There have been experiments with UBI in other contexts, and although the outcomes have not been clear, they are worth examining. For example, in 2017, Finland began a UBI program in which 2,000 unemployed people were paid 560 euros ($635) a month, with no deduction from benefits they were already receiving. The goal of the program was to allow them the freedom to find jobs, even low-paid or temporary work. The program was not successful in terms of increasing employment, but the well-being of recipients increased. They were happier and healthier, and some reported greater self-confidence and creativity.[23] A similar three-year program was begun for 4,000 low-income individuals and families in Ontario, Canada, in 2017. Participants were given $16,989 (US$12,876) for individuals and $24,027 (US$18,211) for couples annually; 50 percent of earned income was subtracted, and those with disabilities received an extra $500 (US$379) each month. The plan was terminated after a year, when the Liberal premier was replaced by a Progressive Conservative. The results included better physical and mental health (e.g., less migraines, fatigue, depression, symptoms of fibromyalgia and celiac disease or IBS) and abatement of food insecurity for half of the participants.[24]

Imagine a contemporary proposal, with wide debate in the public auditorium for universal basic income, so that every citizen and resident of the United States had enough money for food, shelter, clothing, health care, and education, regardless of their wealth or income. The government would provide these funds, through taxation, on the premise that these goods were fundamental human entitlements. Either the government would simply provide lump sums in electronic deposits or people would get tax credits, up to designated amounts, for the first amounts of money they spent on food, shelter, clothing, health care, and education. The goods and services would be available in the normal marketplace, and if citizens and residents made mistakes, it would be their problem, although counselors and advisors would be freely available.

Assume those who were very wealthy would not object, because arguments could be made that the UBI funds would immediately be spent, thereby bolstering the entire economy. But imagine that there would be objections to such a policy from those whose earned income is already close to the UBI. Their main objection would be that so long as they had to work, it was not fair that others received free subsistence. But if they got the same amount of money, it would no longer be unfair. Suppose they would still object because the money going to those who need it is unearned. Would they forego their own unearned payments of UBI? And if they object to the unearned nature of UBI, then do they object to wealthy people receiving unearned money through investments or inheritance? My guess is that those who currently earn incomes close to what an UBI would be and object to an UBI do not object to the unearned income of wealthy people. At any rate, they either do or do not object to the unearned income of the wealthy. If they do, then their position is consistent. But if they do not object to the unearned income of the wealthy, then they are only objecting to unearned income for the poor, and that is discriminatory and unfair, which can, of course, be pointed out. Indeed, the identities of poor and homeless people remain vastly undertheorized and without voice or advocacy, so on the societal side, especially within academia, there remains much work to be done there.

One participant in the 2017 Finnish program, a former editor, summed up his experience this way: "I am still without a job," he explained. "I can't say that the basic income has changed a lot in my life. OK, psychologically yes, but financially—not so much."[25] In 1965, Erich Fromm examined the psychological aspects of guaranteed income (what I am calling UBI) for those who would receive it.[26] He began by noting that the history of humankind was until recently plagued by real scarcity and the threat of starvation. But, in the present period of abundance, this has changed in material terms:

> Guaranteed income would not only establish freedom as reality rather than a slogan, it would also establish a principle deeply rooted in Western religious and humanist tradition: man has the right to live, regardless! This right to live, to have food, shelter, medical care, education, etc., is an intrinsic human right that cannot be restricted by any condition, not even the one that he must be socially "useful." . . . A psychology of scarcity produces anxiety, envy, egotism. . . . A psychology of abundance produces initiative, faith in life, solidarity.[27]

By a psychology of abundance, Fromm means something different from the physical conditions of abundance, because he claimed that the psychology appropriate to human species past still dominated contemporary perspectives on scarcity. He was undoubtedly correct on this claim, because food insecurity is now well known to be a problem of distribution. Surplus food is not comprehensively distributed, because there may be reluctance to give away something with monetary value. But the monetary value of surplus presupposes scarcity. The situation is more complicated with shelter insecurity, but it is also well known that local real estate interests restrict the construction of affordable and cheap housing through zoning regulations. Fromm deflected possible objections that under a UBI people would lose their incentive to work by pointing out that physically and mentally creative work is not pursued from necessity. He reasoned that a UBI would free up opportunities to pursue that kind of work, as well as intellectual, spiritual, and moral development, as well as human flourishing more generally.[28]

The Finnish and Canadian experiments with UBI would seem to corroborate Fromm's aspirational aims. There is reason to believe that giving poor people money with no strings attached will make them healthier, happier, and likely more creative as well. But this is still a consequentialist approach, inviting balance against the goal of increasing employment. The difficult question is whether people have a right to the wherewithal for basic subsistence, and, if they do, whether the government is obligated to fulfill the conditions of recognizing that right. That the government is the only entity able to acknowledge and fulfill such a right is indisputable, because the government, state or federal, is the only entity with the command of resources and administrative capability to do so. But government resources in democratic nonpredatory societies are based on taxation. So this question amounts to the question of whether citizens are morally obligated to recognize the right of others in their state or nation to basic subsistence. Such obligation would not be political, and it is morally debatable. But it might be a humanitarian obligation.

Before further consideration of this question of a right to subsistence, it should be noted that if enough already exists for everyone, but the poor can't afford it, it is a plausible solution to tax the rich more to fund a UBI that would mainly benefit the poor. But what if problems with surplus food distribution and housing regulation, as well as waste in the health-care system, could be corrected through greater efficiency, so that the poor could afford these goods? In that case, the need for a UBI program looks different. Under situations of existing inefficient or unjust distributional policies, a UBI would allow poor people to join that existing system, without large increases in cost. With some increase of money in circulation, after a UBI program was implemented, there would be no incentive for suppliers, providers, and government regulators to make substantial budgetary changes. There is therefore a more general policy decision before the design and implementation of UBI policy—namely, can and should the present system be made more affordable?

The big question of whether people have a right to bare subsistence intersects with the question of efficiency, because fulfillment of such a right through greater efficiency would be just as good as the results of a UBI that did not change efficiency—many more people would get what they need in either case. There would probably be less moral and economic disruption and disagreement with the increased-efficiency UBI policy than a UBI without efficiency reform. But in either case, the question of whether there is a right to subsistence adds a vector of urgency to whichever policy is chosen and applied.

The US Constitution is not a source of the positive rights that advocates for UBI claim. But the 1948 United Nations Declaration of Universal Human Rights added a full spectrum of social and economic rights to its reiteration of more established social and political rights.

The Declaration addressed both rights and freedoms: articles 1 and 2 asserted universal human equality to all rights and freedoms, articles 3–13 asserted individual liberties and rights to life and security, and articles 14–21 asserted political and civil rights. From article 1 through article 21, there is nothing in the document beyond customary political and civil rights in democratic nation-states, except that the rights are claimed internationally and recognized as universal rights by the fifty nations that originally signed UDHR. Articles 22–28, however, proclaim rights to individual development, rewarding employment, education, social security, and community participation: Article 25 proclaims rights of security for the ill, unemployed, aged, and disabled, and special regard for mothers and children. Article 29 states that individuals have duties to their communities, based on their abilities. Article 30 proclaims the validity of all rights and freedoms listed, in that there is to be no implication that they may be violated. The political and civil rights of articles 1–21 represent explicit claims against governments, which, as noted, already formally existed in some nation-states. By contrast, it is not clear who is responsible for the fulfillment of the rights listed in articles 21–29, particularly article 24, which proclaims everyone's right to rest and leisure, including paid holidays, but especially article 25, 1:

> Everyone has the right to a standard of living adequate for the health and well-being of himself and of his family, including food, clothing, housing and medical care and necessary social services, and the right to security in the event of unemployment, sickness, disability, widowhood, old age or other lack of livelihood in circumstances beyond his control.[29]

The political and civil liberties vouchsafed in articles 1–21 already formally existed in the first fifty member states, and the United Nations had no power to interfere in their sovereignty regarding them. Nor did the United Nations have a mechanism for enforcing these rights and freedoms in nations that did not formally recognize them. The rights of social and economic equality, particularly the rights to minimal material well-being, remain idealistic goals in the early twenty-first century, not only throughout the world but also in its richest nations.[30]

In the 1960s, while the idea of universal human rights was still fresh, and before the half-century of neoconservativism that was to follow, as well as current conservative populism that goes after the basic civil rights of racial and ethnic minority groups, it was possible to credibly speak and write about humanitarian psychological goals, as Fromm did. Robert Theobald, the editor of the volume in which the essay by Fromm discussed here appeared, included in the appendix to that text his own essay, previously published in *Free Men and Free Markets*, "The Guaranteed Income Proposal."[31] Theobald does not argue for the beneficial consequences of his guaranteed income proposal as a justification for it. Rather, he seeks to "break the link between jobs and income." He simply asserts that there is an absolute right to human subsistence, viz:

> In order to ensure that government concern with the total socioeconomic system would not outweigh its responsibility to every member of society, a due-income from government should be given as an *absolute constitutional right*; for unless this is guaranteed, the government would have the possibility of developing the most extreme form of tyranny imaginable.[32]

Theobald thus made guaranteed income a condition for the assurance of freedom. Of course, any form of government has "the possibility of developing the most extreme form of tyranny imaginable." And the possibility of a constitutional amendment for UBI policy isn't even on the horizon. But what is important here is the claim of absolute right, concerning government. It's possible in a democratic society that such a right would come to be recognized. Health care is (before the election of 2020) close to being recognized as an absolute right, and some now speak of higher education in those terms. But we are not there yet for any of these cases. A right, especially an absolute right that is not guaranteed by binding documents (and even then), is not the kind of thing for which there can be empirical evidence beyond a consensus that such a right exists.

While evidence-based policy is not the worst form of policy in the sense that Winston Churchill said democracy is the worst form of government except for all the others, evidence-based policy is not easy. It is not easy to persuade politicians and the public to rely on the best available evidence according to experts whom they may disdain as a class, and not easy to adjust when expert evidence is inaccurate or incomplete, or does not mean what it is taken to mean. What we could say is that evidence-based policy is the best policy we know of, although it is not always good enough. And we can also modify Theodore Roosevelt, who counseled acceptance of failure while "daring greatly," because the reality is that we also have to accept failure on the most pedestrian levels, in fulfillment of the most basic tasks and needs. This would especially be true were the balm of anonymous or identity-free government to be combined with a commitment to evidence-based public policy, because evidence is a rose garden shot through with thorns.

CONCLUSION

Evidence-based public policy has problems in theoretical justification of inductive and causal reasoning and problems in recognizing when imperfect evidence calls for decisions. The upshot is that an empirical commitment requires plodding through imperfect evidence. However, political, emotional, and self-interested obstructions to policies based on evidence also need to be recognized and addressed in evidence-based ways. Where empiricism cannot be followed, because there is no evidence for what some think would be good public policy, more broad humanitarian commitments may lead to the design and implementation of new policies, the success of which will be assessed after the fact.

Conclusion

PROGRESSIVE ANONYMITY: REVIEW AND LOOSE ENDS

> We the People of the United States, in Order to form a more perfect Union, establish Justice, insure domestic Tranquility, provide for the common defence, promote the general Welfare, and secure the Blessings of Liberty to ourselves and our Posterity, do ordain and establish this Constitution for the United States of America.
>
> —Preamble to the Constitution of the United States

Chapter 1 established the need for identity politics as a focus on victims of oppression. Intellectually, this need was evident in the post–World War II diagnoses of oppressors that neglected the nature and needs of those oppressed. Chapter 2 was a discussion of the political limits of identity groups for political groups based on them, because opposition to any identity group with governmental power would lead to strife, in place of government fulfilling its obligations. This thesis carried into chapter 3, which sought to resurrect universalism for progressive goals. Chapter 4 was a necessary pause to examine why, concerning racism, progress has been intermittent. The answer was the persistence of white racial status, making racial equality impossible without the elimination of race. Chapter 5 established that evidence-based government faces the obstacle of public preference for emotional motivation, not to mention the preference of intellectuals for ideology. Chapter 6 sought to come to terms with the imperfections of evidence, which are perhaps matched only by the imperfections of democracy.

Overall, this book has been deflationary concerning both identities and rationally motivated anonymous government. Both evidence-based government and democracy are deeply flawed, but they must be balanced as ideals so as to preserve the social-compact idea that government exists for the benefit of all those governed.

I have been using the term "progressive" to mean change that makes things better for people within a nation, the United States. "Anonymity" means that public policy is worded and applied without regard to social identities of gender, race, religion, national origin, wealth and income, culture, education, and ability, either as stand-alone identities or as intersected identities. In the spirit of John Rawls's "veil of ignorance," the veil is drawn between government policies and all of those governed. Unlike Rawls's veil, however, this is not a thought experiment but a practical proposal. Policies are anonymous in their wordings and descriptions of those to whom they apply, but policy designers continue to know who they are. Government candidates and officials know how their constituents and members of their bases are likely to benefit from proposed policies, and under anonymous government, they will implicitly campaign on that basis, as they always have.

The difference of progressive anonymity from an identity-politics system within government is that changes through evidence-based policy benefit those better off, as well as those worse off. People who are comparatively worse off as members of disadvantaged identity groups may benefit comparatively more than those more advantaged at the outset—for instance, people of color benefit more than whites from policies against racial discrimination and those who are poor benefit more than the affluent from government payouts. So, everyone won't benefit to the same extent, but everyone will benefit. If they are not spiteful, people will support policies that benefit others, as well as themselves, on account of the benefit to themselves. If the rational, self-interested subject of classical economics is not the average subject of politics, then it falls to leaders and educators to patiently explain how certain policies will benefit everyone. This is a long and tedious labor, but it is the price for freedom as afforded by democracy. The people have a tendency to squander their political freedom to select their government by voting for candidates who entertain or scare them. But appeals to such motives should not be manipulated by progressives through nudges, because taking democracy seriously means respecting the autonomy of members of the electorate.

The idea of anonymity within government, from government, and for the beneficiaries of government is not a vision to be brought to people in aspirational terms, but an emphasis on the purpose and functioning of good government. Good government is government of all the people that is fair and impartial. Corrections of past unfairness or bias may look as though it is just to target some groups for the benefit of others (for example, raising taxes on the rich to fund universal health care or free college). But that is a faulty presentation. When progressive new proposals are first presented, they are often met with the question "How will you pay for that?" That is a trap for those presenting or proposing the new policy. Any program that is added on will expand government budgets if the other parts of the budget are not changed by the elimination of existing programs, reallocations, cutting waste, or even increasing deficits. Policy design or redesign should be expected to result in changes throughout the budget.

As discussed in chapter 5, Karl Popper wanted government to be empirical, and he emphasized the importance of government by law in democracies. He alluded to piecemeal public policies aimed at correcting specific problems and eschewed ideas of utopia. His fundamentally deflationary or "negative utilitarian" approach to ideals for government was explicitly expressed in "Public and Private Values." Popper began this paper with "While misery is a matter for public policy, happiness is not." And he ended with "The attempt to plan for progress must mean the end of it." In between, Popper argued that there is a public duty to fight against avoidable miseries, which has the greatest moral urgency. His reasoning was that striving for goods ought to be a private matter, because if the attainment of such goods becomes the agenda of public policy, then some inflict their values on others.

Popper thought that the socialist view that the state has a duty to take care of citizens who cannot take care of themselves and the liberal view of distrust of state intervention could be reconciled on the ground of his (negative utilitarian) proposal. The socialist does not think that totalitarianism is inevitable under socialism; the liberal believes liberalism can meet the dangers of misery, injustice, exploitation, and the absence of equal opportunity.[1] The ills that each side claims it can avoid are recognized as ills by more people than those who support each side, because often both sides agree on what social evils are. It is easier for both sides to agree on an agenda to combat social ills than to agree about social goods. Popper also claimed that his agenda for public policy was consistent with the minimal utilitarian doctrine of "minimize pain" and that it allowed for more diverse opinions than the classical "maximize happiness."[2]

Still, there will also always be disagreement on what should count as pain that ought to be minimized. For example, the concept of *microaggression* encompasses detailed remarks or small actions that are experienced as disrespectful, demeaning, or hostile by members of racial minority groups. Such speech and expression is experienced as harm and may be cumulatively distressing and wearing for recipients. But microaggression is difficult to prove and those unwilling to analyze events in daily life in detailed ways may be unable to recognize it or take responsibility for it. Another example is prison reform. Prison reform efforts have accompanied the institution of incarceration throughout the modern period, but especially in the eighteenth century.[3] But those who believe that prisons are necessary for social order and that inmates deserve what happens to them as prisoners may not be willing or able to consider reform.

For cases where different mind-sets or social conceptual schemes are opposed, factual evidence may have no effect toward progressive change. If the government rejects the use of "nudges" or the manipulation of behavior by cues and suggestions that activate strong motivations that are not rationally attuned to evidence, then such impasses should be worked out in the social sphere. Popper's general thesis that misery should be minimized lends itself to government benefit as progress, without invoking identities and objection and dissent based on counter-identities. His claim that the agendas of public policy ought not to be plans for progress only seems at odds with this idea, since he conceded that the elimination of pain can viewed as a good and new goods constitute progress. The idea that government should benefit those governed is general enough to include planning for this kind of progress. What is important is that planners not take it upon themselves to decide what kind of society there should be, as a whole. Planning public policy is piecemeal, because public policy is piecemeal.

The American electoral public is believed to have an unquenchable thirst for presidential visions such as "The New Deal" (Franklin Delano

Roosevelt), "The New Frontier" (John F. Kennedy), "The Great Society" (Lyndon B. Johnson), "The Shining City on a Hill" (Ronald Reagan), "Compassionate Conservatism" (George W. Bush), "Yes We Can" (Barack Obama), or "Make America Great Again" (Donald Trump). These visions help "brand" candidates and administrations.[4] If this thirst exists, and if the ability to slake it is dispositive for electoral victory, it would be problematic for any deflationary presentation of government as evidence-based public policy. But the causal link from strong visions and slogans to how people actually vote has not been established. Cultural critics and analysts typically take it for granted that a candidate with a strong vision and slogan who wins does so in large part because of their vision and slogan. Yet to be undertaken are empirical studies about the electoral effectiveness of visions and slogans. Chants and enthusiasm at political rallies certainly show enthusiasm, but it is not known how representative such participants are of a wider electorate or whether those who chant and enthuse do all (or most) vote for the candidate they are cheering. It is possible that many are still voting based on what they believe issues are and that they dismiss visions and slogans as either unavoidable advertising or merely celebration. It is possible that chanting and cheering exhausts the political energy of activist political supporters.

We assume, after the fact, that the visions and slogans of winning candidates were important factors in their victories. But the visions only fire up about 30 percent of the voting population, about half of those who vote, who are about 60 percent of the voting population in close presidential elections. And the total voting population is about 70 percent of the total population, so less than 15 percent of the total population could have their voting choices decided by visions and slogans.[5]

The success of the Republican party since Ronald Reagan has been based on platforms to minimize government. The 40 percent of eligible voters who do not vote has disengaged with government in a more conclusive way. Something profound may have changed in the United States since the Reagan years. Government is distrusted, or else dismissed, on all sides. As Mark Lilla tells this story in his 2017, post–Trump election analysis and exhortation, *The Once and Future Liberal: After Identity Politics*, Reagan Republicans and the Tea Party movement that followed, along with the extreme right, have been successful in creating alienation from government in general. The result has been a shift in public attention from civic matters to private life (and, I would add, private consumption and electronic solitude). Among Democrats, a different kind of depoliticization has occurred over the same time, through the development of ever-narrowing identities. Lilla caps his analysis with the claim "Identity is Reaganism for Lefties." Lilla thinks that the American people need a new vision and a broad identity that can be shared. His suggestion is civic involvement through political projects and the identity of "Citizen." Citizen status can be recognized across differences in identities and Lilla thinks it could and should be cultivated and valorized through civic education that revitalizes "we" and what we owe one another—in other words, civic duty.[6] Lilla's diagnosis is a resonant and plausible interpretation of recent history, but his prescription may be irrelevant. It may be too late for successful and effective political visions and slogans. We may be entering an historical period in which the majority of Americans are done with government as an institution they can trust, which is worth obeying and honoring for its own sake. The majority of Americans may no longer be inspired by government. On a federal level, it is true that citizenship is something that citizens share, but not all residents are citizens. Citizenship is a status that individuals have in relation to government and its main privilege could be eligibility for benefiting from the federal government. But citizenship and civic involvement in itself is probably not sufficient to create excitement about government and renewed desire for good government. Only appealing public policies could do that, policies that address specific miseries in ways that also benefit those who are not suffering from such miseries. This is a tall order. The miseries have to be identified and publicized and inclusive solutions to them need to be crafted. Public consensus must be built in society, before new legislation is proposed.

The idea of citizen or citizenship may not be exciting enough to motivate visions (assuming they are still politically necessary) or civic participation. Something else that citizens and noncitizens share is nationality. Citizenship is an identity, attached to individuals, while nationality is a shared attribute. Citizenship imposes obligations on individuals, whereas nationality takes them as they are. One is a citizen, but one has the attribute of nationality. Nationality is a fact about persons and need not be connected to nationalisms. It is not accidental that since Lyndon B. Johnson, presidents begin and conclude their State of the Union addresses with the salutation "My Fellow Americans"[7] and not "My fellow citizens" or "My fellow American citizens." Again, we do not know that such rhetoric is necessary for political support. But if it is, shared American nationality could work as a vision theme, either sparking new enthusiasm for government or addressing people in their indifference. If vision is unnecessary or no longer as necessary, political engagement could be more directly based on how government benefits and serves those governed. This would consistent of a fundamental change in broad ideas of the US federal government, from a quasi-sacred guardian of society and its values to a transactional institution. If people pay taxes and obey the laws, that might be enough to fulfill their part of a contract with government that benefits and serves them. Interestingly enough, this means that evidence-based public policy is the whole or major part of domestic government.

Nationality may be a concept of government that shrinks government, as Republicans have been demanding, but also benefits and serves people, as Democrats still advocate. Instead of JFK's "Ask what you can do for your country," we would have "Ask what your country can do for you." In line with Popper's goal of uniting socialists and liberals, government without hoopla, and without visions about how the whole society should be, would, in minimizing misery without seeking to promote happiness, be leaner than attempts to do both. The minimization of misery would increase the sphere of justice, because those worse off would benefit disproportionately and their circumstances would closer approximate those already better off.

Finally, we may not need to give up on happiness, as a benefit of government. Policies that lessen misery, such as universal basic income or greater efficiency in health care or surplus food distribution, will increase happiness as an "unintended consequence." This was evident in pilot UBI programs in Finland and Canada, as discussed in chapter 6. Such positive unintended consequences of anti-misery programs are a matter of grace. Grace through government is ineffable and cannot be legislated or directly administered. But empirically based experimental public policy is inconclusive enough to allow for it.

POSTSCRIPT

Like many who were shocked and distressed, I became addicted to constant political news after Trump was elected president. It seemed to me that my news sources (*Washington Post*, *New York Times*, *Huffington Post*, *National Public Radio*, CNN, ABC, and PBS) were delivering objective accounts of growing fascism, as well as derangement in the presidential persona. I personally found Trump extremely offensive. However, my perspective moved to a meta level during the Democratic impeachment investigation and through the trial in the US Senate.

Each side was accusing the other of violating rules of law and government, as set forth in the US Constitution. Democrats claimed that Trump had abused his power in withholding military aid from Ukraine pending an investigation of his presumptive political rival and that he had obstructed the congressional investigation of this matter by not allowing members of his administration to testify. Republicans claimed that the president had not been proved to have abused his power and that the congressional investigation had not followed certain legally required procedures. Republicans did not accept that the congressional investigation was in good faith, claiming it was merely part of an ongoing effort to repudiate the election of Trump; Democrats accused Republicans of a cover-up, because they needed Trump's political support for their forthcoming individual elections. Each side accused the other of having politicized constitutional issues for purely political motives.

I realized that they were both right! Democrats, as well as Republicans, made accusations for political motives, to increase or keep political power. Each side was quite adept at doing this, and as of this writing, I expect it to carry into the general election. This means that the US government at this time has been rendered dysfunctional by politics and contest, based on political identities and the demographic identities that draw people to this or that party or who party leaders claim to be representing.

We are thereby living through the antithesis of evidence-based anonymous government. And it may not be coincidental that although many sectors of the population have cause for complaint, we are also living through a time of extreme economic prosperity. If we take seriously that political upheaval is usually a reaction to economic downturns, then this political upheaval must have another cause. My own view is that it is an expression of excess—namely, a form of decadence. Enough people have become satisfied as consumers and owners, and there are enough consumers and owners, so that the belief that government is superfluous has become the main underlying assumption. Enough people believe that they no longer need things from government. So government has become hard entertainment. I call it "hard" because it is less like romcoms, musicals, sitcoms, historical period pieces, or even good documentaries and more like horror movies, crime stories, and other kinds of "thrillers."

February 12, 2020

What a difference two months has made! The political struggle during President Trump's impeachment trial has morphed into a politicized existential struggle. Democrats have not approved of the president's leadership during the US COVID-19 pandemic, whereas Republicans have approved. Democratic states (California and New York) were among the first to practice social distancing and closures, while a handful of Republican states held out after this policy became all but national. But now every state has declared a state of disaster.

It is too soon to write about this disaster with the knowledge and dispassion it merits, except to say that political identities and all of their baggage from the "Culture Wars" have so proved to be even more

POSTSCRIPT

adherent than racial identities. The disproportionate number of black deaths has been broadcast as a social problem by all, including white leaders at all levels of society.

April 12, 2020

NOTES

INTRODUCTION AND CHAPTER OVERVIEW

1. Naomi Zack, *Reviving the Social Compact: Inclusive Citizenship in an Age of Extreme Politics* (Lanham, MD: Rowman & Littlefield, 2018), chapter 8, "Homelessness and Monetization," 131–46; ibid., reprinted as "Homelessness, Philosophy and Public Policy," in G. John M. Abbarno, ed., *The Ethics of Homelessness* (Leiden, Boston: Brill Rodopi, 2020), 175–91.

2. Zack, *Reviving the Social Compact*. In chapter 3, I claim that the extreme disagreements between the two major US political parties, together with instant electorates manufactured through social media, have all but broken the federal government because politics as competition has distracted from governmental functions.

3. John Rawls, *A Theory of Justice* (Cambridge, MA: Harvard University Press, 1971), 11, 13, 60–61, 76.

4. Raymond Williams, *The Long Revolution* (Cardigan, UK: Parthian, 1961/2011), 387.

5. Some public policy theorists have claimed that US public school officials are not attentive to parents, because they are focused on the government entities that provide their funding. See Kevin B. Smith and Christopher W. Larimer, *The Public Policy Theory Primer* (New York: Routledge, 2019), 60–66.

6. In 2019, the US economy was broadly judged to be 68 percent consumer driven. See Kimberly Amadeo, "US Economy Demand Consumer Spending Trends and Current Statistics, Consumer Spending Up 2.5%," *The Balance*, https://www.thebalance.com/consumer-spending-trends-and-current-statistics-3305916.

7. See C. K. Jacobson, "Resistance to Affirmative Action: Self-Interest or Racism?" *Journal of Conflict Resolution* 29, no. 2 (1985): 306–29, https://doi.org/10.1177/0022002785029002007; Peter Schmidt, "Supreme Court Shows Increased Skepticism toward Affirmative Action," *Chronicle of Higher Education* 53, no. 17 (2006), A20.

8. Linda Benesch, "New Polling on Social Security, Medicare, and Prescription Drug Prices," Polling Social Security, *Social Security Works*, March 16, 2018, https://socialsecurityworks.org/2018/03/16/new-polling-social-security/.

9. Mary Bernstein, "Identity Politics," *Annual Review of Sociology* 31, no. 1 (2005): 47–74, esp. 48.

10. Weiyi Cai and Simone Landon, "Attacks by White Extremists Are Growing. So Are Their Connections," *New York Times*, April 3, 2019, https://www.nytimes.com/interactive/2019/04/03/world/white-extremist-terrorism-christchurch.html.

11. For discussion of the claims of injustice by the "white mass recently politicized" during the 2016 US presidential election rhetoric, see Naomi Zack, "Contemporary Claims of Political Injustice: History and the Race to the Bottom," *Res Philosophica*, published online first: October 18, 2017, https://doi.org/10.11612/resphil.1613.

12. Adam Serwer, "The Terrorism That Doesn't Spark a Panic: Americans Should React to Violence from Religious and Ethnic Minorities with the Same Sense of Proportion They Reserve for Far-Right Extremists," *The Atlantic*, January 28, 2019, https://www.theatlantic.com/ideas/archive/2019/01/homegrown-terrorists-2018-were-almost-all-right-wing/581284/.

13. Jewish Virtual Library, "Encyclopedia Judaica: Blood Libel," https://www.jewishvirtuallibrary.org/blood-libel.

14. Amy Russo, "Pete Buttigieg Warns 'White Identity Politics' Launching Nation into 'Crisis,'" *Huff Post*, May 12, 2019, https://www.huffpost.com/entry/pete-buttigieg-white-identity-politics-crisis-of-belonging_n_5cd86ca5e4b054da4e8b316a?guccounter=1.

1. POLITICAL DIAGNOSES IN THE POST–WORLD WAR II ERA AND THE NEED FOR IDENTITY POLITICS

1. Roger Errera and Hannah Arendt, "The Last Interview," in *The Last Interview and Other Conversations*, trans. Andrew Brown (Brooklyn, NY: Melville House, 2013), 133.

2. Philip Hallie, "From Cruelty to Goodness," *The Hastings Center Report* 11, no. 3 (June 1981), 25.

NOTES

3. See S. Overgaard, "On Levinas' Critique of Husserl," in *Metaphysics, Facticity, Interpretation*, eds. D. Zahavi, S. Heinämaa, and H. Ruin, Contributions to Phenomenology, vol. 49 (Dordrecht, Netherlands: Springer, 2003), 115–38.

4. See Peter Atterton, Matthew Calarco, and Maurice Friedman, eds., *Levinas and Buber: Dialogue and Difference* (Philadelphia, PA: Duquesne University Press, 2004).

5. See Martin Heidegger, "Letter on Humanism," in *Basic Writings: Nine Key Essays, Plus the Introduction to Being and Time,* trans. David Farrell Krell (London: Routledge, 1978), 213–66.

6. For a more recent critique of the persistence of subject-object metaphysics, see Jacques Derrida, "The Ends of Man," *Philosophy and Phenomenological Research* 30, no. 1 (1969): 31–57.

7. His description of the nonintentional process resembles a practice of meditation, consisting of trying not to think of anything. One wonders whether Levinas himself was able to achieve that state; did he practice meditation? See Leah Kalmanson, Frank Garrett, and Sarah Mattice, eds., *Levinas and Asian Thought* (Philadelphia, PA: Duquesne University Press, 2013).

8. Emmanuel Levinas, "Ethics as First Philosophy"/"Justifications de l'Ethique" (Bruxelles: Editions de l'Universite de Bruxelles, 1984), 41–51. From *The Levinas Reader*, ed. Sean Hand (Oxford and Cambridge: Blackwell, 1989), 75–85, quotation 79. This passage is ambiguous. I have read it as Levinas's invitation to consider nonintentional consciousness. But others, such as Robert Farrell, my colleague in a Levinas reading group at Lehman College during the fall 2019 semester, may interpret it as Levinas's characterization of Husserlian phenomenological analysis. If Levinas was referring to the Husserlian tradition by his use of "philosophy" as issuing an invitation, then he would have meant to criticize that tradition for treating nonintentional consciousness as an object for the intentional subject. At any rate, for Levinas, nonintentional consciousness is not an object intended by consciousness, because he posits it as that state of consciousness prior to, or beyond intentionality.

9. Ibid., 80.
10. Ibid., 82.
11. Ibid., 83.
12. Ibid.
13. Ibid.
14. Ibid., 86.
15. Jonathan Bennett, "The Conscience of Huckleberry Finn," *Philosophy* 49 (1974), 123–24 (discussion 5–6). Quotation of Himmler from William L. Shirer, *The Rise and Fall of the Third Reich* (New York, 1960), 937–38, 966.
16. Ibid., 5–6.

17. See Jean-Paul Sartre, *Being and Nothingness: A Phenomenological Essay on Ontology*, trans. Hazel E. Barnes (New York: Washington Square Press, 1956/1984). For the two regions of being, present consciousness and everything else, see 56–85; for bad faith, see 36–118. See also Jean-Paul Sartre, *Existentialism Is a Humanism*, trans. Carol Macomber (New Haven, CT: Yale University Press, 1947/1996/2007).

18. Sartre, *Existentialism Is a Humanism*, 22.

19. Jean-Paul Sartre, *Anti-Semite and Jew*, trans. George J. Becker (New York: Schocken Books, 1965), 23.

20. Ibid., 24.

21. Ibid., 72.

22. Sartre wrote of the French anti-Semite, "The Jew only serves him as a pretext; elsewhere his counterpart will make use of the Negro or the man of yellow skin." Sartre, *Anti-Semite and Jew*, 54.

23. Sartre, *Anti-Semite and Jew*, 60.

24. Lublin/Majdanek was a German concentration and extermination camp built and operated by the SS outside of Lublin during the German occupation of Poland. Lublin had 7 gas chambers, 2 wooden gallows, and 227 structures overall. Lublin was the first concentration camp to be liberated, and approximately 78,000 people were killed there. See *Holocaust Encyclopedia*, "Lublin/Majdanek Concentration Camp: Conditions," United States Holocaust Memorial and Museum, https://encyclopedia.ushmm.org/content/en/article/lublin-majdanek-concentration-camp-conditions.

25. Sartre, *Anti-Semite and Jew*, 71.

26. Karl Popper, "Anti-Semitism in Austria: A Letter to Friedrich Hayek (1969)," in *Popper, After the Open Society: Selected Social and Political Writings*, eds. Jeremy Shearmur and Piers Norris Turner (London and New York: Routledge, 2012), 36.

27. Sartre, *Anti-Semite and Jew*, 80–92.

28. Ibid., 93–96, 109, 119.

29. Ibid., 150.

30. Frantz Fanon, *Black Skin, White Masks*, trans. Charles L. Markham (New York: Grove, 1967), quotation from 1952, page 88.

31. Hannah Arendt, *The Origins of Totalitarianism* (New York: Harcourt, Brace, Jovanovich, 1951–1973).

32. Arendt said of her adventure:

> In the end I did not leave in such a peaceful way. And I must say that gives me a certain satisfaction. I was arrested, and had to leave the country illegally . . . and that was instant gratification for me. I

thought at least I had done something! At least I am not "innocent." No one could say that of me! . . .

We were very poor, we were hunted down, we had to flee, by hook or by crook we somehow had to get through, and whatever. That's how it was. But we were young. I even had a little fun with it—I can't deny it.

From Hannah Arendt, "What Remains? The Language Remains: A Conversation with Günter Gaus," trans. Joan Stambaugh, *Zur Person*, ZDF TV, Germany, October 28, 1964, printed in *The Last Interview and Other Conversations* (Brooklyn, NY: Melville House, 2013), 9 and 23.

33. Hannah Arendt and Martin Heidegger, *Letters, 1925–1975*, trans. Andrew Shields (Orlando, FL: Harcourt, 2004).

34. See Gunther Neske and Emil Kettering, eds., *Martin Heidegger and National Socialism* (New York: Paragon House, 1990).

35. Arendt, "What Remains?" 19.

36. Hannah Arendt, *Eichmann in Jerusalem: A Report on the Banality of Evil* (New York: Penguin, 1963/2006); Hannah Arendt, "Eichmann Was Outrageously Stupid," interview by Joachim Fest, *Das Thema*, SWR TV, Germany, November 9, 1964, printed in *The Last Interview and Other Conversations* (Brooklyn, NY: Melville House, 2013), 41–65.

37. Ibid., 62.

38. Arendt, "What Remains?" 4.

39. Ibid.

40. See Virginia Held, reply by Alfred Kazin, "Feminism & Hannah Arendt," To the Editors, *New York Review of Books*, October 21, 1982 (in response to *Woman in Dark Times* from the June 24, 1982, issue), https://www.nybooks.com/articles/1982/10/21/feminism-hannah-arendt/; Bonnie Honig, ed., *Feminist Interpretations of Hannah Arendt* (University Park: Pennsylvania State University Press, 1995).

41. Arendt, "What Remains?" 5.

42. On Arendt and political philosophy, see Seyla Benhabib, ed., *Politics in Dark Times: Encounters with Hannah Arendt* (Cambridge: Cambridge University Press, 2010).

43. Jewish Virtual Library, "Documenting Numbers of Victims of the Holocaust and Nazi Persecution," United States Holocaust Memorial and Museum, February 4, 2019, https://www.jewishvirtuallibrary.org/documenting-numbers-of-victims-of-the-holocaust.

44. *Holocaust Encyclopedia*, "Blacks During the Holocaust Era," United States Holocaust Memorial and Museum, https://encyclopedia.ushmm.org/content/en/article/blacks-during-the-holocaust-era.

45. For this philosophical history of false universalism, see Naomi Zack, *The Ethics and Mores of Race: Equality After the History of Philosophy* (Lanham, MD: Rowman & Littlefield, 2011).

46. For discussion of the idea of universal human rights pertaining to UDHR, in the context of race, see Zack, *The Ethics and Mores of Race*, 141–62.

47. There is a broad consensus about this interpretation of Popper's idea of falsification as the hallmark of science compared to pseudoscience. The primary work is Karl Popper, *The Logic of Scientific Discovery* (Hutchinson Education, 1959–2000). For a distillation, see William Groton, "Karl Popper: Political Philosophy," *Internet Encyclopedia of Philosophy*, https://www.iep.utm.edu/popp-pol/.

48. Karl Popper, *Conjectures and Refutations* (London: Routledge and Kegan Paul, 1963–1989), 361. Recognition of injustice has occurred throughout history in the absence of well-formed ideas of justice. For discussion of this issue, see Naomi Zack, *Reviving the Social Compact: Inclusive Citizenship in an Age of Extreme Politics* (Lanham, MD: Rowman & Littlefield, 2018), 52, 84–84, and Naomi Zack, *Applicative Justice: A Pragmatic Empirical Approach to Racial Injustice* (Lanham, MD: Rowman & Littlefield, 2016), 65–88.

49. See Karl Popper, dedication and "Historical Note," *The Poverty of Historicism* (London and New York: Routledge, 1957), ix–x.

50. Ibid., "Historical Note."

2. FROM SOCIETY TO GOVERNMENT: PROBLEMS WITH IDENTITY POLITICS

1. https://www.philosophytalk.org/blog/identity-politics.

2. The forbearance part is a negative right, the resource provision an entitlement or positive right. See Globalization101, "Negative vs. Positive Rights," Project of SUNY Levin Institute, http://www.globalization101.org/negative-vs-positive-rights/.

3. Political candidates and parties may even go further than this and in effect create or construct "bases" or groups of followers. This effect occurred among white working-class people who voted for Donald Trump in the 2016 US presidential election. See Naomi Zack, *Reviving the Social Compact: Inclusive Citizenship in an Age of Extreme Politics* (Lanham, MD: Rowman & Littlefield, 2018), chapter 3, "The Political Creation of Class," 43–58.

4. Sarah Bryner and Grace Haley, "Race, Gender, and Money in Politics: Campaign Finance and Federal Candidates in the 2018 Midterms," Center for Responsive Politics, https://www.pgpf.org/sites/default/files/US-2050-Race-

Gender-and-Money-in-Politics-Campaign-Finance-and-Federal-Candidates-in-the-2018-Midterms.pdf.

5. James McClellan, "Liberty, Order, and Justice: An Introduction to the Constitutional Principles of American Government," Rule of Law & US Constitutionalism, Online Library of Liberty, 2000, https://oll.libertyfund.org/pages/rule-of-law-us-constitutionalism.

6. Thomas Hobbes, *Leviathan* (1651), Second Part, Chap XVIII, 151–52.

7. John Locke, *Second Treatise of Government* (1689), © Jonathan Bennett 2017, Early Modern Texts, 2018, http://www.earlymoderntexts.com/assets/pdfs/locke1689a.pdf, Locke, 1689/2017, IX, 124.

8. Michael R. Powers, "From Hunter to Prisoner: Hurricane Katrina and the Social Contract," *Journal of Risk Finance* 7, issue 1 (2006), https://doi.org/10.1108/jrf.2006.29407aaa.001.

9. Donald E. Pease, *The New American Exceptionalism* (Minneapolis: University of Minnesota Press, 2009), 97.

10. Josh Freedman and Michael Lind, "The Past and Future of America's Social Contract," *The Atlantic,* December 19, 2013, https://www.theatlantic.com/business/archive/2013/12/the-past-and-future-of-americas-social-contract/282511/.

11. John Myhill, "The Native Speaker, Identity, and the Authenticity Hierarchy," *Language Sciences* 25, issue 1 (January 2003): 77–97.

12. See Georg G. Iggers, *The German Conception of History: The National Tradition of Historical Thought from Herder to the Present* (Scranton, PA: Harper and Row, 1984); Janne Mende, *A Human Right to Culture and Identity: The Ambivalence of Group Rights*, trans. Jochen Gahrau (London: Rowman & Littlefield, 2016), 19–48.

13. Charles Taylor, *The Ethics of Authenticity* (Cambridge, MA: Harvard University Press, 1991).

14. Ibid., 26.

15. Ibid., 43.

16. Theo W. A. de Wit, "'My Way': Charles Taylor on Identity and Recognition in a Secular Democracy," *Stellenbosch Theological Journal* 4, no. 1 (2018), 157.

17. Ibid., 56–60. Thus, recognition itself is recognized when it is not forthcoming, just as reactions to injustice are prior to well-formed ideas about justice. For more about such recognition and protest in the breach, see Naomi Zack, "Starting from Injustice: Justice, Applicative Justice, and Injustice Theory," *Harvard Review of Philosophy*, online first, June 10, 2017, https://www.pdcnet.org/harvardreview/onlinefirst.

18. Ibid., 61.

19. See Maria P.P. Root, "Bill of Rights for Racially Mixed People," https://www.safehousealliance.org/wp-content/uploads/2012/10/A-Bill-of-Rights-for-Racially-Mixed-People.pdf.

20. US state laws on changing gender identity from gender assigned at birth are not uniform. See Transgender Law Center, "State-by-State Overview: Changing Gender Markers on Birth Certificates," https://transgenderlawcenter.org/resources/id/state-by-state-overview-changing-gender-markers-on-birth-certificates.

21. See Spencer Case, "What Philosophers Must Learn from the Transracialism Meltdown," *Quillette*, May 26, 2017, https://quillette.com/2017/05/26/philosophers-must-learn-transracialism-meltdown/.

22. Barbara "Shining Woman" Warren, "Who Is an Indian," PowerSource, http://www.powersource.com/cocinc/ancest/whois.htm.

23. See Brenda Lyshaug, "Authenticity and the Politics of Identity: A Critique of Charles Taylor's Politics of Recognition," *Contemporary Political Theory* 3 (2004): 300–320, https://doi.org/10.1057/palgrave.cpt.9300125; Radical Philosophy Identity Archive, https://www.radicalphilosophy.com/tag/identity; Janice Peck, "Itinerary of a Thought: Stuart Hall, Cultural Studies, and the Unresolved Problem of the Relation of Culture to 'Not Culture,'" *Cultural Critique*, no. 48 (2001): 200–249, www.jstor.org/stable/1354401.

24. W. E. Cross Jr. and B. J. Vandiver, "Nigrescence Theory and Measurement: Introducing the Cross Racial Identity Scale (CRIS)," in *Handbook of Multicultural Counseling*, eds. J. G. Ponterotto, J. M. Casas, L. A. Suzuki, and C. M. Alexander (Thousand Oaks, CA: Sage, 2001), 371–93.

25. Madonna G. Constantine, Tina Q. Richardson, Eric M. Benjamin, and John W. Wilson, "An Overview of Black Racial Identity Theories: Limitations and Considerations for Future Theoretical Conceptualizations," *Applied & Preventive Psychology* 7:95–99 (1998), https://pdfs.semanticscholar.org/83b5/4af29e543446fe7a8d48b5780608c8b6d36a.pdf.

26. See de Wit, "'My Way.'"

27. See Andrew Schaap, "Political Reconciliation Through a Struggle for Recognition?" *Social & Legal Studies* 13, no. 4 (December 2004): 523–40, DOI: 10.1177/0964663904047332.

28. Frantz Fanon, *Black Skin, White Masks* (London: Pluto Press, 1952/1986/2008).

29. Ibid., 102.

30. Francis Fukuyama, *Identity: The Demand for Dignity and the Politics of Resentment* (London: Profile Books, 2018), 7–8.

31. Ibid., 32.

32. See Miriam Meyerhoff, "Gender Performativity," *The International Encyclopedia of Human Sexuality*, first edition, eds. Patricia Whelehan and Anne Bolin (Chichester: John Wiley & Sons, 2015).

33. See Joseph Raz, *The Morality of Freedom* (Oxford and New York: Oxford University Press, 1986), 165–216, 245–63, esp. 207–9 and 166 on group rights and duties. Cited by Peter Jones, "Human Rights, Group Rights, and Peoples' Rights," *Human Rights Quarterly* 21, no. 1 (February 1999): 80–107, citation 83.

34. For a preliminary bibliography, see Peter Jones, "Group Rights," *The Stanford Encyclopedia of Philosophy* (Summer 2016 Edition), ed. Edward N. Zalta, https://plato.stanford.edu/archives/sum2016/entries/rights-group/.

35. Catharine MacKinnon, *Feminism Unmodified: Discourses on Life and Law* (Cambridge, MA: Harvard University Press, 1987), chapter 2, "Difference and Dominance: On Sex Discrimination."

36. ADL (Anti Defamation League), "New Hate and Old: The Changing Face of American White Supremacy: A Report from the Center on Extremism," https://www.adl.org/new-hate-and-old (consulted April 2019).

37. Barbara Harff, *Ethnic Conflict in World Politics*, 2nd edition (New York: Routledge, 2018).

38. That is, the language of the Bill of Rights, the Sixteenth Amendment to the Constitution, and the civil rights movement–era legislation about discrimination, voting, and immigration, as well as US Supreme Court rulings on affirmative action, all refer to what individuals are entitled to and what cannot be done to them regardless of distinct identities, instead of recognizing distinct groups that do or do not have rights. The same is true of the 1948 United Nations Universal Declaration of Human Rights. Concerning international law, see Jochen von Bernstorff, "The Changing Fortunes of the Universal Declaration of Human Rights: Genesis and Symbolic Dimensions of the Turn to Rights in International Law," *European Journal of International Law* 19, issue 5 (November 2008): 903–24, https://doi.org/10.1093/ejil/chn069. The subject of individual rights has a vast literature and usually discussion centers on the rights of specific individuals, types of individuals, and which government entity can protect them. It seems to go without saying that the subject or recipient of rights is an individual and not a group. See, for instance, William J. Brennan Jr., "State Constitutions and the Protection of Individual Rights," *Harvard Law Review* 90, no. 3 (1976–1977), https://heinonline.org/HOL/LandingPage?handle=hein.journals/hlr90&div=30&id=&page.

39. Todd Gitlin, *The Twilight of Common Dreams: Why America Is Wracked by Culture Wars* (New York: Metropolitan Books, 1995).

40. See Julie E. Maybee, *Making and Unmaking Disability: The Three-Body Approach* (Lanham, MD: Rowman & Littlefield, 2019), chapter 7.

41. See Chelsea Whyte, "Green New Deal Proposal Includes Free Higher Education and Fair Pay," *New Scientist*, February 12, 2019, https://www.newscientist.com/article/2193592-green-new-deal-proposal-includes-free-higher-education-and-fair-pay/. For the document itself, see Green New Deal Group, "A Green New Deal: Joined-Up Policies to Solve the Triple Crunch of the Credit Crisis, Climate Change and High Oil Prices," First Report of the Green New Deal Group, Technical Report, New Economics Foundation, December 2007, https://www.researchgate.net/publication/271506210_A_Green_New_Deal_Joined-up_Policies_to_Solve_the_Triple_Crunch_of_the_Credit_Crisis_Climate_Change_and_High_Oil_Prices.

42. See Tom Flanagan, "Will Mounting Costs of Reconciliation Benefit Indigenous People?" *The Globe and Mail*, November 6, 2018, https://www.theglobeandmail.com/opinion/article-will-mounting-costs-of-reconciliation-benefit-indigenous-people/.

43. For a more comprehensive statement of these problems, see Naomi Zack, "Reparations and the Rectification of Race," *Journal of Ethics*, Special Issue: *Race, Racism and Reparations* 3 (2003): 139–51.

44. Rodney C. Roberts, "Race, Rectification, and Apology," in Naomi Zack, ed. *Oxford Handbook of Race and Philosophy* (New York: Oxford University Press, 2017/2019), 516–25.

45. Bilal Qureshi, "From Wrong to Right: A U.S. Apology for Japanese Internment," *All Things Considered*, NPR, August 9, 2013, https://www.npr.org/sections/codeswitch/2013/08/09/210138278/japanese-internment-redress.

46. Martin Pengelly, "Georgetown Students Vote to Pay Reparations for Slaves Sold by University," *The Guardian*, April 15, 2019, https://www.theguardian.com/world/2019/apr/15/georgetown-students-reparations-vote-slaves-sold-by-university.

3. UNIVERSALISM OR FORCE: INCLUSION OR DOMINATION

1. Emmanuel Levinas and Seán Hand, "Reflections on the Philosophy of Hitlerism," *Critical Inquiry* 17, no. 1 (Autumn 1990): 62–71.

2. For the first part of this paragraph, concerning equality, see Naomi Zack, "Philosophical Theories of Justice, Inequality, and Racial Inequality," *Graduate Faculty Philosophy Journal*, Special Issue on Race in the History of Philosophy, vol. 35, no. 1–2 (2014): 353–68, and Naomi Zack, "Equality," in *Wiley-Blackwell Encyclopedia of Race, Ethnicity, and Nationalism*, eds. John Stone, Rutledge Dennis, Polly Rizova, Anthony D. Smith, and Xiaoshuo Hou (published online: December 30, 2015), http://onlinelibrary.wiley.com/book/

10.1002/9781118663202. For a fuller exposition of the last sentence in the paragraph, see Naomi Zack, *White Privilege and Black Rights: The Injustice of US Police Racial Profiling and Homicide* (Lanham, MD: Rowman & Littlefield, 2015), chapter 1.

3. For the seminal article that opened up the question of the biological foundation of race, see Anthony Appiah, "'But Would That Still Be Me?' Notes on Gender, 'Race,' Ethnicity, as Sources of 'Identity,'" *Journal of Philosophy* 87, no. 10 (1990): 493–99. See also K. Anthony Appiah, "Race, Culture, Identity: Misunderstood Connections," Tanner Lectures on Human Value, delivered at University of California at San Diego, October 27 and 28, 1994, https://philpapers.org/archive/apprci.pdf. There were at least two very intense conferences on the subject: "Race: Its Meaning and Significance," Department of Philosophy, Rutgers University, November 1994, and "The Race Debates: From Philosophy to Biomedical Research," University of San Francisco, April, 2014. For an examination of scientific foundations for race, see Naomi Zack, *Philosophy of Science and Race* (New York: Routledge, 2002). For more contemporary writings on this issue, see the essays by Albert Atkin, Michael O. Hardimon, John H. Relethford, Joshua Glasgow, and Jorge J. E. Gracia in Part III, "Metaphysics and Philosophy of Science," in Naomi Zack, ed., *The Oxford Handbook of Philosophy and Race* (New York: Oxford University Press, 2017/2019), 135–90.

4. For discussion of this issue, see Zack, *Philosophy of Science and Race*, 77–78.

5. Booker T. Washington, "Booker T. Washington's Atlanta Exposition Speech, September 18, 1895," State Historical Society of Iowa, https://iowaculture.gov/history/education/educator-resources/primary-source-sets/reconstruction-and-its-impact/booker-t.

6. Ibid.

7. For discussion of Du Bois's contribution to empirical sociology, see Aldon Morris, *The Scholar Denied: W. E. B. Du Bois and the Birth of Modern Sociology* (Berkeley: University of California Press, 2017). It cannot be claimed that Du Bois was contradicting himself at the time of his Conservation address, because the study was not then complete. But it does not seem a stretch to assume that he was then open to, if not directly entertaining, his thesis that the causes of African American ills were at least as much in their societal circumstances as their own moral traits.

8. Wilson J. Moses, "W. E. B. Du Bois's 'The Conservation of Races' and Its Context: Idealism, Conservatism and Hero Worship," *Massachusetts Review* 34, no. 2 (1993): 275–94.

9. Robert Wortham, ed., *The Sociological Souls of Black Folk: Essays by W. E. B. Du Bois* (Lanham, MD: Lexington Books, 2011), 115.

10. Lee A. Mcbride, "Insurrectionist Ethics and Racism," in Naomi Zack, ed., *The Oxford Handbook of Philosophy and Race* (New York: Oxford University Press, 2017/2019), 225–34.

11. Lucius Outlaw, "Africana Philosophy," *Journal of Ethics* 1, no. 3 (1997): 265–90, www.jstor.org/stable/25115551.

12. Chike Jeffers, "The Cultural Theory of Race: Yet Another Look at Du Bois's 'The Conservation of Races,'" *Ethics* 123, no. 3 (April 2013): 403–26, https://doi.org/10.1086/669566

13. Beginning in January 2019, there has been considerable speculation about how racial identities will determine how people vote: Anthony Cilluffo and Richard Fry, "An Early Look at the 2020 Electorate," Pew Research Center, January 30, 2019, Social & Demographic Trends, https://www.pewsocialtrends.org/essay/an-early-look-at-the-2020-electorate/; Ronald Brownstein, "2020 Democrats Face the Most Diverse Electorate in History," CNN Politics, February 12, 2019, https://www.cnn.com/interactive/2019/02/politics/dem-primaries-exit-polls/.

14. See Ida B. Wells, "Southern Horrors" (1892) in *On Lynchings* (Mineola, NY: Dover Books, 2014); *The Crisis, NAACP Magazine*, 1910–1923, http://www.paperlessarchives.com/the_crisis.html.

15. See, for instance, Andrew MacDonald/William Luther Pierce, *The Turner Diaries* (Hillsboro, WV: National Vanguard Books, 1978/1999).

16. Levinas and Hand, "Reflections on the Philosophy of Hitlerism," 64.

17. Ibid., 66.

18. Ibid.

19. Jean-Paul Sartre was to offer a similar critique of Marxism, although he began with a completely secular view, not of reason, but of consciousness. See Jean-Paul Sartre, *Search for A Method*, trans. Hazel Barnes (New York: Knopf, 1963).

20. In his *Myth of the Twentieth Century* (2891–PS), Rosenberg stated, "Today, a new faith is awakening—the Myth of the Blood, the belief that the divine being of mankind generally is to be defended with the blood. The faith embodied by the fullest realization, that the Nordic blood constitutes that mystery which has supplanted and overwhelmed the old sacraments" (114). See Jewish Virtual Library, "Nuremberg Trial Defendants: Alfred Rosenberg," https://www.jewishvirtuallibrary.org/nuremberg-trial-defendants-alfred-rosenberg.

21. Levinas and Hand, "Reflections on the Philosophy of Hitlerism," 78.

22. Ibid., 70. For Sartre's parallel analysis, see *Anti-Semite and Jew*, trans. George J. Becker (New York: Schocken Books, 1944).

23. Levinas and Hand, "Reflections on the Philosophy of Hitlerism," 70.

24. Howard Caygill, "Levinas's Political Judgement: The Esprit Articles," *Radical Philosophy*, issue 104 (November/December 2000), https://www.radicalphilosophy.com/article/levinass-political-judgement.

25. Siep Stuurman, "François Bernier and the Invention of Racial Classification," *History Workshop Journal*, no. 50 (Autumn 2000): 1–21.

26. See W. E. B. Du Bois, "The Conservation of Races," in *The Problem of the Color Line at the Turn of the Twentieth Century: The Essential Early Essays*, ed. Nahum Dimitri Chandler (New York: Fordham University Press, 2015), 51–65, on numbers of races, 51–54; reprint of "The Conservation of Races" (Washington, DC: American Negro Academy, 1897).

27. The United Nations, Universal Declaration of Human Rights, https://www.un.org/en/universal-declaration-human-rights/.

28. See United Nations, Declarations, https://search.un.org/results.php?ie=utf8&output=xml_no_dtd&oe=utf8&Submit=Search&_ga=GA1.2.1860660212.1568062408&_gid=GA1.2.836267279.1568062408&_gali=searchfrm&query=declarations&tpl=un&lang=en&rows=10. For a longer discussion of this impracticality of the Universal Declaration of Human Rights, see Naomi Zack, *The Ethics and Mores of Race: Equality After the History of Philosophy* (Lanham, MD: Rowman and Littlefield, 2011), 150–58.

29. The main intellectual problem with Rawlsian ideal theory is that no one takes it seriously as ideal theory, removed from reality. See Naomi Zack, *Applicative Justice: A Pragmatic Empirical Approach to Racial Injustice* (Lanham, MD: Rowman & Littlefield, 2016), 9–34; Zack, *Philosophy of Science and Race*, 73–86.

30. Levinas and Hand, "Reflections on the Philosophy of Hitlerism," 70.

31. See Zack, *Applicative Justice*, 9–22.

32. Gottlob Frege, "The Thought: A Logical Inquiry," *Mind* LXV, no. 259 (July 1956): 289–311.

33. John Rawls, *A Theory of Justice* (Chicago: University of Chicago Press, 1971), 3.

4. WHITE SUPREMACY AND STATUS: THE RACISM OF RACE

1. Jennifer Eberhardt, "Can Airbnb Train Hosts Not to Be Racists?" *The Daily Beast* June 12, 2019, https://www.thedailybeast.com/can-airbnb-train-hosts-not-to-be-racists. From Jennifer L. Eberhardt, *Biased* (New York: Viking, Penguin Random House, 2019).

2. Stephen Hawkins, Daniel Yudkin, Míriam Juan-Torres, and Tim Dixon, "Hidden Tribes: A Study of America's Polarized" (New York: More in Common, 2018), https://www.moreincommon.com/hidden-tribes.

3. J. L. A. Garcia, "The Heart of Racism," *Journal of Social Philosophy* 27, issue 1 (March 1996), https://doi.org/10.1111/j.1467-9833.1996.tb00225.x.

4. J. L. Matthews and T. Matlock, "Understanding the Link between Spatial Distance and Social Distance," *Social Psychology* 42 (2011): 185–92, DOI: 10.1027/1864-9335/a000062.

5. D. R. Williams, N. Priest, and N. B. Anderson, "Understanding Associations among Race, Socioeconomic Status, and Health: Patterns and Prospects," *Health Psychology* 35, no. 4 (2016): 407–11, https://www.ncbi.nlm.nih.gov/pubmed/27018733.

6. Equal Justice Initiative, "Resistance to Civil Rights," September 2019, https://eji.org/racial-justice/resistance-civil-rights.

7. Belatedly, but nonetheless worthy of note, the US Department of Homeland Security declared White Supremacist terrorism as great a threat as foreign terrorism in September 2019. See Ellen Nakashima, "DHS: Domestic Terrorism, Particularly White-Supremacist Violence, as Big a Threat as ISIS, al-Qaeda," *Washington Post*, September 20, 2019, https://www.washingtonpost.com/national-security/domestic-terror--particularly-white-supremacist-violence--as-big-a-threat-as-isis-al-qaeda-dhs-says/2019/09/20/dff8aa4e-dbad-11e9-bfb1-849887369476_story.html.

8. However, the relationship is not direct or simple because the famous Brazilian lightening effect of money is only evident among educated blacks who have married whites. See Luisa Farah Schwartzman, "Does Money Whiten? Intergenerational Changes in Racial Classification," *American Sociological Review* 72, no. 6 (December 2007): 940–63.

9. On every class level, whites do better than nonwhites; see Raj Chetty, Nathaniel Hendren, Maggie Jones, and Sonya R. Porter, "Race and Economic Opportunity in the United States: An Intergenerational Study," Equality of Opportunity Project (March 2018), http://www.equality-of-opportunity.org/assets/documents/race_paper.pdf.

10. See David Roediger, *The Wages of Whiteness: Race and the Making of the American Working Class*, revised edition (New York: Verso, 1999); Walter Benn Michaels, *Our America: Nativism, Modernism, and Pluralism* (Durham, NC: Duke University Press, 1995).

11. See Nicholas Carnes and Noam Lupu, "It's Time to Bust the Myth: Most Trump Voters Were Not Working Class," *Washington Post*, June 5, 2017, https://www.washingtonpost.com/news/monkey-cage/wp/2017/06/05/its-time-to-bust-the-myth-most-trump-voters-were-not-working-class/; Jane Mayer, "The Reclusive Hedge-Fund Tycoon Behind the Trump Presidency: How

NOTES 167

Robert Mercer Exploited America's Populist Insurgency," *New Yorker Magazine*, March 17, 2018, https://www.newyorker.com/magazine/2017/03/27/the-reclusive-hedge-fund-tycoon-behind-the-trump-presidency.

12. A 2016 Brookings Institute study found that low-income whites are less concerned about the racial achievement gap than about the gap between rich and poor. See Jon Valant and Daniel Newark, "Race, Class, and Americans' Perspectives of Achievement Gaps," Brown Center Chalkboard, January 16, 2017, https://www.brookings.edu/blog/brown-center-chalkboard/2017/01/16/race-class-and-americans-perspectives-of-achievement-gaps/.

13. Juliana Menasce Horowitz, Anna Brown, and Kiana Cox, "Views of Racial Inequality," *Race in America*, Pew Research Center, April 9, 2019, https://www.pewsocialtrends.org/2019/04/09/views-of-racial-inequality/.

14. Derald Wing Sue, Christina M. Capodilupo, Gina C. Torino, Jennifer M. Bucceri, Aisha M. B. Holder, Kevin L. Nadal, and Marta Esquilin, "Racial Microaggressions in Everyday Life: Implications for Clinical Practice," in *American Psychologist* 62, no. 4 (May–June 2007): 271–86, DOI: 10.1037/0003-066X.62.4.271.

15. See Robin DiAngelo, *White Fragility: Why It's Hard for White People to Talk about Racism* (New York: Random House, 2018).

16. Max Weber, "Status Groups and Classes," in *The Theory of Social and Economic Organization*, trans A. M. Henderson and Talcott Parsons (New York: Simon and Schuster, 1947/1975), 424–29, quotation from 427.

17. See Sue et al., "Racial Microaggressions."

18. For recent changes, see Hansi Lo Wang, "National 2020 Census to Keep Racial, Ethnic Categories Used in 2010," January 26, 2018, NPR, https://www.npr.org/2018/01/26/580865378/census-request-suggests-no-race-ethnicity-data-changes-in-2020-experts-say. For historical changes, see Tanvi Misra, "A Complete History of Census Race Boxes," CityLab, https://www.citylab.com/life/2015/11/a-complete-history-of-census-race-boxes/413716/.

19. For discussion of race (specifically black race) as exactly that kind of wild card that is more disruptive than an "intersection," see Naomi Zack, *Reviving the Social Compact: Inclusive Citizenship in an Age of Extreme Politics* (Lanham, MD: Rowman & Littlefield, 2018), chapter 2, "The Junction of Race," 27–42.

20. W. D. Jordan, "Historical Origins of the One-Drop Racial Rule in the United States," *Journal of Critical Mixed Race Studies* 1, no. 1 (2014), https://escholarship.org/uc/item/91g761b3.

21. See F. James Davis, *Who Is Black: One Nation's Definition* (University Park: Pennsylvania State Press, 1991), and Naomi Zack, *Race and Mixed Race* (Philadelphia, PA: Temple University Press, 1992/1993), 95–111.

22. See Naomi Zack, "The Fluid Symbol of Mixed Race," *Hypatia*, 25th Anniversary Issue, 25, no. 4 (Fall 2010): 875–90.

23. See Vincent N. Pham, "Our Foreign President Barack Obama: The Racial Logics of Birther Discourses," *Journal of International and Intercultural Communication* 8, issue 2 (2015): 86–107.

24. Much of the material in this section appeared in Naomi Zack, *Philosophy of Race: An Introduction* (Cham, Switzerland: Palgrave Macmillan, 2018), chapters 1 and 2. However, in that book, I had not developed the idea of status in terms of racial hierarchies and relied on the anachronistic use of the concept of racism to characterize the science of race and its philosophical contributions from the seventeenth through the nineteenth centuries.

25. Siep Stuurman, "François Bernier and the Invention of Racial Classification," *History Workshop Journal*, no. 50 (2000): 1–21.

26. Audrey Smedley and Brian D. Smedley, *Race in North America: Origin and Evolution of a Worldview*, 4th edition (Boulder, CO: Westview Press, 2011), 218–19.

27. Stephen Jay Gould, "The Geometer of Race," *Discover* 15, no. 11 (1994): 65–69.

28. William Max Nelson, "Making Men: Enlightenment Ideas of Racial Engineering," *American Historical Review* 115, no. 5 (2010): 1364–94.

29. Philippa Levine, *Eugenics: A Very Short Introduction* (New York: Oxford University Press, 2017).

30. Georges Cuvier, *The Animal Kingdom: Arranged in Conformity with its Organization*, ed. H. McMurtrie (New York: G&C&H. Carvill, 1831), 50, https://archive.org/details/animalkingdomar03graygoog.

31. Nelson, "Making Men."

32. Apparently Agassiz was so wealthy that it is difficult to enumerate, much less change, the buildings and honoraria that bear his name. See Juliet E. Isselbacher, "Agassiz Name on Harvard Campus Honors Not Louis Agassiz, But Wife and Son," *Harvard Crimson*, April 4, 2019, https://www.thecrimson.com/article/2019/4/4/agassiz-name-and-legacy/.

33. Stephen Jay Gould, *The Mismeasure of Man* (London and New York: Norton, 1996), 78 and 79.

34. Gould, *The Mismeasure of Man*, 80–82.

35. Melvin Richter, "The Study of Man: A Debate on Race," *Commentary*, February 1, 1958, https://www.commentarymagazine.com/articles/the-study-of-man-a-debate-on-race/.

36. See US State Department, "The Immigration Act of 1924 (The Johnson-Reed Act)," Office of the Historian, https://history.state.gov/milestones/1921-1936/immigration-act; Nicholas W. Gillham, "Sir Francis Galton and the Birth of Eugenics," *Annual Review of Genetics* 35, no. 1 (2001): 83–101.

37. David Hume, "Of National Characters," in *The Philosophical Works*, ed. Thomas Hill Green and Thomas Hodge Grose (Darmstadt, West Germany: Scientia Verlag Aalen, 1964), 4 vols., 3:252 n. 1.

38. David Hume, "Of the Populousness of Ancient Nations," in *Essays Moral, Political and Literary*, eds. T. H. Green and T. H. Grose (London: Longmans, Green, 1875), Essay XI, p. 382.

39. Immanuel Kant, "On the Different Races of Man," or "On the Different Races of Human Beings," in *This Is Race: An Anthology Selected from the International Literature on the Races of Man*, ed. Earl W. Count (New York: Schuman, 1950), 19.

40. Emmanuel Chukwudi Eze, "The Color of Reason: The Idea of 'Race' in Kant's Anthropology," in *Anthropology and the German Enlightenment*, ed. Katherine Faull (London: Bucknell and Associates Press, 1994), vol. 8, chapter IV, reprinted in Eze, ed., *Race and the Enlightenment: A Reader* (Cambridge, MA: Blackwell, 1997), 117.

41. Immanuel Kant, *Observations on the Feeling of the Beautiful and the Sublime*, trans. John T. Goldthwait (Berkeley: University of California Press, 1965), 110–11.

42. Immanuel Kant, *Anthropology from a Pragmatic Point of View*, trans. Hans H. Rudnick, ed. Victor Lyle Dowdell (Carbondale: Southern Illinois University Press, 1996), 55–56.

43. Kant, "On the Different Races of Man," or "On the Different Races of Human Beings," 16–24.

44. Robert Bernasconi, "Kolb's Pre-Racial Encounter with the Hottentots and Its Impact on Buffon, Kant, and Rousseau," *Graduate Faculty Philosophy Journal*, Special Issue on Race in the History of Philosophy, New School University (2014): 101–24.

45. Georg Wilhelm Fredrich Hegel, "Geographical Bases of World History," from "Lectures on the Philosophy of World History," in Emmanuel Chukwudi Eze, ed., *Race and the Enlightenment: A Reader* (Cambridge, MA: Blackwell, 1997), 124.

46. Hume had plenty of objections and criticisms from both monogenists and those such as James Beattie who were more open minded about the achievements and abilities of non-Europeans (Popkin, 1977–1978). Beattie noted that Europeans had only been civilized for about two thousand years and that Hume did not know enough about Negro civilizations to draw the generalization he did (Beattie, 1997). Hume could have preserved both tolerance and consistency in his moral theory by at least suggesting that, as members of the human species, "n"egroes (the word had a small "n" until about 1930) also developed distinct cultures from moral causes, even if those moral causes were influenced by extremes of climate. But despite numerous opportunities to do

that, he did not change his assessment. I think we can say without anachronism that Hume's views of human races were deeply prejudiced because of the radical change in the methods he used to describe the histories of blacks and whites. However, he also disparaged Amerindians, writing that their difference from European whites was as great as the difference of animals. See Aaron Garrett and Silvia Sebastiani, "David Hume on Race," in *Oxford Handbook of Philosophy and Race*, ed. Naomi Zack (New York: Oxford University Press, 2017/2019), 31–43.

47. See Chike Jeffers, "DuBois, Appiah, and Outlaw on Racial Identity," in *Oxford Handbook of Philosophy and Race*, ed. Naomi Zack (New York: Oxford University Press, 2017/2019), 204–13.

5. EVIDENCE-BASED GOVERNMENT AND ITS OBSTACLES

1. Plato, *The Republic*, 342e.

2. Daniel Burke, "Does God Really Want Donald Trump to Be President?" CNN, February 1, 2019, https://edition.cnn.com/2019/02/01/us/sanders-trump-god/index.html.

3. Karl Popper, "Democracy in America," *The Economist*, January 1, 2016, reprinted from April 23, 1988, https://www.economist.com/democracy-in-america/2016/01/31/from-the-archives-the-open-society-and-its-enemies-revisited.

4. Plato failed to convert the ruler of Syracuse to being a philosopher-king, although that was not his fault. See Livius.org, "Plato on Sicily," https://www.livius.org/sources/content/plato/letter-7/plato-on-sicily/.

5. However, commentators have found his references and explication of this kind of wisdom somewhat enigmatic. See Zena Hitz, "Plato on the Sovereignty of Law," in *A Companion to Greek and Roman Political Thought*, ed. Ryan K. Balot (Malden, MA: Blackwell, 2009), 389–403.

6. *The Republic*, 341c4-d10.

7. For a recent list, see Ian J. Stark, "Celebrities Turned Politicians," *Newsweek*, April 14, 2017, https://www.newsday.com/entertainment/celebrities/celebrities-turned-politicians-1.12571047.

8. See Louis Fisher, *From Presidential Wars to American Hegemony: The Constitution After 9/11* (New York: Palgrave Macmillan, 2006).

9. See Robin I. Dunbar, *Grooming, Gossip and the Evolution of Language* (London: Faber and Faber, 1996).

10. Joseph E. Ledoux, "Cognitive-Emotional Interactions in the Brain," *Cognition and Emotion* 3, issue 4 (1989): 267–89; published online January 7, 2008, https://www.tandfonline.com/doi/abs/10.1080/02699938908412709.

11. David Hume, *A Treatise of Human Nature (1739–40)*, in *Hume Texts Online*, eds. Amyas Merivale and Peter Millican (Selby-Bigge edition with Nidditch notes), Book 2, Part 3, Section 3.1, p. 413 (https://davidhume.org/texts/t/2/3/3).

12. Any cognitive theory of the emotions is not likely to hold that beliefs create emotions, rather they evoke them. There is some evidence that there are universal human emotions, across cultures. Beliefs evoke emotions in the sense that emotional reactions can be changed with changes in beliefs. For example, a person who believes a stranger has a gun would be afraid, but if they see it is a cell phone, their fear would subside. (See Jesse Prinz, "Which Emotions Are Basic?" in *Emotion, Evolution, and Rationality*, eds. D. Evans and P. Cruse [London: Oxford University Press, 2004], 69–88.)

13. Chief Justice Roberts called for civic education in his 2019 report on the US judiciary. See John G. Roberts Jr., "2019 Year-End Report on the Federal Judiciary," December 31, 2019, https://www.supremecourt.gov/publicinfo/year-end/2019year-endreport.pdf.

14. Popper, "Democracy in America."

15. Benjamin Carter Hett, *The Death of Democracy: Hitler's Rise to Power and the Downfall of the Weimar Republic* (New York: St. Martin's Griffin, 2019).

16. Michael J. Gerhardt, "Lessons of Impeachment History," *George Washington Law Review* 67 (1998–1999): 603–25, https://scholarship.law.unc.edu/cgi/viewcontent.cgi?article=1077&context=faculty_publications.

17. Jean-Paul Sartre, *Search for a Method*, trans. Hazel Barnes (New York: Vintage Books, 1968), 3–34.

18. Karl Popper, "Uniting the Camp of Humanitarianism (1942–47)," in *Popper, After the Open Society: Selected Social and Political Writings*, eds. Jeremy Shearmur and Piers Norris Turner (London and New York: Routledge, 2012), 113–17.

19. On presentations of the different candidates' positions on health care, see Elizabeth Thomas, "Medicare for All or Single Payer: Here's How the 2020 Democrats Differ on Health Care," ABC News, September 12, 2019, https://abcnews.go.com/Politics/2020-democrats-differ-health-care/story?id=64636048. See also Dylan Scott, "The Real Differences between the 2020 Democrats' Health Care Plans, Explained," *Vox*, https://www.vox.com/policy-and-politics/2019/12/19/21005124/2020-presidential-candidates-health-care-democratic-debate.

20. Carol M. Kopp, "Income Inequality," *Investopedia*, updated November 7, 2019, https://www.investopedia.com/terms/i/income-inequality.asp.

21. Thomas Piketty, *Capital in the Twenty-First Century*, trans. Arthur Goldhammer (Cambridge, MA: Harvard University Press, 2014).

22. See Ganesh Sitaraman, *The Crisis of the Middle-Class Constitution: Why Economic Inequality Threatens Our Republic* (New York: Alfred A. Knopf, 2017).

23. Richard P. F. Holt and Daphne T. Greenwood, "Negative Trickle-Down and the Financial Crisis of 2008," *Journal of Economic Issues* 46, no. 2 (2012): 363–70, DOI: 10.2753/JEI0021-3624460211.

24. "Capitalism and Its Critics: A Modern Marx," *The Economist*, May 3, 2014, https://www.economist.com/leaders/2014/05/03/a-modern-marx.

25. For journalistic accounts and scholarly sources, see Wikipedia, "Occupy Wall Street," https://en.wikipedia.org/wiki/Occupy_Wall_Street.

26. See Daniel Chomsky, "A Distorting Mirror: Major Media Coverage of Americans' Tax Policy Preferences," *Institute for New Economic Thinking Working Paper Series*, no. 73 (April 17, 2018), http://dx.doi.org/10.2139/ssrn.3228781.

27. Nancy Cartwright and Jeremy Hardie, *Evidence-Based Policy: A Practical Guide for Doing It Better* (New York: Oxford University Press, 2012), esp. 2–9 for an overview of effectiveness.

28. Karl Popper, "The Open Society after Five Years: Prefaces to the American Edition of *The Open Society* (1948–50)," in *Popper, After the Open Society: Selected Social and Political Writings*, eds. Jeremy Shearmur and Piers Norris Turner (London and New York: Routledge, 2012), 170.

29. Cartwright and Hardie, *Evidence-Based Policy*. (Much of this book is devoted to nests of these kinds of problems.)

30. Lydia Saad, "Abortion Is Threshold Issue for One in Six U.S. Voters: Nearly as Many Single-Issue Abortion Voters Are Pro-Choice as Pro-Life," Gallup, October 4, 2012, https://news.gallup.com/poll/157886/abortion-threshold-issue-one-six-voters.aspx.

31. For extended discussion of the successful development of immigration restriction as a determining electoral issue during the 2016 US presidential campaign, see Naomi Zack, *Reviving the Social Compact: Inclusive Citizenship in an Age of Extreme Politics* (Lanham, MD: Rowman & Littlefield, 2018), 47–48.

32. See Tom K. Wong, *The Politics of Immigration: Partisanship, Demographic Change, and American National Identity* (New York: Oxford University Press, 2017).

33. Kevin B. Smith and Christopher W. Larimer, *The Public Policy Theory Primer* (New York: Routledge, 2018, 2019), x–xi and 1–22, quotation x–xi.

NOTES

34. Ibid.

35. Smith and Larimer, *The Public Policy Theory Primer*, 46–49; H. A. Simon, "Bounded Rationality," in *Utility and Probability*, eds. J. Eatwell, M. Milgate, and P. Newman, New Palgrave (London: Macmillan, 1990), 15–18.

36. Otto A. Davis, M. A. H. Dempster, and Aaron Wildavsky, "A Theory of the Budgetary Process," *American Political Science Review* 60, no. 3 (September 1966): 529–47, https://www.cmu.edu/dietrich/sds/docs/davis/A%20 Theory%20of%20the%20Budgetary%20Process.pdf.

37. Smith and Larimer, *Public Policy Theory Primer*, 196–200. See also Leda Cosmides and John Tooby, "Cognitive Adaptations for Social Exchange," in *The Adapted Mind: Evolutionary Psychology and the Generation of Culture*, eds. Jerome H. Barkow, Leda Cosmides, and John Tooby (Oxford: Oxford University Press, 1992), 163–228; Leda Cosmides and John Tooby, "Better than Rational: Evolutionary Psychology and the Invisible Hand," *American Economic Review* 84, no. 2 (May 1994): 327–32, https://www.jstor.org/stable/2117853?seq=1.

38. Smith and Larimer, *Public Policy Theory Primer*, 49–50 and 54–55.

39. Smith and Larimer, *Public Policy Theory Primer*, 54–55; M. Charles Tiebout, "A Pure Theory of Local Expenditures," *Journal of Political Economy* 64 (1956): 414–24.

40. Smith and Larimer, *Public Policy Theory Primer*, 52–59; Mark Schneider and Jack Buckley, "What Do Parents Want from Schools? Evidence from the Internet," *Education Evaluation and Policy Analysis* 24, no. 2 (June 1, 2002): 133–44, https://doi.org/10.3102/01623737024002133.

41. Bryan Caplan, *The Myth of the Rational Voter: Why Democracies Choose Bad Policies* (Princeton, NJ: Princeton University Press, 2007), and Ilya Somin, *Democracy and Political Ignorance: Why Smaller Government Is Smarter* (Stanford, CA: Stanford University Press, 2013).

42. See Richard H. Thaler and Cass R. Sunstein, *Nudge: Improving Decisions about Health, Wealth, and Happiness* (New York: Penguin, 2009), and David Halpern, *Inside the Nudge Unit* (New York: Penguin, 2016). The tax and attic examples are from Halpern's book, whereas the behavioral theory behind this policy is described by Thaler and Cass.

43. Robert Krulwich, "There's a Fly in My Urinal," NPR, December 19, 2009, https://www.npr.org/templates/story/story.php?storyId=121310977.

44. For discussion of the ethical aspects of "Nudge," with additional sources, see Christian Schubert, "A Note on the Ethics of Nudges," CEPR Policy Portal, *Vox*, January 22, 2016, https://voxeu.org/article/note-ethics-nudges.

6. THE PROBLEMS WITH EVIDENCE AND UNIVERSAL BASIC INCOME

1. Winston S. Churchill, *Winston S. Churchill: His Complete Speeches, 1897–1963*, vol. 7, ed. Robert Rhodes James (1974), 7566, from Bartleby.com, https://www.bartleby.com/73/417.html.

2. Theodore Roosevelt, "The Man in the Arena/Citizenship in a Republic," April 23, 2010, Sorbonne, Paris, from Theodore Roosevelt Center, Dickinson State University, https://www.theodorerooseveltcenter.org/Learn-About-TR/TR-Encyclopedia/Culture-and-Society/Man-in-the-Arena.aspx.

3. FindLaw, "What Is a Wrongful Death Lawsuit?" https://hirealawyer.findlaw.com/choosing-the-right-lawyer/wrongful-death-plaintiff.html.

4. Jurors may also end up making policy. See Gary J. Jacobsohn, "Citizen Participation in Policy-Making: The Role of the Jury," *Journal of Politics* 39, no. 1 (February 1977): 73–96.

5. See Nelson Goodman on "The New Riddle of Induction," in *Fact, Fiction, and Forecast* (Cambridge, MA: Harvard University Press, 1955); 2nd edition (Indianapolis: Bobbs-Merrill, 1965); 3rd edition (Indianapolis: Bobbs-Merrill, 1973); 4th edition (Cambridge, MA: Harvard University Press, 1983), 74. See also Daniel Cohnitz and Marcus Rossberg, "Nelson Goodman," *The Stanford Encyclopedia of Philosophy*, ed. Edward N. Zalta (Summer 2019 Edition), https://plato.stanford.edu/archives/sum2019/entries/goodman/, section 5, "The Old and the New Riddle of Induction and Their Solutions."

6. For induction, see David Hume of *A Treatise of Human Nature*, Book 1, part iii, section 6; for causation, see David Hume, *An Enquiry Concerning Human Understanding*, 5.1.6/44, both in *Hume Texts Online*, eds. Amyas Merivale and Peter Millican (Selby-Bigge edition with Nidditch notes), https://davidhume.org.

7. There is also the methodological convention of beginning with "the null hypothesis." See Deborah J. Rumsey, "What a p-Value Tells You about Statistical Data," https://www.dummies.com/education/math/statistics/what-a-p-value-tells-you-about-statistical-data/; *Statistics for Dummies*, 2nd edition; Deborah J. Rumsey, "Null Hypothesis Definition and Examples, How to State," *Statistics, How to*, https://www.statisticshowto.datasciencecentral.com/probability-and-statistics/null-hypothesis/.

8. Stephen S. Hall, "Scientists on Trial: At Fault?" *Nature* 477 (2011): 264–69, DOI:10.1038/477264a, https://www.nature.com/news/2011/110914/full/477264a.html?WT.mc_id=TWT_NatureNews; Michael Ray, "L'Aquila Earthquake of 2009," ITALY, Briticannica.com, https://www.britannica.com/event/LAquila-earthquake-of-2009.

9. Hall, "Scientists on Trial."

10. Erin McCarthy, "Why Can't We Predict Earthquakes?" *Mental Floss*, November 12, 2012, https://www.mentalfloss.com/article/12997/why-cant-we-predict-earthquakes.

11. David Bressan, "April 6, 2009: The L Aquila Earthquake," *Scientific American*, https://blogs.scientificamerican.com/history-of-geology/april-6-2009-the-laquila-earthquake/.

12. I have written about the moral and political obligation of disaster preparation and will not repeat that work here. Please see Naomi Zack, "Philosophy and Disaster," *Homeland Security Affairs Journal* II, no. 1, article 5 (April 2006), https://www.hsaj.org/articles/176; Naomi Zack, "Ethics of Disaster Planning," *Philosophy of Management*, Special Issue, *Ethics of Crisis*, ed. Per Sandin, vol. 8, no. 2 (2009): 53–64; Naomi Zack, *Ethics for Disaster* (Lanham, MD: Rowman & Littlefield, 2009).

13. On presentations of the different candidates positions on health care, see Elizabeth Thomas, "Medicare for All or Single Payer: Here's How the 2020 Democrats Differ on Health Care 2020," ABC News, September 12, 2019, https://abcnews.go.com/Politics/2020-democrats-differ-health-care/story?id=64636048; Dylan Scott, "The Real Differences between the 2020 Democrats' Health Care Plans, Explained," *Vox*, https://www.vox.com/policy-and-politics/2019/12/19/21005124/2020-presidential-candidates-health-care-democratic-debate.

14. John Mirowsky and Catherine E. Ross, *Education, Social Status, and Health* (New York: Routledge, 2003).

15. Students remember visual material better than content. See Erin O'Connor, "What Do Students Remember? David Head Asked the Question in His Classes—and Considers What He Learned," *Inside HigherEd*, March 1, 2011, https://www.insidehighered.com/views/2011/03/01/what-do-students-remember.

16. Naomi Priest, Natalie Slopen, Susan Woolford, Jeny Tony Philip, Dianne Singer, Anna Daly Kauffman, Kathryn Mosely, Matthew Davis, Yusuf Ransome, David Williams, "Stereotyping across Intersections of Race and Age: Racial Stereotyping among White Adults Working with Children," *Plos*, September 12, 2018, https://journals.plos.org/plosone/article?id=10.1371/journal.pone.0201696.

17. R. A. Moffitt, "The Deserving Poor, the Family, and the U.S. Welfare System," *Demography* 52 (2015): 729–49, https://doi.org/10.1007/s13524-015-0395-0.

18. Yannick Vanderborght and Philippe Van Parijs, "The History of Basic Income," in *L'allocation universelle*, chapter 1 (expanded English published by Harvard University Press, 2017), web version edited and abridged by Simon

Birnbaum and Karl Widerquist, 2005, Basic Income Earth Network (BIEN), https://basicincome.org/basic-income/history/.

19. See My Property Guide, "What Is Ground Rent?" http://www.mypropertyguide.co.uk/articles/display/10107/what-is-ground-rent.htm.

20. From Thomas Paine, *The Age of Reason* (1794–1796), Tradition Classics, vol. iv (2012), 611, 612–13, cited in Vanderborght and Van Parijs, "The History of Basic Income."

21. For the range of this contemporary support, see Annie Lowrey, *Give People Money: How a Universal Basic Income Would End Poverty, Revolutionize Work, and Remake the World* (New York: Crown, 2018).

22. For the conservative support, see James Varney, "Universal Basic Income: Even Conservative Economist Says It's 'Our Best Hope,'" *Washington Times*, July 29, 2018; Charles Murray, "A Plan to Replace the Welfare State," *FOCUS* 24, no. 2 (Spring-Summer 2006):1–4, https://pdfs.semanticscholar.org/f3b1/2f13ab571e7fbb8579ae4c4d14fc069c167a.pdf; Milton Friedman, "The Case for a Negative Income Tax: A View from the Right," in "Excerpts from Friedman, M. (1968)," in *Issues in American Public Policy*, ed. J.H. Bunzel (Englewood Cliffs, NJ: Prentice-Hall, 1968), 111–20; Noah J. Gordon, "The Conservative Case for a Guaranteed Basic Income: Creating a Wage Floor Is an Effective Way to Fight Poverty—and It Would Reduce Government Spending and Intrusion," *The Atlantic*, August 6, 2014, https://www.theatlantic.com/politics/archive/2014/08/why-arent-reformicons-pushing-a-guaranteed-basic-income/375600/.

23. Janne Körkkö, "Finland's Basic Income Trial Boosts Happiness, but Not Employment," *New York Times*, February 9, 2019, https://www.nytimes.com/2019/02/09/world/europe/finland-basic-income.html.

24. Mike Brown, "It's Called Universal Basic Income," Inverse.com, February 21, 2019, https://www.inverse.com/article/53466-basic-income-canada-s-trial-had-a-huge-effect-on-people-s-health.

25. Ashitha Nagesh, "Finland Basic Income Trial Left People 'Happier but Jobless,'" *BBC News*, February 8, 2019, https://www.bbc.com/news/world-europe-47169549.

26. Erich Fromm, "The Psychological Aspects of the Guaranteed Income," in *The Guaranteed Income: Next Step in Economic Evolution?*, ed. Robert Theobald (New York: Doubleday, 1965/1966), 175–84.

27. Ibid., 176.

28. Ibid.

29. United Nations, "Universal Declaration of Human Rights," December 10, 1948, https://www.un.org/en/universal-declaration-human-rights/.

30. The wording in this section on the United Nations draws from chapter 7 of Naomi Zack, *The Ethics and Mores of Race: Equality after the History of*

Philosophy (Lanham, MD: Rowman & Littlefield, 2011), 154–55. See also United Nations, "Universal Declaration of Human Rights."

31. Robert Theobald, "The Guaranteed Income Proposal as Set Out in *Free Men and Free Markets*," in *The Guaranteed Income*, appendix, 227–33. From Theobald, *Free Men and Free Markets* (New York: C.N. Potter, 1963).

32. Ibid., 227–28.

CONCLUSION. PROGRESSIVE ANONYMITY: REVIEW AND LOOSE ENDS

1. D. W. Sue, C. M. Capodilupo, G. C. Torino, J. M. Bucceri, A. M. B. Holder, K. L. Nadal, and M. Esquilin, "Racial Microaggressions in Everyday Life: Implications for Clinical Practice," *American Psychologist* 62, no. 4 (2007): 271–86, https://doi.org/10.1037/0003-066X.62.4.271.

2. Karl Popper, "Public and Private Values (1946?)," in *Popper, After the Open Society: Selected Social and Political Writings*, eds. Jeremy Shearmur and Piers Norris Turner (London and New York: Routledge, 2012), 118 and 131.

3. See Jack Lynch, "Cruel and Unusual: Prisons and Prison Reform," *CW Journal* (Summer 2011), https://www.history.org/Foundation/journal/Summer11/prison.cfm.

4. Robert North Roberts, Scott John Hammond, and Valerie A. Sulfaro, eds., *Presidential Campaigns, Slogans, Issues, and Platforms: The Complete Encyclopedia* (Santa Barbara, CA: Greenwood, 2012).

5. Drew DeSilver, "U.S. Trails Most Developed Countries in Voter Turnout," FactTank, Pew Research Center, May 21, 2018, https://www.pewresearch.org/fact-tank/2018/05/21/u-s-voter-turnout-trails-most-developed-countries/.

6. See Mark Lilla, *The Once and Future Liberal: After Identity Politics* (New York: HarperCollins, 2017), 93.

7. History First, "My Fellow Americans: A Brief History of the State of the Union," https://history-first.com/2018/02/01/my-fellow-americans-a-brief-history-of-the-sotu/.

SELECT BIBLIOGRAPHY

GENERAL SOURCES

ADL (Anti Defamation League). "New Hate and Old: The Changing Face of American White Supremacy: A Report from the Center on Extremism." https://www.adl.org/new-hate-and-old (consulted April 2019).
Amadeo, Kimberly. "US Economy Demand Consumer Spending Trends and Current Statistics, Consumer Spending Up 2.5%." *The Balance*. https://www.thebalance.com/consumer-spending-trends-and-current-statistics-3305916.
Benesch, Linda. "New Polling on Social Security, Medicare, and Prescription Drug Prices." Polling Social Security. *Social Security Works*, March 16, 2018. https://socialsecurityworks.org/2018/03/16/new-polling-social-security/.
Bressan, David. "April 6, 2009: The L Aquila Earthquake." *Scientific American*. https://blogs.scientificamerican.com/history-of-geology/april-6-2009-the-laquila-earthquake/.
Brown, Mike. "It's Called Universal Basic Income." Inverse.com, February 21, 2019. https://www.inverse.com/article/53466-basic-income-canada-s-trial-had-a-huge-effect-on-people-s-health.
Brownstein, Ronald. "2020 Democrats Face the Most Diverse Electorate in History." CNN Politics, February 12, 2019. https://www.cnn.com/interactive/2019/02/politics/dem-primaries-exit-polls/.
Bryner, Sarah, and Grace Haley. "Race, Gender, and Money in Politics: Campaign Finance and Federal Candidates in the 2018 Midterms." Center for Responsive Politics. https://www.pgpf.org/sites/default/files/US-2050-Race-Gender-and-Money-in-Politics-Campaign-Finance-and-Federal-Candidates-in-the-2018-Midterms.pdf.
Burke, Daniel. "Does God Really Want Donald Trump to Be President?" CNN, February 1, 2019. https://edition.cnn.com/2019/02/01/us/sanders-trump-god/index.html.
Cai, Weiyi, and Simone Landon. "Attacks by White Extremists Are Growing. So Are Their Connections." *New York Times*, April 3, 2019. https://www.nytimes.com/interactive/2019/04/03/world/white-extremist-terrorism-christchurch.html.
"Capitalism and Its Critics: A Modern Marx." *Economist*, May 3, 2014. https://www.economist.com/leaders/2014/05/03/a-modern-marx.
Carnes, Nicholas, and Noam Lupu. "It's Time to Bust the Myth: Most Trump Voters Were Not Working Class." *Washington Post*, June 5, 2017. https://www.washingtonpost.com/news/monkey-cage/wp/2017/06/05/its-time-to-bust-the-myth-most-trump-voters-were-not-working-class/.

SELECT BIBLIOGRAPHY

Case, Spencer. "What Philosophers Must Learn from the Transracialism Meltdown." *Quillette*, May 26, 2017. https://quillette.com/2017/05/26/philosophers-must-learn-transracialism-meltdown/.

Chetty, Raj, Nathaniel Hendren, Maggie Jones, and Sonya R. Porter. "Race and Economic Opportunity in the United States: An Intergenerational Study." Equality of Opportunity Project, March 2018. http://www.equality-of-opportunity.org/assets/documents/race_paper.pdf.

Churchill, Winston S. *Winston S. Churchill: His Complete Speeches, 1897–1963.* Volume 7. Ed. Robert Rhodes James (1974) from Bartleby.com. https://www.bartleby.com/73/417.html.

Cilluffo, Anthony, and Richard Fry. "An Early Look at the 2020 Electorate." Pew Research Center, January 30, 2019. https://www.pewsocialtrends.org/essay/an-early-look-at-the-2020-electorate/.

The Crisis, NAACP Magazine. 1910–1923. http://www.paperlessarchives.com/the_crisis.html.

DeSilver, Drew. "U.S. Trails Most Developed Countries in Voter Turnout." FactTank, Pew Research Center, May 21, 2018. https://www.pewresearch.org/fact-tank/2018/05/21/u-s-voter-turnout-trails-most-developed-countries/.

DiAngelo, Robin. *White Fragility: Why It's Hard for White People to Talk about Racism.* New York: Random House, 2018.

Eberhardt, Jennifer. "Can Airbnb Train Hosts Not to Be Racists?" *The Daily Beast*, April 8, 2019. https://www.thedailybeast.com/can-airbnb-train-hosts-not-to-be-racists.

Equal Justice Initiative. "Resistance to Civil Rights." September 2019. https://eji.org/racial-justice/resistance-civil-rights.

FindLaw. "What Is a Wrongful Death Lawsuit?" https://hirealawyer.findlaw.com/choosing-the-right-lawyer/wrongful-death-plaintiff.html.

Flanagan, Tom. "Will Mounting Costs of Reconciliation Benefit Indigenous People?" *The Globe and Mail*, November 6, 2018. https://www.theglobeandmail.com/opinion/article-will-mounting-costs-of-reconciliation-benefit-indigenous-people/.

Fraga, Kaleena. History First. "My Fellow Americans: A Brief History of the State of the Union." https://history-first.com/2018/02/01/my-fellow-americans-a-brief-history-of-the-sotu/.

Freedman, Josh, and Michael Lind. "The Past and Future of America's Social Contract." *The Atlantic*, December 19, 2013. https://www.theatlantic.com/business/archive/2013/12/the-past-and-future-of-americas-social-contract/282511/.

Gordon, Noah J. "The Conservative Case for a Guaranteed Basic Income: Creating a Wage Floor Is an Effective Way to Fight Poverty—and It Would Reduce Government Spending and Intrusion." *The Atlantic*, August 6, 2014. https://www.theatlantic.com/politics/archive/2014/08/why-arent-reformicons-pushing-a-guaranteed-basic-income/375600/.

Green New Deal Group. "A Green New Deal: Joined-up Policies to Solve the Triple Crunch of the Credit Crisis, Climate Change and High Oil Prices." First report of the Green New Deal Group, Technical Report, New Economics Foundation, December 2007. https://www.researchgate.net/publication/271506210_A_Green_New_Deal_Joined-up_Policies_to_Solve_the_Triple_Crunch_of_the_Credit_Crisis_Climate_Change_and_High_Oil_Prices.

Hall, Stephen S. "Scientists on Trial: At Fault?" *Nature* 477 (2011): 264–69. https://www.nature.com/news/2011/110914/full/477264a.html?WT.mc_id=TWT_NatureNews.

Hawkins, Stephen, Daniel Yudkin, Míriam Juan-Torres, and Tim Dixon. "Hidden Tribes: A Study of America's Polarized." New York: More in Common, 2018. https://www.moreincommon.com/media/nhplchwt/hidden_tribes_report.pdf.

Holocaust Encyclopedia. "Blacks During the Holocaust Era." United States Holocaust Memorial and Museum. https://encyclopedia.ushmm.org/content/en/article/blacks-during-the-holocaust-era.

Holocaust Encyclopedia. "Lublin/Majdanek Concentration Camp: Conditions." United States Holocaust Memorial and Museum. https://encyclopedia.ushmm.org/content/en/article/lublin-majdanek-concentration-camp-conditions.

SELECT BIBLIOGRAPHY

Jewish Virtual Library. "Documenting Numbers of Victims of the Holocaust and Nazi Persecution." United States Holocaust Memorial and Museum, February 4, 2019. https://www.jewishvirtuallibrary.org/documenting-numbers-of-victims-of-the-holocaust.

Jewish Virtual Library. "Encyclopedia Judaica: Blood Libel." https://www.jewishvirtuallibrary.org/blood-libel.

Jewish Virtual Library. "Nuremberg Trial Defendants: Alfred Rosenberg." https://www.jewishvirtuallibrary.org/nuremberg-trial-defendants-alfred-rosenberg.

Kopp, Carol M. "Income Inequality." Economy, Economics. *Investopedia*. Updated November 7, 2019. https://www.investopedia.com/terms/i/income-inequality.asp.

Körkkö, Janne. "Finland's Basic Income Trial Boosts Happiness, but Not Employment." *New York Times*, February 9, 2019. https://www.nytimes.com/2019/02/09/world/europe/finland-basic-income.html.

Krulwich, Robert. "There's a Fly in My Urinal." NPR, December 19, 2009. https://www.npr.org/templates/story/story.php?storyId=121310977.

Lo Wang, Hansi. "National 2020 Census to Keep Racial, Ethnic Categories Used in 2010." NPR, January 26, 2018. https://www.npr.org/2018/01/26/580865378/census-request-suggests-no-race-ethnicity-data-changes-in-2020-experts-say.

Lowrey, Annie. *Give People Money: How a Universal Basic Income Would End Poverty, Revolutionize Work, and Remake the World*. New York: Crown, 2018.

Lynch, Jack. "Cruel and Unusual: Prisons and Prison Reform." *CW Journal* (Summer 2011). https://www.history.org/Foundation/journal/Summer11/prison.cfm.

Mayer, Jane. "The Reclusive Hedge-Fund Tycoon Behind the Trump Presidency: How Robert Mercer Exploited America's Populist Insurgency." *New Yorker Magazine*, March 17, 2018. https://www.newyorker.com/magazine/2017/03/27/the-reclusive-hedge-fund-tycoon-behind-the-trump-presidency.

McCarthy, Erin. "Why Can't We Predict Earthquakes?" *Mental Floss*, November 12, 2012. https://www.mentalfloss.com/article/12997/why-cant-we-predict-earthquakes.

Menasce, Juliana, Anna Brown Horowitz, and Kiana Cox. "Views of Racial Inequality." Pew Research Center, April 9, 2019. https://www.pewsocialtrends.org/2019/04/09/views-of-racial-inequality/.

Misra, Tanvi. "A Complete History of Census Race Boxes." CityLab. https://www.citylab.com/life/2015/11/a-complete-history-of-census-race-boxes/413716/.

Murray, Charles. "A Plan to Replace the Welfare State." *FOCUS* 24, no. 2 (Spring-Summer 2006): 1–4. https://pdfs.semanticscholar.org/f3b1/2f13ab571e7fbb8579ae4c4d14fc069c167a.pdf.

Nakashima, Ellen. "DHS: Domestic Terrorism, Particularly White-Supremacist Violence, as Big a Threat as ISIS, al-Qaeda." *Washington Post*, September 20, 2019. https://www.washingtonpost.com/national-security/domestic-terror--particularly-white-supremacist-violence--as-big-a-threat-as-isis-al-qaeda-dhs-says/2019/09/20/dff8aa4e-dbad-11e9-bfb1-849887369476_story.html.

O'Connor, Erin. "What Do Students Remember? David Head Asked the Question in His Classes—and Considers What He Learned." *Inside Higher Ed*, March 1, 2011. https://www.insidehighered.com/views/2011/03/01/what-do-students-remember.

Pengelly, Martin. "Georgetown Students Vote to Pay Reparations for Slaves Sold by University." *The Guardian*, April 15, 2019. https://www.theguardian.com/world/2019/apr/15/georgetown-students-reparations-vote-slaves-sold-by-university.

Priest, Naomi, Natalie Slopen, Susan Woolford, Jeny Tony Philip, Dianne Singer, Anna Daly Kauffman, Kathryn Mosely, Matthew Davis, Yusuf Ransome, and David Williams. "Stereotyping across Intersections of Race and Age: Racial Stereotyping among White Adults Working with Children." *Plos*, September 12, 2018. https://journals.plos.org/plosone/article?id=10.1371/journal.pone.0201696.

Qureshi, Bilal. "From Wrong to Right: A U.S. Apology for Japanese Internment." *All Things Considered*, NPR, August 9, 2013. https://www.npr.org/sections/codeswitch/2013/08/09/210138278/japanese-internment-redress.

Radical Philosophy Identity Archive. https://www.radicalphilosophy.com/tag/identity.

Ray, Michael. "L'Aquila Earthquake of 2009." Italy, Briticannica.com. https://www.britannica.com/event/LAquila-earthquake-of-2009.

Richter, Melvin. "The Study of Man: A Debate on Race." *Commentary*, February 1, 1958. https://www.commentarymagazine.com/articles/the-study-of-man-a-debate-on-race/.

Roosevelt, Theodore. "The Man in the Arena"/"Citizenship in a Republic." April 23, 2010, Sorbonne, Paris, from Theodore Roosevelt Center, Dickenson State University. https://www.theodorerooseveltcenter.org/Learn-About-TR/TR-Encyclopedia/Culture-and-Society/Man-in-the-Arena.aspx.

Root, Maria P. P. "A Bill of Rights for Racially Mixed People." https://www.safehousealliance.org/wp-content/uploads/2012/10/A-Bill-of-Rights-for-Racially-Mixed-People.pdf.

Rumsey, Deborah J. "Null Hypothesis Definition and Examples, How to State." *Statistics, How to*. https://www.statisticshowto.datasciencecentral.com/probability-and-statistics/null-hypothesis/.

Rumsey, Deborah J. "What a p-Value Tells You about Statistical Data." https://www.dummies.com/education/math/statistics/what-a-p-value-tells-you-about-statistical-data/.

Russo, Amy. "Pete Buttigieg Warns 'White Identity Politics' Launching Nation into 'Crisis.'" *Huff Post*, May 12, 2019. https://www.huffpost.com/entry/pete-buttigieg-white-identity-politics-crisis-of-belonging_n_5cd86ca5e4b054da4e8b316a?guccounter=1.

Saad, Lydia. "Abortion Is Threshold Issue for One in Six U.S. Voters: Nearly as Many Single-Issue Abortion Voters Are Pro-Choice as Pro-Life." Gallup, October 4, 2012. https://news.gallup.com/poll/157886/abortion-threshold-issue-one-six-voters.aspx.

Schubert, Christian. "A Note on the Ethics of Nudges." CEPR Policy Portal. *Vox*, January 22, 2016. https://voxeu.org/article/note-ethics-nudges.

Scott, Dylan. "The Real Differences between the 2020 Democrats' Health Care Plans, Explained." *Vox*. https://www.vox.com/policy-and-politics/2019/12/19/21005124/2020-presidential-candidates-health-care-democratic-debate.

Serwer, Adam. "The Terrorism That Doesn't Spark a Panic: Americans Should React to Violence from Religious and Ethnic Minorities with the Same Sense of Proportion They Reserve for Far-Right Extremists." *The Atlantic*, January 28, 2019. https://www.theatlantic.com/ideas/archive/2019/01/homegrown-terrorists-2018-were-almost-all-right-wing/581284/.

Stark, Ian J. "Celebrities Turned Politicians." *Newsweek*, April 14, 2017. https://www.newsday.com/entertainment/celebrities/celebrities-turned-politicians-1.12571047.

Thomas, Elizabeth. "Medicare for All or Single Payer: Here's How the 2020 Democrats Differ on Health Care." ABC News, September 12, 2019. https://abcnews.go.com/Politics/2020-democrats-differ-health-care/story?id=64636048.

Transgender Law Center. "State-by-State Overview: Changing Gender Markers on Birth Certificates." https://transgenderlawcenter.org/resources/id/state-by-state-overview-changing-gender-markers-on-birth-certificates.

United Nations. "Universal Declaration of Human Rights." December 10, 1948. https://www.un.org/en/universal-declaration-human-rights/.

US State Department. "The Immigration Act of 1924 (The Johnson-Reed Act)." Office of the Historian. https://history.state.gov/milestones/1921-1936/immigration-act.

Valant, Jon, and Daniel Newark. "Race, Class, and Americans' Perspectives of Achievement Gaps." Brown Center Chalkboard, January 16, 2017. https://www.brookings.edu/blog/brown-center-chalkboard/2017/01/16/race-class-and-americans-perspectives-of-achievement-gaps/.

Varney, James. "Universal Basic Income: Even Conservative Economist Says It's 'Our Best Hope.'" *Washington Times*, July 29, 2018.

Whyte, Chelsea. "Green New Deal Proposal Includes Free Higher Education and Fair Pay." *New Scientist*, February 12, 2019. https://www.newscientist.com/article/2193592-green-new-deal-proposal-includes-free-higher-education-and-fair-pay/.

Wikipedia. "Occupy Wall Street." https://en.wikipedia.org/wiki/Occupy_Wall_Street.

SCHOLARLY PUBLICATIONS

Appiah, K. Anthony. "'But Would That Still Be Me?' Notes on Gender, 'Race,' Ethnicity, as Sources of 'Identity.'" *Journal of Philosophy* 87, no. 10 (1990): 493–99.
Appiah, K. Anthony. "Race, Culture, Identity: Misunderstood Connections." The Tanner Lectures on Human Value, delivered at University of California at San Diego, October 27 and 28, 1994. https://philpapers.org/archive/apprci.pdf.
Arendt, Hannah. *Eichmann in Jerusalem: A Report on the Banality of Evil*. New York: Penguin, 1963/2006.
Arendt, Hannah. "Eichmann Was Outrageously Stupid." Interview by Joachim Fest, *Das Thema*. SWR TV, Germany, November 9, 1964. Printed in *The Last Interview and Other Conversations*, 41–65. Brooklyn, NY: Melville House, 2013.
Arendt, Hannah. "What Remains? The Language Remains: A Conversation with Günter Gaus." Trans. Joan Stambaugh, *Zur Person*. ZDF TV, Germany, October 28, 1964. Printed in *The Last Interview and Other Conversations*, 3–38. Brooklyn, NY: Melville House, 2013.
Arendt, Hannah, and Martin Heidegger. *Letters, 1925–1975*. Trans. Andrew Shields. Orlando, FL: Harcourt, 2004.
Atterton, Peter, Matthew Calarco, and Maurice Friedman, eds. *Levinas and Buber: Dialogue and Difference*. Philadelphia, PA: Duquesne University Press, 2004.
Benhabib, Seyla, ed. *Politics in Dark Times: Encounters with Hannah Arendt*. Cambridge: Cambridge University Press, 2010.
Bennett, Jonathan. "The Conscience of Huckleberry Finn." *Philosophy* 49 (1974): 123–24.
Bernasconi, Robert. "Kolb's Pre-Racial Encounter with the Hottentots and Its Impact on Buffon, Kant, and Rousseau." *Graduate Faculty Philosophy Journal*. Special Issue on Race in the History of Philosophy, New School University (2014): 101–24.
Bernstein, Mary. "Identity Politics." *Annual Review of Sociology* 31, no. 1 (2005): 47–74. https://www.annualreviews.org/doi/abs/10.1146/annurev.soc.29.010202.100054.
Bernstorff, Jochen von. "The Changing Fortunes of the Universal Declaration of Human Rights: Genesis and Symbolic Dimensions of the Turn to Rights in International Law." *European Journal of International Law* 19, issue 5 (November 2008): 903–24. https://doi.org/10.1093/ejil/chn069.
Brennan, William J., Jr. "State Constitutions and the Protection of Individual Rights." *Harvard Law Review* 90, no. 3 (1976–1977). https://heinonline.org/HOL/LandingPage?handle=hein.journals/hlr90&div=30&id=&page.
Caplan, Bryan. *The Myth of the Rational Voter: Why Democracies Choose Bad Policies*. Princeton, NJ: Princeton University Press, 2007.
Cartwright, Nancy, and Jeremy Hardie. *Evidence-Based Policy: A Practical Guide for Doing It Better*. New York: Oxford University Press, 2012.
Caygill, Howard. "Levinas's Political Judgement: The Esprit Articles." *Radical Philosophy*, issue 104 (November/December 2000). https://www.radicalphilosophy.com/article/levinass-political-judgement.
Chomsky, Daniel. "A Distorting Mirror: Major Media Coverage of Americans' Tax Policy Preferences." *Institute for New Economic Thinking Working Paper Series*, no. 73 (April 17, 2018). http://dx.doi.org/10.2139/ssrn.3228781.
Constantine, Madonna G., Tina Q. Richardson, Eric M. Benjamin, and John W. Wilson. "An Overview of Black Racial Identity Theories: Limitations and Considerations for Future Theoretical Conceptualizations." *Applied & Preventive Psychology* 7 (1998): 95–99. https://pdfs.semanticscholar.org/83b5/4af29e543446fe7a8d48b5780608c8b6d36a.pdf.
Cosmides, Leda, and John Tooby. "Cognitive Adaptations for Social Exchange." In *The Adapted Mind: Evolutionary Psychology and the Generation of Culture*, eds. Jerome H. Barkow, Leda Cosmides, and John Tooby. Oxford: Oxford University Press, 1992.
Cross, W. E., Jr., and B. J. Vandiver. "Nigrescence Theory and Measurement: Introducing the Cross Racial Identity Scale (CRIS)." In *Handbook of Multicultural Counseling*, eds. J. G. Ponterotto, J. M. Casas, L. A. Suzuki, and C. M. Alexander, 371–93. Thousand Oaks, CA: Sage, 2001.

Cuvier, Georges. *The Animal Kingdom: Arranged in Conformity with Its Organization*. Ed. H. McMurtrie. New York: G&C&H. Carvill, 1831. https://archive.org/details/animalkingdomar03graygoog.

Davis, F. James. *Who Is Black: One Nation's Definition*. University Park: Pennsylvania State Press, 1991.

Davis, Otto A., M. A. H. Dempster, and Aaron Wildavsky. "A Theory of the Budgetary Process." *American Political Science Review* 60, no. 3 (September 1966): 529–47. https://www.cmu.edu/dietrich/sds/docs/davis/A%20Theory%20of%20the%20Budgetary%20Process.pdf.

Derrida, Jacques. "The Ends of Man." *Philosophy and Phenomenological Research* 30, no. 1 (1969): 31–57.

Du Bois, W. E. B. "The Conservation of Races." In *The Problem of the Color Line at the Turn of the Twentieth Century: The Essential Early Essays*, ed. Nahum Dimitri Chandler, 51–65. New York: Fordham University Press, 2015. (Reprint of "The Conservation of Races." Washington, DC: American Negro Academy, 1897.)

Dunbar, Robin I. *Grooming, Gossip and the Evolution of Language*. London: Faber and Faber, 1996.

Eberhardt, L., and Gary J. Jacobsohn. "Citizen Participation in Policy-Making: The Role of the Jury." *Journal of Politics* 39, no. 1 (February 1977): 73–96.

Errera, Roger, and Hannah Arendt. "The Last Interview." In *The Last Interview and Other Conversations*, trans. Andrew Brown. Brooklyn, NY: Melville House, 2013.

Eze, Emmanuel Chukwudi. "The Color of Reason: The Idea of 'Race' in Kant's Anthropology." In *Anthropology and the German Enlightenment*, ed. Katherine Faull. London: Bucknell and Associates Press, 1994.

Fanon, Frantz. *Black Skin, White Masks*. Trans. Charles Lamb Markham. New York: Grove, 1967; United Kingdom: Pluto Press, 1952/1986/2008.

Fisher, Louis. *From Presidential Wars to American Hegemony: The Constitution after 9/11*. New York: Palgrave Macmillan, 2006.

Frege, Gottlob. "The Thought: A Logical Inquiry." *Mind* LXV, no. 259 (July 1956): 289–311.

Friedman, Milton. "The Case for a Negative Income Tax: A View from the Right." In *Issues in American Public Policy*, ed. J. H. Bunzel, 111–20. Englewood Cliffs, NJ: Prentice-Hall, 1968.

Fromm, Erich. "The Psychological Aspects of the Guaranteed Income." In *The Guaranteed Income: Next Step in Economic Evolution?*, ed. Robert Theobald, 175–84. New York: Doubleday, 1965/1966.

Fukuyama, Francis. *Identity: The Demand for Dignity and the Politics of Resentment*. London: Profile Books, 2018.

Garcia, J. L. A. "The Heart of Racism." *Journal of Social Philosophy* 27, issue 1. https://onlinelibrary.wiley.com/doi/abs/10.1111/j.1467-9833.1996.tb00225.x.

Garrett, Aaron, and Silvia Sebastiani. "David Hume on Race." In *Oxford Handbook of Philosophy and Race*, ed. Naomi Zack, 31–43. New York: Oxford University Press, 2017.

Gerhardt, Michael J. "Lessons of Impeachment History." *George Washington Law Review* 67 (1998–1999): 603–25. https://scholarship.law.unc.edu/cgi/viewcontent.cgi?article=1077&context=faculty_publications.

Gillham, Nicholas W. "Sir Francis Galton and the Birth of Eugenics." *Annual Review of Genetics* 35, no. 1 (2001): 83–101.

Gitlin, Todd. *The Twilight of Common Dreams: Why America Is Wracked by Culture Wars*. New York: Metropolitan Books, 1995.

Globalization101. "Negative vs. Positive Rights." A Project of SUNY Levin Institute. http://www.globalization101.org/negative-vs-positive-rights/.

Goodman, Nelson. "On the New Riddle of Induction." In *Fact, Fiction, and Forecast*, 4th edition. Cambridge, MA: Harvard University Press, 1983.

Gorton, William. "Karl Popper: Political Philosophy." *Internet Encyclopedia of Philosophy*. https://www.iep.utm.edu/popp-pol/.

Gould, Stephen Jay. "The Geometer of Race." *Discover* 15, no. 11 (1994): 65–69.

Gould, Stephen Jay. *The Mismeasure of Man*. London and New York: Norton, 1996.

Hallie, Philip. "From Cruelty to Goodness." *The Hastings Center Report* 11, no. 3 (June 1981): 23–28. https://www.jstor.org/stable/3561320.
Halpern, David. *Inside the Nudge Unit.* New York: Penguin, 2016.
Harff, Barbara. *Ethnic Conflict in World Politics.* 2nd edition. New York: Routledge, 2018.
Hegel, Georg Wilhelm Friedrich. "Geographical Bases of World History." From "Lectures on the Philosophy of World History." In *Race and the Enlightenment: A Reader,* ed. Emmanuel Chukwudi Eze. Cambridge, MA: Blackwell, 1997.
Heidegger, Martin. "Letter on Humanism." In *Basic Writings: Nine Key Essays, Plus the Introduction to Being and Time,* trans. David Farrell Krell, 213–66. London: Routledge, 1978.
Held, Virginia, reply by Alfred Kazin. "Feminism & Hannah Arendt." To the Editors. *New York Review of Books,* October 21, 1982. (In response to *Woman in Dark Times* from the June 24, 1982, issue.) https://www.nybooks.com/articles/1982/10/21/feminism-hannah-arendt/.
Hett, Benjamin Carter. *The Death of Democracy: Hitler's Rise to Power and the Downfall of the Weimar Republic.* New York: St. Martin's Griffin, 2019.
Hobbes, Thomas. *Leviathan.* 1651. https://www.earlymoderntexts.com/authors/hobbes.
Holt, Richard P. F., and Daphne T. Greenwood. "Negative Trickle-Down and the Financial Crisis of 2008." *Journal of Economic Issues* 46, no. 2 (2012): 363–70. DOI: 10.2753/JEI0021-3624460211.
Honig, Bonnie, ed. *Feminist Interpretations of Hannah Arendt.* University Park: Pennsylvania State University Press, 1995.
Hume, David. *An Enquiry Concerning Human Understanding.* In *Hume Texts Online,* eds. Amyas Merivale and Peter Millican. https://davidhume.org/texts/e/ (Selby-Bigge edition with Nidditch notes).
Hume, David. *A Treatise of Human Nature (1739–40).* In *Hume Texts Online,* eds. Amyas Merivale and Peter Millican. https://davidhume.org/texts/t/ (Selby-Bigge edition with Nidditch notes).
Hume, David. "Of National Characters." In *The Philosophical Works,* eds. Thomas Hill Green and Thomas Hodge Grose. 4 vols. Darmstadt, West Germany: Scientia Verlag Aalen, 1964.
Hume, David. "Of the Populousness of Ancient Nations." In *Essays Moral, Political and Literary,* eds. T. H. Green and T. H. Grose. London: Longmans, Green, 1875.
Iggers, Georg G. *The German Conception of History: The National Tradition of Historical Thought from Herder to the Present.* Scranton, PA: Harper and Row, 1984.
Isselbacher, Juliet E. "Agassiz Name on Harvard Campus Honors Not Louis Agassiz, but Wife and Son." *Harvard Crimson,* April 4, 2019. https://www.thecrimson.com/article/2019/4/4/agassiz-name-and-legacy/.
Jacobson, C. K. "Resistance to Affirmative Action: Self-Interest or Racism?" *Journal of Conflict Resolution* 29, no. 2 (1985): 306–29. https://doi.org/10.1177/0022002785029002007.
Jeffers, Chike. "The Cultural Theory of Race: Yet Another Look at Du Bois's 'The Conservation of Races.'" *Ethics* 123, no. 3 (April 2013): 403–26. https://doi.org/10.1086/669566.
Jeffers, Chike. "DuBois, Appiah, and Outlaw on Racial Identity." In *Oxford Handbook of Philosophy and Race,* ed. Naomi Zack, 204–13. New York: Oxford University Press, 2017.
Jones, Peter. "Group Rights." In *The Stanford Encyclopedia of Philosophy* (Summer 2016 Edition), ed. Edward N. Zalta. https://plato.stanford.edu/archives/sum2016/entries/rights-group/.
Jones, Peter. "Human Rights, Group Rights, and Peoples' Rights." *Human Rights Quarterly* 21, no. 1 (February 1999): 80–107.
Jordan, W. D. "Historical Origins of the One-Drop Racial Rule in the United States." *Journal of Critical Mixed Race Studies* 1, no. 1 (2014). Retrieved from https://escholarship.org/uc/item/91g761b3.
Kalmanson, Leah, Frank Garrett, and Sarah Mattice, eds. *Levinas and Asian Thought.* Philadelphia, PA: Duquesne University Press, 2013.
Kant, Immanuel. *Anthropology from a Pragmatic Point of View.* Trans. Hans H. Rudnick, ed. Victor Lyle Dowdell. Carbondale: Southern Illinois University Press, 1996.

Kant, Immanuel. *Observations on the Feeling of the Beautiful and the Sublime*. Trans. John T. Goldthwait. Berkeley: University of California Press, 1965.

Kant, Immanuel. "On the Different Races of Man," or "On the Different Races of Human Beings." In *This Is Race: An Anthology Selected from the International Literature on the Races of Man*, ed. Earl W. Count, 16–24. New York: Schuman, 1950.

Ledoux, Joseph E. "Cognitive-Emotional Interactions in the Brain." *Cognition and Emotion* 3, issue 4 (1989): 267–89. Published online: January 7, 2008. https://www.tandfonline.com/doi/abs/10.1080/02699938908412709.

Levinas, Emmanuel. "Ethics as First Philosophy"/"Justifications de l'Ethique" (Bruxelles: Editions de l'Universite de Bruxelles, 1984). From *The Levinas Reader*, ed. Seán Hand. Oxford and Cambridge: Blackwell, 1989.

Levinas, Emmanuel, and Seán Hand. "Reflections on the Philosophy of Hitlerism." *Critical Inquiry* 17, no. 1 (Autumn 1990): 62–71.

Levine, Philippa. *Eugenics: A Very Short Introduction*. New York: Oxford University Press, 2017.

Lilla, Mark. *The Once and Future Liberal: After Identity Politics*. New York: HarperCollins, 2017.

Locke, John. *Second Treatise of Government*. 1689. © Jonathan Bennett 2017, Early Modern Texts, 2018. http://www.earlymoderntexts.com/assets/pdfs/locke1689a.pdf.

Lucius, Outlaw. "Africana Philosophy." *Journal of Ethics* 1, no. 3 (1997): 265–90. www.jstor.org/stable/25115551.

Lyshaug, Brenda. "Authenticity and the Politics of Identity: A Critique of Charles Taylor's Politics of Recognition." *Contemporary Political Theory* 3 (2004): 300. https://doi.org/10.1057/palgrave.cpt.9300125.

MacDonald, Andrew, and William Luther Pierce. *The Turner Diaries*. Hillsboro, WV: National Vanguard Books, 1978/1999.

MacKinnon, Catharine. "Difference and Dominance: On Sex Discrimination." In *The Moral Foundations of Civil Rights*, eds. R. K. Fullinwider and C. Mills, 144–58. Maryland Studies in Public Philosophy. Totowa, NJ: Rowman & Littlefield, 1986.

MacKinnon, Catharine. *Feminism Unmodified: Discourses on Life and Law*. Cambridge, MA: Harvard University Press, 1987.

Matthews, J. L., and T. Matlock. "Understanding the Link between Spatial Distance and Social Distance." *Social Psychology* 42 (2011): 185–92. https://psycnet.apa.org/doiLanding?doi=10.1027%2F1864-9335%2Fa000062.

Maybee, Julie E. *Making and Unmaking Disability: The Three-Body Approach*. Lanham, MD: Rowman & Littlefield, 2019.

Mcbride, Lee A. "Insurrectionist Ethics and Racism." In *The Oxford Handbook of Philosophy and Race*, ed. Naomi Zack, 225–34. New York: Oxford, 2017.

McClellan, James. "Liberty, Order, and Justice: An Introduction to the Constitutional Principles of American Government." *Rule of Law & US Constitutionalism*. Online Library of Liberty, 2000. https://oll.libertyfund.org/pages/rule-of-law-us-constitutionalism.

Mende, Janne. *A Human Right to Culture and Identity: The Ambivalence of Group Rights*. Trans. Jochen Gahrau. London: Rowman & Littlefield, 2016.

Meyerhoff, Miriam. "Gender Performativity." *The International Encyclopedia of Human Sexuality*. First Edition. Eds. Patricia Whelehan and Anne Bolin. Chichester: John Wiley & Sons, 2015.

Michaels, Walter Benn. *Our America: Nativism, Modernism, and Pluralism*. Durham, NC: Duke University Press, 1995.

Mirowsky, John, and Catherine E. Ross. *Education, Social Status, and Health*. New York: Routledge, 2003.

Moffitt, R. A. "The Deserving Poor, the Family, and the U.S. Welfare System." *Demography* 52 (2015): 729–49. https://doi.org/10.1007/s13524-015-0395-0.

Morris, Aldon. *The Scholar Denied: W. E. B. Du Bois and the Birth of Modern Sociology*. Berkeley: University of California Press, 2017.

Moses, Wilson J. "W. E. B. Du Bois's 'The Conservation of Races' and Its Context: Idealism, Conservatism and Hero Worship." *Massachusetts Review* 34, no. 2 (1993): 275–94.

SELECT BIBLIOGRAPHY

Myhill, John. "The Native Speaker, Identity, and the Authenticity Hierarchy." *Language Sciences* 25, issue 1 (January 2003): 77–97.
Nelson, William Max. "Making Men: Enlightenment Ideas of Racial Engineering." *American Historical Review* 115, no. 5 (2010): 1364–94.
Neske, Gunther, and Emil Kettering, eds. *Martin Heidegger and National Socialism*. New York: Paragon House, 1990.
Overgaard, S. "On Levinas' Critique of Husserl." In *Metaphysics, Facticity, Interpretation*, eds. D. Zahavi, S. Heinämaa, and H. Ruin, 115–38. Contributions to Phenomenology, vol. 49. Dordrecht, Netherlands: Springer, 2003.
Pease, Donald E. *The New American Exceptionalism*. Minneapolis: University of Minnesota Press, 2009.
Peck, Janice. "Itinerary of a Thought: Stuart Hall, Cultural Studies, and the Unresolved Problem of the Relation of Culture to 'Not Culture.'" *Cultural Critique*, no. 48 (2001): 200–249. www.jstor.org/stable/1354401.
Pham, Vincent N. "Our Foreign President Barack Obama: The Racial Logics of Birther Discourses." *Journal of International and Intercultural Communication* 8, issue 2 (2015): 86–107. Published online: April 2, 2015. https://nca.tandfonline.com/doi/abs/10.1080/17513057.2015.1025327#.Xj3N1zFKjcs.
Piketty, Thomas. *Capital in the Twenty-First Century*. Trans. Arthur Goldhammer. Cambridge, MA: Harvard University Press, 2014.
Popper, Karl. "Anti-Semitism in Austria: A Letter to Friedrich Hayek (1969)." In *Popper, After the Open Society: Selected Social and Political Writings*, eds. Jeremy Shearmur and Piers Norris Turner. London and New York: Routledge, 2012.
Popper, Karl. *Conjectures and Refutations*. London: Routledge and Kegan Paul, 1963–1989.
Popper, Karl. "Democracy in America." *The Economist*, January 1, 2016. Reprinted from April 23, 1988. https://www.economist.com/democracy-in-america/2016/01/31/from-the-archives-the-open-society-and-its-enemies-revisited.
Popper, Karl. *The Logic of Scientific Discovery*. Hutchinson Education, 1959–2000.
Popper, Karl. "The Open Society after Five Years: Prefaces to the American Edition of *The Open Society* (1948–50)." In *Popper, After the Open Society: Selected Social and Political Writings*, eds. Jeremy Shearmur and Piers Norris Turner, 169–81. London and New York: Routledge, 2012.
Popper, Karl. *The Poverty of Historicism*. London and New York: Routledge, 1957.
Popper, Karl. "Public and Private Values (1946?)." In *Popper, After the Open Society: Selected Social and Political Writings*, eds. Jeremy Shearmur and Piers Norris Turner, 118–31. London and New York: Routledge, 2012.
Popper, Karl. "Uniting the Camp of Humanitarianism (1942–47)." In *Popper, After the Open Society: Selected Social and Political Writings*, eds. Jeremy Shearmur and Piers Norris Turner, 113–17. London and New York: Routledge, 2012.
Powers, Michael R. "From Hunter to Prisoner: Hurricane Katrina and the Social Contract." *Journal of Risk Finance* 7, issue 1 (2006). https://doi.org/10.1108/jrf.2006.29407aaa.001.
Prinz, Jesse. "Which Emotions Are Basic?" In *Emotion, Evolution, and Rationality*, eds. D. Evans and P. Cruse, 69–88. London: Oxford University Press, 2004.
Rawls, John. *A Theory of Justice*. Chicago: University of Chicago Press, 1971.
Raz, Joseph. *The Morality of Freedom*. Oxford and New York: Oxford University Press, 1986.
Roberts, John G., Jr. "Year-End Report on the Federal Judiciary." December 31, 2019. https://www.supremecourt.gov/publicinfo/year-end/2019year-endreport.pdf.
Roberts, Robert North, Scott John Hammond, and Valerie A. Sulfaro, eds. *Presidential Campaigns, Slogans, Issues, and Platforms: The Complete Encyclopedia*. Santa Barbara, CA: Greenwood, 2012.
Roberts, Rodney C. "Race, Rectification, and Apology." In *Oxford Handbook of Race and Philosophy*, ed. Naomi Zack, 516–25. New York: Oxford University Press, 2017/2019.
Roediger, David. *The Wages of Whiteness: Race and the Making of the American Working Class*. Revised edition. New York: Verso, 1999.
Sartre, Jean-Paul. *Anti-Semite and Jew*. Trans. George J. Becker. New York: Schocken Books, 1965.

Sartre, Jean-Paul. *Being and Nothingness: A Phenomenological Essay on Ontology.* Trans. Hazel E. Barnes. New York: Washington Square Press, 1956/1984.
Sartre, Jean-Paul. *Existentialism Is a Humanism.* Trans. Carol Macomber. New Haven, CT: Yale University Press, 1947/1996/2007.
Sartre, Jean-Paul. *Search for a Method.* Trans. Hazel Barnes. New York: Knopf, 1963.
Schaap, Andrew. "Political Reconciliation through a Struggle for Recognition?" *Social & Legal Studies* 13, no. 4 (December 2004): 523–40. https://journals.sagepub.com/doi/10.1177/0964663904047332.
Schmidt, Peter. "Supreme Court Shows Increased Skepticism toward Affirmative Action." *Chronicle of Higher Education* 53, no. 17 (2006): A20.
Schneider, Mark, and Jack Buckley. "What Do Parents Want from Schools? Evidence from the Internet." *Education Evaluation and Policy Analysis* 24, no. 2 (June 1, 2002): 133–44. https://doi.org/10.3102/01623737024002133.
Schwartzman, Luisa Farah. "Does Money Whiten? Intergenerational Changes in Racial Classification." *American Sociological Review* 72, no. 6 (December 2007): 940–63.
Simon, H. A. "Bounded Rationality." In *Utility and Probability*, eds. J. Eatwell, M. Milgate, and P. Newman, 15–18. The New Palgrave. London: Macmillan, 1990.
Sitaraman, Ganesh. *The Crisis of the Middle-Class Constitution: Why Economic Inequality Threatens Our Republic.* New York: Alfred A. Knopf, 2017.
Smedley, Audrey, and Brian D. Smedley. *Race in North America: Origin and Evolution of a Worldview.* 4th edition. Boulder, CO: Westview Press, 2011.
Smith, Kevin B., and Christopher W. Larimer. *The Public Policy Theory Primer.* New York: Routledge, 2018, 2019.
Somin, Ilya. *Democracy and Political Ignorance: Why Smaller Government Is Smarter.* Stanford, CA: Stanford University Press, 2013.
Stuurman, Siep. "François Bernier and the Invention of Racial Classification." *History Workshop Journal*, no. 50 (2000): 1–21.
Sue, Derald Wing, Christina M. Capodilupo, Gina C. Torino, Jennifer M. Bucceri, Aisha M. B. Holder, Kevin L. Nadal, and Marta Esquilin. "Racial Microaggressions in Everyday Life: Implications for Clinical Practice." In *American Psychologist* 62, no. 4 (May–June 2007): 271–86. https://doi.org/10.1037/0003-066X.62.4.271.
Taylor, Charles. *The Ethics of Authenticity.* Cambridge, MA: Harvard University Press, 1991.
Thaler, Richard H., and Cass R. Sunstein. *Nudge: Improving Decisions about Health, Wealth, and Happiness.* New York: Penguin, 2009.
Theobald, Robert. "The Guaranteed Income Proposal as Set Out in Free Men and Free Markets." In *The Guaranteed Income*, 227–33. From Theobald, *Free Men and Free Markets.* New York: C.N. Potter, 1963.
Tiebout, M. Charles. "A Pure Theory of Local Expenditures." *Journal of Political Economy* 64 (1956): 414–24.
Vanderborght, Yannick, and Philippe Van Parijs. "The History of Basic Income." In *L'allocation universelle.* chapter 1 (expanded English published by Harvard University Press, 2017), web version edited and abridged by Simon Birnbaum and Karl Widerquist, 2005, Basic Income Earth Network (BIEN). https://basicincome.org/basic-income/history/.
Warren, Barbara "Shining Woman." "Who Is an Indian." PowerSource. http://www.powersource.com/cocinc/ancest/whois.htm.
Washington, Booker T. "Booker T. Washington's Atlanta Exposition Speech, September 18, 1895." State Historical Society of Iowa. https://iowaculture.gov/history/education/educator-resources/primary-source-sets/reconstruction-and-its-impact/booker-t.
Weber, Max. "Status Groups and Classes." In *The Theory of Social and Economic Organization*, trans. A. M. Henderson and Talcott Parsons, 424–29. New York: Simon and Schuster, 1947/1975.
Wells, Ida B. "Southern Horrors" (1892). In *On Lynchings.* Mineola, NY: Dover Books, 2014.

Williams, D. R., N. Priest, and N. B. Anderson. "Understanding Associations among Race, Socioeconomic Status, and Health: Patterns and Prospects." *Health Psychology* 35, no. 4 (2016): 407–11. https://www.ncbi.nlm.nih.gov/pubmed/27018733.

Williams, Raymond. *The Long Revolution*. Cardigan, UK: Parthian, 1961/2011.

Wit, Theo W. A. de. "'My Way': Charles Taylor on Identity and Recognition in a Secular Democracy." *Stellenbosch Theological Journal* 4, no. 1 (2018): 153–78.

Wong, Tom K. *The Politics of Immigration: Partisanship, Demographic Change, and American National Identity*. New York: Oxford University Press, 2017.

Wortham, Robert, ed. *The Sociological Souls of Black Folk: Essays by W. E. B. Du Bois*. Lanham, MD: Lexington Books, 2011.

Zack, Naomi. *Applicative Justice: A Pragmatic Empirical Approach to Racial Injustice*. Lanham, MD: Rowman & Littlefield, 2016.

Zack, Naomi. "Contemporary Claims of Political Injustice: History and the Race to the Bottom." *Res Philosophica*. Published online first: October 18, 2017. https://doi.org/10.11612/resphil.1613.

Zack, Naomi. "Equality." In *Wiley-Blackwell Encyclopedia of Race, Ethnicity, and Nationalism*, eds. John Stone, Rutledge Dennis, Polly Rizova, Anthony D. Smith, and Xiaoshuo Hou. Published online: December 30, 2015. http://onlinelibrary.wiley.com/book/10.1002/9781118663202.

Zack, Naomi. *The Ethics and Mores of Race: Equality After the History of Philosophy*. Lanham, MD: Rowman & Littlefield, 2011.

Zack, Naomi. *Ethics for Disaster*. Lanham, MD: Rowman & Littlefield, 2009.

Zack, Naomi. "Ethics of Disaster Planning." *Philosophy of Management*. Special Issue: *Ethics of Crisis*. Ed. Per Sandin. Vol. 8, no. 2 (2009): 53–64.

Zack, Naomi. "The Fluid Symbol of Mixed Race." *Hypatia*, 25th Anniversary Issue, 25, no. 4 (Fall 2010): 875–90.

Zack, Naomi, ed. *The Oxford Handbook of Philosophy and Race*. New York: Oxford University Press, 2017/2019.

Zack, Naomi. "Philosophical Theories of Justice, Inequality, and Racial Inequality." *Graduate Faculty Philosophy Journal*. Special Issue on Race in the History of Philosophy, New School University, vol. 35, no. 1–2 (2014): 353–68.

Zack, Naomi. "Philosophy and Disaster." *Homeland Security Affairs Journal* II, no. 1, article 5 (April 2006). https://www.hsaj.org/articles/176.

Zack, Naomi. *Philosophy of Race: An Introduction*. Cham, Switzerland: Palgrave Macmillan, 2018.

Zack, Naomi. *Philosophy of Science and Race*. New York: Routledge, 2002.

Zack, Naomi. *Race and Mixed Race*. Philadelphia, PA: Temple University Press, 1992/1993.

Zack, Naomi. "Reparations and the Rectification of Race." *Journal of Ethics*. Special Issue: *Race, Racism and Reparations* 3 (2003): 139–51.

Zack, Naomi. *Reviving the Social Compact: Inclusive Citizenship in an Age of Extreme Politics*. Lanham, MD: Rowman & Littlefield, 2018.

Zack, Naomi. "Starting from Injustice: Justice, Applicative Justice, and Injustice Theory." *Harvard Review of Philosophy*, June 10, 2017. https://www.pdcnet.org/harvardreview/content/harvardreview_2017_0024_0079_0095.

Zack, Naomi. *White Privilege and Black Rights: The Injustice of US Police Racial Profiling and Homicide*. Lanham, MD: Rowman & Littlefield, 2015.

INDEX

abstract idea of race, 68–69
abuse of power, 149
accommodationist, 61
affirmative action, 8, 161n38
Affordable Care Act, 127
African Americans: black culture of, 63; black identity of, 74–75; #Black Lives Matter and, 45, 132; black racial destiny of, 65, 74; Hume and civilizations of, 169n46; Marxist theory and, 42; minority exploitation and, 77; universal Negro identity of, 43; in US, 62; white people identifying as, 40
Africans, 94
Agassiz, Louis, 90, 91–92
"Age of Discovery," 95
Alexander, Michelle, 78
algorithms, people learning, 12
American Negro Academy, 60, 62
anonymity, 4, 97, 142
Anti-Semite and Jew (Sartre), 21, 22–23, 24, 27
anti-Semitism, 22–25
L'Aquila, Italy, 124–127
Arendt, Hannah: adventure of, 26, 156n32; on Eichmann, 26; feminism neglected by, 28; gender exclusion by, 27; philosophy idealization by, 21, 27; post–World War II literature and, 15, 25–29; tyranny comments of, 13
authenticity, 39

bad conscience, 19–21
bad faith, 22, 23, 25
bad government, 104
Beattie, James, 169n46
behaviors, dominant, 48–49
beliefs, 171n12
Bennett, Jonathan, 20
Bernasconi, Robert, 94
Bernier, François, 68, 69, 88–89, 96
biological race, 60, 61
birther claims, 88
black culture, 63
black identity, 74–75
#Black Lives Matter, 45, 132
Black Power movement, 40
black racial destiny, 65, 74
Blumenbach, Johann Friedrich, 89–90
bounded rationality, 112–113
Brazil, effect of money in, 82, 166n8
Brown, Michael, 45
Buber, Martin, 16
budgeting, zero-based, 113
Buffon, George-Louis Leclerc, Comte de, 90
bureaucracy, permanent, 106
Butler, Judith, 46

candidates, election, 35
Capital in the Twenty-First Century (Piketty), 108, 109

capitalism, 106; consumers pleased with, 6; crony, 6–7; goods distribution in, 5–6; marketplace efficiency in, 6; patrimony, 108; regulation of, 7; social compact theory and, 3–4
capital punishment, 129
Caplan, Bryan, 115
Caygill, Howard, 68
celebrities, 41
Christianity, 66
Churchill, Winston, 121, 138
citizens: dignity and rights of, 70; equality of, 58; evidence expectations of, 123; government benefiting, 37–38, 142, 146; government's social contract with, 37; leadership chosen by, 12; progressive anonymity for, 4; progressive policies benefiting, 51–52; rights of, 161n38; social compact theory benefiting, 37–38, 103
civil liberties, 38, 137
civil rights, 58, 80
climate change, 7, 54
Clinton, Bill, 37
Clinton, Hillary, 132
closeness, of the Other, 17–18
coercive behavioral techniques, 129
cognitive theory, 102–103, 171n12
collective knowledge, 31
collective problems, 8
college education, 127
colonialism, 95
colonizers, 42
concentration camps. *See* Lublin/Majdanek concentration camp
consciousness: Levinas on, 17; nonintentional pre-reflective, 19; oneself created through, 21–22; Sartre's theory of, 21–22. *See also* intentional consciousness
"The Conservation of the Races" (Du Bois), 60, 61–62, 163n7
constant conjunction theory of causation (Hume), 122–123
Constitution, US, 33, 34, 36, 100, 141
consumers, 6
cost-benefit analyses, 133
courtrooms, 122

COVID-19, 8; bounded rationality and, 113; Democrat and Republican legislation for, 5; leadership during, 150; minorities influenced by, 47; political struggle over, 31; social distancing and, 37, 111; stay-home directives from, 5; in US, 54–55
Crania Americana (Morton), 90–91
criminal justice, 114
crony capitalism, 6–7
Cross, William E., Jr., 40
Crummell, Alexander, 62
Cuvier, Georges, 90–91

Les damnés de la terre (Fanon), 41
Davenport, Charles, 92
death penalty, 114
decision making, from evidence, 123, 126–127
Defense Production Act, 8, 55
democracy: electorate autonomy in, 143; law obedience in, 2; legal structures in, 35–36; liberal, 57; political theories in, 109; rule by law in, 103–104; as worst form of government, 121, 138
Democracy and Political Ignorance (Somin), 115
Democrats, 150; and common ground with Republicans, 78–79; COVID-19 legislation and, 5; government politicization by, 54–55; ideology and, 107; progressive tax from, 110
De Wit, Theo, 39
dialogic identity formation, 45
DiAngelo, Robin, 85
difference principle (Rawls), 4
disabled people, 51
discrimination: in housing, 2; against minorities, 82, 98; racial, 86
diversity, 35–36
dominant behaviors, 48–49
Douglass, Frederick, 61–62
Du Bois, W. E. B., 72, 87, 96; black racial destiny, 65, 74–75; on black struggle, 64–65; "The Conservation of the Races" by, 60, 61–62, 163n7; idealist metaphysics of, 63; race ideas of, 62–63
duty ethics (deontology), 118

INDEX

earthquakes, 124–126
economic inequality, 108
economic prosperity, 150
economic systems, 5
education, 127–129
egoism, 11–12, 16
Eichmann, Adolf, 26
elected officials, 106
electorate, 3, 143
eliminativism, 60–61
elitist technocrats, 114
emotions, 171n12
empiricism, 104–105, 122
employment, 127
Enlightenment universalism, 64, 72, 73
entertainment, government as, 150
entities, in identity groups, 34
environmental protections, 52
equality: of citizens, 58; economic, 108; gender, 46; human, 54, 72, 137; human rights and, 95–96; income, 107–108; inequalities and, 51; racial, 58, 80, 80–81, 86, 141; racism and, 58, 59
An Essay on the Inequality of the Human Races (Gobineau), 92
The Ethics of Authenticity (Taylor), 39
eugenics movement, 90, 92
evidence: citizens' expectations from, 123; decisions from, 123, 126–127; imperfections of, 141
evidence-based government, 3, 102, 104–111
evidence-based public policies, 102, 103, 111–115, 116, 119, 123, 129, 139
evil doers, 20
existentialism, 22, 43, 105

Fanon, Frantz: *Les damnés de la terre* by, 41; on ontological resistance of blacks, 25; and quarrel with Sartre, 42; on universal Negro identity, 43
Farrell, Robert, 155n8
feminism, 28, 29, 39
Finland, 133, 147
food insecurity, 5, 130, 135
free enterprise, 6
free-floating variable, 49
Free Men and Free Markets (Theobald), 138

Frege, Gottlob, 60, 73
Friedman, Milton, 132
Fromm, Erich, 134–135, 138
Fukuyama, Francis, 43, 44, 50

Galton, Francis, 92
gender: equality, 46; exclusion, 27; minorities and problems of, 47
genealogical race, 68–69
genocide, 14, 28
Georgetown University, 53
Germany, 67, 69
Gingrich, Newt, 37
Gitlin, Todd, 51
global prosperity, 8
Gobineau, Joseph Arthur de, 90, 92
God, invocation of, 65
good faith, 24
good government, 143
goods distribution, 5–6
Gould, Stephen Jay, 90, 91
government: bad, 104; change approach of, 3; citizens benefiting from, 37–38, 142, 146; citizens' social contract with, 37; coercive behavioral techniques used by, 129; collective problems and, 8; democracy as worst form of, 121, 138; Democrat and Republican politicization of, 54–55; empirical approach to, 103–104; evidence-based, 3, 102, 104–111; good, 143; as hard entertainment, 150; identity flux and, 46; identity politics in, 1; ideological-based, 104–111; justice from, 98; Locke and purpose of, 37; permanent bureaucracy in, 106; public schools funding and, 153; reason in, 101; Republicans contracting, 145; social compact benefiting citizens and, 37–38, 103; society separate from, ix; totalitarian, 31, 104, 115–116, 129; universalism in, 57–58; white male property owners in, 34, 35
Green New Deal, 38, 52
Grotius, 26
ground ownership, 132
ground rent, 132
groups: identities of, 46, 48–49; in identity politics, 33; indigenous, 52;

marginalized, 46; politics through membership in, 11; racial conflict, 49–50; rights, 44–48, 48–50
"The Guaranteed Income Proposal" (Theobald), 138

Hallie, Philip, 13
happiness, from UBI, 147
hate, objects of, 23
hate crimes, 49
Hayek, Friedrich, 23, 105
health care, 107; mental health and, 119; need for, 128; rights to, 138; wealth and education in, 127–129
Hegel, Georg Wilhelm Fredrich, 92, 95
Heidegger, Martin, 16, 26
Herder, Johann Gottfried, 38
"Hidden Tribes" (report), 78
Himmler, Heinrich, 20–21
Histoire Naturelle (Buffon), 90
Hitler, Adolf, 65
Hitlerism, 64–70, 72
Hobbes, Thomas, 36
Holocaust, 25–26
homelessness, 3
Homo sapiens, types of, 89
housing discrimination, 2
Hulliung, Mark, 36–37
human beings: equality of, 54, 72, 137; no predetermined nature of, 22; as species, 93; white supremacy and, 54
humanitarianism, 105
human rights: equality and, 95–96; UBI for, 135; UN for, 14; universal, 136–138; in US, 133
Hume, David: constant conjunction theory of causation, 122–123; inductive reasoning and, 122; Negro civilizations and, 169n46; racial differences and, 92–93; racial hierarchy and, 95; on reason as slave to passions, 102; *Treatise* by, 101
Hurricane Katrina, 37
Husserlian intentionality, 15, 155n8
hypodescent, 87

idealist metaphysics, 63
ideal theory, 14
identity flux, 46

identity groups: citizen rights and, 161n38; colonizers and, 42; entities in, 34; group rights and, 44–48; individuals in, 45; language used in, 39; membership in, 40; oppressed, 64; progressive policies and, 51–52; shared traits in, 53–54; universal humanity and, 42, 43; universal Negro, 43; victimization in, 9–10
identity-neutral egalitarianism, 8–9
identity politics: electorate's interests in, 3; global prosperity and, 8; in government, 1; group interests in, 33; intellectual void filled by, 29; oppression victims in, 14, 141; problems with, 9, 38–44; shared interests in, 50–52
ideological-based government, 104–111
ideology, 106–107, 109
immigration restrictions, 110
impeachment, 104, 150
inclusivity, 2, 81
income: earned and unearned, 134; education increasing, 127; equal, 107–108; white people with low, 167n12. *See also* universal basic income
incrementalism, 113
indigenous group, 52
indigenous lands, 53
individualism, 39
inductive reasoning, 122
inherent dignity, 70
institutional racism, 82–83, 86, 88
instrumental rationality, 111
intellectual void politics, 29
intentional consciousness, 155n8; ego at center of, 16; Levinas on, 15–16; the Other and, 19
isolation, 95
Italian earthquake, 124–127
I-thou analysis, 16

Jeffers, Chike, 63
Jews, 22–26, 28
Jim Crow, 78
Johnson, Lyndon B., 146
Johnson-Reed Immigration Act (1924), 92

INDEX

justice: criminal, 114; from government, 98; for minorities, 77–78; race-based, 74; Rawls's view on, 72–73, 74; recognition of, 159n17; universalism and, 72–74

Kant, Immanuel, 92, 93–94
King, Martin Luther, 132
knowledge, lived experience as a source of, 17

language, relation to identity, 39
Larimer, Christopher, 112–114
law, 2, 122
laziness, stereotype of, 130
leadership, 12
learning, practice of, 128
legal structures, in democracy, 35–36
legislation, civil rights, 58
Levinas, Emmanuel, 59–60, 155n7; bad conscience escaped and, 21; on consciousness experience, 17; on Enlightenment universalism, 72; Germany remarks of, 67; on Hitlerism, 64–70; on intentional consciousness, 15–16; liberalism and, 67; Marxist theory claims of, 67; nonintentional consciousness and, 155n8; nonintentional pre-reflective consciousness and, 19; post–World War II literature of, 15–21; "Reflections on the Philosophy of Hitlerism" by, 64; subject-object relation and, 16; universalism claim of, 66, 71; universality and, 57
Levy, Hyman, 105
liberal arts, 128
liberalism: in democracy, 57; Levinas and, 67; universal humanistic, 71
libertarian paternalism, 116
Lilla, Mark, 145–146
Linnaeus, Carolus (Carl), 89
literature, post–World War II, 15–29
Locke, John, 36, 37
"looks like me" factor, 46
Lublin/Majdanek concentration camp, 23, 156n24

Machiavelli, Niccolò, 111

MacKinnon, Catharine, 48
magical thinking, 12
Magna Carta, 36
Maguire, Laura, 33
marginalized group identities, 46
marketplace efficiency, 6
Marx, Karl, 7
Marxist theory: African Americans and, 42; falsification of, 30; ideology of, 106; Levinas claims about, 67; Popper's criticism of, 31, 105; Sartre on, 27
mass expression, 44–45
master identity, 87–88
mauvaise conscience, 17, 20
media coverage, 44–45
Mein Kampf (Hitler), 65
Mende, Janne, 39
mental health, 119
meritocracy, 12
metaphysics, 16, 63–64
microaggression, 84, 86, 96, 144
minorities: African Americans exploitation and, 77; COVID-19 influencing, 47; discrimination against, 82, 98; gender problems and, 47; inclusivity for whites and, 81; justice for, 77–78; microaggressions against, 84, 144; as objects of hate, 23; policies helping, 8–9; progressivism and, 78; racial, 78, 144; social domains and, 1–2; white people's ignorance of experiences of, 84
Mirowsky, John, 127, 128
misery, reduction of, 147
The Mismeasure of Man (Gould), 91
monogeny, 91, 92–93
moral humanism, 65, 66
morality, basic norms of, 118
More, Thomas, 131
Morton, Samuel, 90–91, 92
Moses, Wilson, 62
Murray, Charles, 132
Myth of the Blood (Rosenberg), 164n20
The Myth of the Rational Voter (Caplan), 115

national identity, 38
nationality, 146–147
Native Americans, 40

natural resources, 7
Nazism: Arendt and, 26; Himmler's view of, 20; Jews and, 25–26, 28; racism in, 66
negative utilitarian approach (Popper), 143
Nigrescence theory, 40–41, 45
nonegalitarian societies, 48
nonideal theory, 99
nonintentional consciousness, 19, 155n8
nonintentional pre-reflective consciousness, 19
"Nouvelle Division de la Terre" (Bernier), 68, 89
Nudge movement, 116–119, 129
nutrition, food insecurity and, 130

Obama, Barack, 78, 87, 127
Occupy Wall Street movement, 29, 45, 108
The Once and Future Liberal (Lilla), 145–146
one-drop rule, 87
Ontario, Canada, 133, 147
"On the Different Races of Human Beings" (Bernasconi), 94
ontological resistance of blacks, 25
The Open Society and its Enemies (Popper), 103
oppression, 31–32; of identity groups, 64; identity politics victims of, 14, 141; resistance to, 45
opt-out models, 116, 117–118
Orbán, Viktor, 44
organs, harvesting, 117–118
The Origins of Totalitarianism (Arendt), 25
the Other, 15; closeness of, 17–18; fear for, 19; unintentional consciousness and, 19
Outlaw, Lucius, 63

Paine, Thomas, 131–132
patrimony capitalism, 108
pension plan, 117
philosophy, 27, 28, 100
physical force, 59
Picuti, Fabio, 124, 125
piecemeal engineering, 109

piecemeal public policies, 143
Piketty, Thomas, 108, 109
"place in the sun," 17
Plato, 99, 100
pluralism, Du Boisian, 60–64
politics: as competition, 153; democracy with theories in, 109; domains of, 1; egoism in, 11–12; through group membership, 11; intellectual void, 29; parties in, 153; philosophy's tensions with, 27; politicization of government, 54–55; of resentment, 44; rule in, 4; social media messaging in, 7; theories in, 106–107
polygeny, 91, 93
Popper, Karl, 15, 23, 99, 119; empirical approach to government of, 103–104; on human misery decrease, 30–31; Marxism abandoned by, 105; Marxist theory criticism by, 31, 105; negative utilitarian approach of, 143; *The Open Society and Its Enemies* by, 103; socialism views of, 143
populism, 138
poverty, caused by race, 58–59
The Poverty of Historicism (Popper), 31
power disparity, 1–2
private property, 37, 131, 132
progressive anonymity, 4, 97, 142
progressive tax, 110
progressivism: lower-class whites and, 83; policies in, 51–52; racial minorities and, 78
property, landed, 132
protests, 38
psychological constitutions, 66
public policies: compliance of, 118; elitist technocrats and, 114; evidence-based, 102, 103, 111–115, 116, 119, 123, 129, 139; human misery in, 30–31; ideology in, 109; minorities helped by, 8–9; piecemeal, 104–105, 143, 144; rational process in, 111; UBI as, 130–138; worldviews blocking, 129
The Public Policy Theory Primer (Smith, K., and Larimer), 112
public schools, 153
public speaking, 101
Putin, Vladimir, 43–44

race: biological, 60, 61; discrimination against, 86; distinctions of, 89–91; Du Bois's ideas on, 62–63; equality of, 58, 80, 141; genealogical and abstract, 68–69; hierarchy of, 97; human worth of, 91–92, 94; Hume on differences in, 92–93; Hume on hierarchy of, 95; identity by, 24, 46; justice based on, 74; as master identity, 87–88; metaphysics of, 63–64; minorities of, 78, 144; modern systems of, 88–95; status system of, 82, 88; universalism and, 67–71; uplifting, 65; US group conflict over, 49–50; US wars of, 65; white supremacy and, 80, 86

"Race Debates," 60, 63–64, 74

racism: inequality of, 58, 59; institutional, 82–83, 86, 88; Nazi, 66; residue of, 79–82; in status system, 168n24; structural, 58, 86, 88; systems favoring whites in, 79–80, 96–97; universality and, 67–69; white antiblack, 40–41; white people's problems of, 10, 96–97

rational-actor model, 118

Rawls, John, 142; difference principle of, 4; ideal theory and, 14; justice view of, 72–73, 74

Read, Herbert, 105

Reagan, Ronald, 108, 145

reasoning: cognitive ideal in, 102–103; in government, 101; as slave to passions, 102

recognition, 50

"Reflections on the Philosophy of Hitlerism" (Levinas), 64

relativism, 39

reparations, 52–53

Republicans, 150; and common ground with Democrats, 78–79; COVID-19 legislation and, 5; government contracted by, 145; government politicization by, 54–55

reverse engineering, 51

Reviving the Social Compact (Zack), ix, x

risk assessment, 124

Roosevelt, Theodore, 121, 139

Rosenberg, Alfred, 67, 164n20

Ross, Catherine E., 127, 128

Rousseau, Jean-Jacques, 44, 94

rule of law, 19, 103–104, 149

Sanders, Sarah, 99

Sartre, Jean Paul: *Anti-Semite and Jew* by, 21, 22–23, 24, 27; consciousness theory of, 21–22; Fanon's quarrel with, 42; Jews and, 22–25; on Marxist theory, 27; post–World War II literature of, 15, 21–25; *Search for a Method* by, 105

school integration, 8

science: evidence standards for, 122; responsibility and, 124–127

Search for a Method (Sartre), 105

self-esteem, 41

self-expression, 18

separatism, 63

SEU. *See* subjective expected utility

shared interests, 50–52

shelter insecurity, 135

single-issue voters, 110

single-payer system (health insurance), 107

slogans, 145

Smith, Adam, 6

Smith, Kevin, 112–114

SNAP. *See* Supplemental Nutrition Assistance Program

social compact theory: capitalism and socialism from, 3–4; government benefiting citizens in, 37–38, 103; Locke as founder of, 36

social distancing, 37, 111

social domains, 1–2

socialism, 106; minimal baselines of, 5; Popper's views on, 143; social compact theory and, 3–4; utopian benefits from, 7

social media, 7, 77, 153

social problems, 35–36

social segregation, 80

societies: government separate from, ix; nonegalitarian, 48; well-ordered, 73; white dominant in, 81

socioeconomic class, 82–83, 85–88

Somin, Ilya, 115

sovereignty, 36

standard of living, 137

State of the Union address, 146–147

states' rights, 55
status system, 85–88; of race, 82, 88; racism in, 168n24; white people in, 95–97
structural racism, 58
subaltern identities, 24
subjective expected utility (SEU), 113
subject-object relation, 16, 18
subsistence rights, 136, 138
substantive rationality, 113
Supplemental Nutrition Assistance Program (SNAP), 130
surplus food distribution, 136

target population, 35
tax policy, 108, 136
Taylor, Charles, 39–40, 45, 50
terrorism, 10
Theobald, Robert, 138
theory of intentionality, 15
A Theory of Justice (Rawls), 74
totalitarian government, 31, 104, 115–116, 129
transmogrification, 61
transsexuals, 40
trickle-down prosperity, 108
Trump, Donald, 149, 150
two-party system, 104
tyranny, 13, 29, 138

UBI. *See* universal basic income
UDHR. *See* Universal Declaration of Human Rights
United Nations (UN), 14, 58, 71, 137. *See also* Universal Declaration of Human Rights
United States (US): African Americans in, 62; Constitution of, 33, 34, 36, 100, 141; COVID-19 in, 54–55; economic inequality in, 108; human rights in, 133; indigenous lands seized in, 53; poverty in, 58–59; progressive policies in, 51–52; race wars in, 65; racial group conflict in, 49–50; social segregation in, 80; socioeconomic class in, 82–83; tax policy in, 108; UBI in, 133–134; white supremacy in, 10–11, 83–84
universal basic income (UBI), 4, 123; in Finland and Ontario, 133; happiness from, 147; for human rights, 135; objections to, 134, 135; psychological aspects of, 134–136; as public policy, 130–138; subsistence rights and, 136; in US, 133–134
Universal Declaration of Human Rights (UDHR), 28, 58, 70–71, 136–137, 161n38
universal housing allowance, 3; universal humanistic liberalism, 71
universal humanity, 42, 43
universal human rights, 136–138
universalism, 60, 75, 141; Enlightenment, 64, 72, 73; genealogy undermining, 69; in government, 57–58; justice and, 72–74; Levinas's claim of, 66, 71; race and, 67–71
universality, 28
universal Negro identity, 43
universal property rights, 131
universal rules of law, 19
Utopia (More), 131
utopian benefits, 7, 105–106
utopian engineering, 109

veil of ignorance, 142
victimization, 9–10
violence, 18; evil doers in, 20; strife from, 50; of White Supremacy, 64, 75
virtue ethics, 118
visions, 145, 146, 147
Vittorini, Vincenzo, 125
Vives, Juan Luis, 131
voting, 38; misinformation of, 115; racial identities in, 46; single-issue, 110; visions and slogans for, 145

Washington, Booker T., 61, 63, 87
Weber, Max, 85
welfare programs, 130
well-being, minimal, 4
"We the People," 33, 37, 58
White Fragility (DiAngelo), 85
white nationalism, 87–88
white people: African American identity and, 40; antiblack racism and, 40–41; low-income, 167n12; minorities wanting inclusivity of, 81; minority experience, ignorance of, 84;

progressivism and lower-class, 83; property owners, 34, 35; racial problems of, 10, 96–97; racism and systems favoring, 79–80, 96–97; societies' dominance by, 81; status of, 95–97
white racial status, 141
White Right, 10, 11
white supremacy/White Supremacy, 43, 65, 78, 96, 166n7; hate crimes from, 49; human equality and, 54; nature of, 82–85; racial equality and, 80, 86; racial hierarchy and, 97; in US, 10–11, 83–84; violence of, 64, 75
Williams, Raymond, 5
Women's March, 45

Xi Jinping, 44

zero-based budgeting, 113

www.ingramcontent.com/pod-product-compliance
Lightning Source LLC
Chambersburg PA
CBHW022012300426
44117CB00005B/152